Additional praise for
PLATFORM REVOLUTION

"Platforms have transformed the economy over the last two decades, but the biggest effects are yet to come. *Platform Revolution* provides the first comprehensive framework for platform strategy and for predicting the winners and losers of future disruptions."
—Susan C. Athey, Stanford University,
former chief economist, Microsoft

"*Platform Revolution* is a manual for the disruption of your industry. You can either read it or try to keep it out of the hands of your competitors—present and future. I think it's an easy call."
—Andrew McAfee, principal research scientist at MIT,
coauthor of *The Second Machine Age*

"*Platform Revolution* provides an exceptional synthesis of cutting-edge research that makes it must-reading for my MBA students. A key insight is that platform strategies can benefit all participants when they understand the underlying economics. Read the book and share it with your business partners. You'll be glad you did."
—Erik Brynjolfsson, MIT Sloan School,
coauthor of *The Second Machine Age*

"Revealing the strategies behind some of today's rising platforms, the authors explain how entrepreneurs—and traditional companies—can thrive in this new world. In cases as diverse as shoes, spices, dating, energy, home appliances and education, *Platform Revolution* provides the essential guide to unlocking the potential of an economic landscape transformed." —Rob Llewellyn, *CXO Weekly*

"In the digital economy, platforms are transforming industries at high speed. *Platform Revolution* is an inspiring guide for business leaders to transform existing businesses to platform businesses."
—Jim Hagemann Snabe, former CEO of SAP

PLATFORM REVOLUTION

HOW NETWORKED MARKETS ARE TRANSFORMING THE ECONOMY— AND HOW TO MAKE THEM WORK FOR YOU

Geoffrey G. Parker,
Marshall W. Van Alstyne, and
Sangeet Paul Choudary

W. W. NORTON & COMPANY
Independent Publishers Since 1923
NEW YORK | LONDON

For information about permission to reproduce selections from this book,
write to Permissions, W. W. Norton & Company, Inc.,
500 Fifth Avenue, New York, NY 10110

For information about special discounts for bulk purchases, please contact
W. W. Norton Special Sales at specialsales@wwnorton.com or 800-233-4830

Manufacturing by Quad Graphics, Fairfield
Book design by BTDnyc
Production manager: Anna Oler

Library of Congress Cataloging-in-Publication Data

Names: Parker, Geoffrey (Geoffrey G.) author. | Van Alstyne, Marshall, author. |
Choudary, Sangeet Paul, author.
Title: Platform revolution : how networked markets are transforming the economy and
how to make them work for you / Geoffrey G. Parker, Marshall W. Van Alstyne, and
Sangeet Paul Choudary.
Description: First Edition. | New York : W. W. Norton & Company, 2016. |
Includes bibliographical references and index.
Identifiers: LCCN 2016001066 | ISBN 9780393249132 (hardcover)
Subjects: LCSH: Internet marketing. | Strategic planning.
Classification: LCC HF5415.1265 .P3674 2016 | DDC 658.8/72—dc23
LC record available at http://lccn.loc.gov/2016001066

ISBN 978-0-393-35435-5 pbk.

W. W. Norton & Company, Inc.
500 Fifth Avenue, New York, N.Y. 10110
www.wwnorton.com

W. W. Norton & Company Ltd.
15 Carlisle Street, London W1D 3BS
1 2 3 4 5 6 7 8 9 0

To the memory of my mother, Mary Lynn Goodrich Parker.

For my A., my X. and my E.

For Devika, for always being there.

CONTENTS

Our goal in writing this book is to solve a number of puzzles posed by the rapid rise of the platform model. These puzzles include:

- How have platform businesses such as Uber and Airbnb managed to disrupt and dominate vast traditional industries within just a few years of their own launch? (We address this question throughout the book, and focus on it especially closely in chapter 4.)
- How can platform businesses outcompete traditional companies while employing just a tiny fraction of the number of people the incumbents employ? (See chapters 1 and 2.)
- How has the rise of the platform transformed the principles governing economic growth and business competition? How do platform businesses resemble the industrial giants of the past—and how do they differ? (See chapters 2 and 4.)
- How and why have specific companies and business leaders soared to the heights of success, plummeted to the depths of failure—or both—as a result of their use, or misuse, of platform business methods? Why did Blackberry fall from 49 percent market share to 2 percent in just four years? How did Steve Jobs fumble his company's platform-model choices in the 1980s . . . and then get them dramatically right in the 2010s? (See chapters 2 and 7.)
- How do some companies solve the challenge of attracting producers and consumers to a new platform simultaneously, while others fail miserably? Why is free pricing sometimes a brilliant business move, and sometimes a fatal error? (See chapters 5 and 6.)
- Why do competitive markets flourish in some platform arenas, while in others winner-take-all markets dominated by a single platform swiftly emerge? (See chapter 10.)
- As platforms grow, they are subject to abuse: customers shopping on eBay can be defrauded, women seeking dates on Match.com can be assaulted, homes rented on Airbnb can be ransacked. Who should pay the price? And how should platform users be protected? (See chapters 8 and 11.)

In answering questions like these, we've sought to create a practical guide to the new economy that is reshaping the world in which

PREFACE

Platform Revolution is our attempt to provide the first clear, complete, authoritative guide to one of the most important economic and social developments of our time—the rise of the platform as a business and organizational model.

The platform model underlies the success of many of today's biggest, fastest-growing, and most powerfully disruptive companies, from Google, Amazon, and Microsoft to Uber, Airbnb, and eBay. What's more, platforms are beginning to transform a range of other economic and social arenas, from health care and education to energy and government. No matter who you are or what you do for a living, it's highly likely that platforms have already changed your life as an employee, a business leader, a professional, a consumer, or a citizen—and are poised to produce even greater changes in your daily life in the years to come.

Over the past two decades, we have come to recognize that powerful economic, social, and technological forces are transforming our world in ways that few people fully understand. We've dedicated ourselves to studying those forces and how they work—how they are disrupting traditional companies, upending markets, and altering careers, and how they are being leveraged by startup businesses that are using them to dominate traditional industries and launch new ones.

Realizing that the platform business model is the leading embodiment of these forces, we began branching out from our academic and corporate backgrounds to work closely with compan that are deeply engaged in creating platform businesses, includ Intel, Microsoft, SAP, Thomson Reuters, Intuit, 500 Startups, F Group, Telecom Italia, and many others. We'll recount their s in the pages that follow.

we all live, work, and play. *Platform Revolution* is an outgrowth of three careers that have been spent immersed in studying and unraveling the mysteries of the platform model.

Two of the authors—Geoff Parker and Marshall Van Alstyne—became interested in the emerging network economy during the dotcom boom of 1997–2000, when both were PhD students at MIT. Those were heady times. The NASDAQ stock index spiked by more than 80 percent as venture capitalists poured investment money into startups boasting cool new technologies and names featuring the prefix *e* or the suffix *com*. With traditional metrics of business success seemingly rendered obsolete, several companies launched hugely successful initial public offerings (IPOs) without ever having made a dime in profit. Students and faculty alike were dropping out of school to launch fledgling technology businesses.

Inevitably, the market came crashing down. Beginning in March 2000, trillions of dollars' worth of paper valuations vanished in a matter of months. Yet amid the rubble, certain companies survived. While Webvan and Pets.com disappeared, Amazon and eBay survived and thrived. Steve Jobs, who had lost Apple to mistakes he made earlier, recovered, returned to Apple, and built it into a juggernaut. Eventually, the online world emerged from the depths of the 2000 downturn to become stronger than ever.

Why were some Internet-based businesses successful while others were not? Were the differences a matter of random luck, or were deeper design principles at work? What are the rules of the new economics of networks? Geoff and Marshall set about trying to answer these questions.

It turned out to be a harder challenge than they expected. They ended up having to develop a new economic theory of two-sided networks. Their *Harvard Business Review* article "Strategies for Two-Sided Markets," coauthored with Harvard professor Thomas R. Eisenmann, laid out what became one of the most widely taught theories of Internet business, one that is still taught in MBA programs around the world. Along with the work of other scholars, Geoff's and Marshall's insights helped to reshape mainstream thinking about business regulation. Later, at the MIT Initiative on the Digital Economy, they furthered their work with such firms as AT&T, Dun & Bradstreet, Cisco, IBM, Intel, Jawbone, Microsoft, Salesforce, SAP, Thomson Reuters, and many others.

The third author of this book, Sangeet Choudary, was a high school student during the dot-com boom of the 1990s, but he was already fascinated by the immense power of the Internet—particularly its power to create business models capable of rapid, scalable growth. Later, while working as the head of innovation and new ventures at Yahoo and Intuit, Sangeet started digging deeper into the factors that spell success or failure for Internet startups. His research on business model failure, coupled with his conversations with venture capitalists and entrepreneurs, helped him identify the increasing importance of a new and massively scalable business model: the platform.

In 2012, Sangeet started focusing on platform businesses fulltime. His premise: as the world becomes increasingly networked, businesses that do a better job of harnessing the power of platform networks will win. Sangeet has offered guidance on platform strategy to a wide range of companies around the world, ranging from startups to Fortune 100 firms, and his popular blog (http://platformed.info) has been featured on leading media globally.

In the spring of 2013, Marshall and Geoff came across Sangeet's work, and we immediately realized the value of a collaboration. Our partnership coalesced in the summer of 2013 when we met for three weeks at MIT to work together on building a cohesive view of platform dynamics. Since then, we've cochaired the MIT Platform Strategy Summit, spoken about platform models at leading world forums such as the G20 summit, Emerce eDay, and TED, taught about platforms at the world's leading universities, and collaborated on implementing platform strategy with business clients around the world.

Now the three of us have written *Platform Revolution*, representing our first attempt to bring together our thinking on platforms in a cohesive, comprehensive fashion.

We've been fortunate enough to have access to the ideas and experiences of some of the greatest firms in the world, having worked with more than a hundred companies in diverse industries on developing and implementing their platform strategies. At the MIT Platform Strategy Summit, leaders of organizations that are building platforms, managing them, or reacting to them, including edX, Samsung, Apigee, Accenture, OkCupid, Alibaba, and many others, have shared their stories with one another and with us. We have also benefited from working with a group of world-class scholars who have dedicated their careers to understanding the digital economy, and who participate in the annual Workshop on Information Systems and Economics (WISE) and the Boston University Platform Strategy Research Symposium, as well as some of the world's leading thinkers in adjacent fields such as behavior design, data science, systems design theory, and agile methodologies.

We have written this book because we believe that digital connectivity and the platform model it makes possible are changing the world forever. The platform-driven economic transformation is producing enormous benefits for society as a whole and for the businesses and other organizations that create wealth, generate growth, and serve the needs of humankind. At the same time, it is creating sweeping changes in the rules that have traditionally governed success and failure. We hope that *Platform Revolution* will help market upstarts, incumbent organizations, regulators and policy-makers, and engaged citizens effectively navigate the challenging new landscape of a world in which platforms win.

GEOFFREY G. PARKER
MARSHALL W. VAN ALSTYNE
SANGEET PAUL CHOUDARY

PLATFORM
REVOLUTION

1

TODAY

Welcome to the
Platform Revolution

I n October 2007, a tiny item appeared in an online newsletter aimed at industrial designers—men and women who shape the appearance of everything from coffee makers to jumbo jets. It referred to an unusual housing option for professionals who planned to attend the upcoming joint convention of two industrial design organizations, the International Congress of Societies of Industrial Design (ICSID) and the Industrial Designers Society of America (IDSA):

> If you're heading out to the ICSID/IDSA World Congress/Connecting '07 event in San Francisco next week and have yet to make accommodations, well, consider networking in your jam-jams. That's right. For "an affordable alternative to hotels in the city," imagine yourself in a fellow design industry person's home, fresh awake from a snooze on the ol' air mattress, chatting about the day's upcoming events over Pop Tarts and OJ.

The hosts for this "networking in your jam-jams" opportunity were Brian Chesky and Joe Gebbia, budding designers who'd moved to San Francisco only to find they couldn't afford the rent on the loft they shared. Strapped for cash, they impulsively decided to make air mattresses and their own services as part-time tour guides available to convention attendees. Chesky and Gebbia attracted three weekend guests and made a thousand bucks, which covered the next month's rent.

Their casual space-sharing experience would launch a revolution in one of the world's biggest industries.

Chesky and Gebbia recruited a third friend, Nathan Blecharczyk, to help them make affordable room rentals a long-term business. Of course, renting space in their San Francisco loft wouldn't yield much revenue. So they designed a website that allowed anyone, anywhere, to make a spare sofa or guest room available to travelers. In exchange, the company—now dubbed Air Bed & Breakfast (Airbnb), after the air mattresses in Chesky and Gebbia's loft—took a slice of the rental fee.

The three partners started out focusing on events for which hotel space was often sold out, scoring their first big hit at the 2008 South by Southwest festival in Austin. But they soon discovered that demand for friendly, affordable accommodations provided by local residents existed year-round and nationwide—and even internationally.

Today, Airbnb is a giant enterprise active in 119 countries, where it lists over 500,000 properties ranging from studio apartments to actual castles and has served over ten million guests. In its last round of investment funding (April 2014), the company was valued at more than $10 billion—a level surpassed by only a handful of the world's greatest hotel chains.

In less than a decade, Airbnb has siphoned off a growing segment of customers from the traditional hospitality industry—all without owning a single hotel room of its own.

It's a tale of dramatic, unexpected change. Yet it's only one in a series of improbable industry upheavals that share a similar DNA:

- Smartphone-based car service Uber was launched in a single city (San Francisco) in March 2009. Less than five years later, it was valued by investors at over $50 billion, and is poised to challenge or replace the traditional taxi business in many of the more than 200 global cities it operates in—all without owning a single car.
- China-based retailing giant Alibaba features nearly a billion different products on just one of its many business portals (Taobao, a consumer-to-consumer marketplace similar to eBay) and has been

dubbed by *The Economist* "the world's biggest bazaar"—all without owning a single item of inventory.

- With over 1.5 billion subscribers visiting regularly to read news, look at photos, listen to music, and watch videos, Facebook garners an estimated $14 billion in annual advertising revenue (2015) and is arguably the world's biggest media company—all without producing a single piece of original content.

How can a major business segment be invaded and conquered in a matter of months by an upstart with none of the resources traditionally deemed essential for survival, let alone market dominance? And why is this happening today in one industry after another?

The answer is the *power of the platform*—a new business model that uses technology to connect people, organizations, and resources in an interactive ecosystem in which amazing amounts of value can be created and exchanged. Airbnb, Uber, Alibaba, and Facebook are just four examples from a list of disruptive platforms that includes Amazon, YouTube, eBay, Wikipedia, iPhone, Upwork, Twitter, KAYAK, Instagram, Pinterest, and dozens more. Each is unique and focused on a distinctive industry and market. And each has harnessed the power of the platform to transform a swath of the global economy. Many more comparable transformations are on the horizon.

The platform is a simple-sounding yet transformative concept that is radically changing business, the economy, and society at large. As we'll explain, practically any industry in which information is an important ingredient is a candidate for the platform revolution. That includes businesses whose "product" is information (like education and media) but also any business where access to information about customer needs, price fluctuations, supply and demand, and market trends has value—which includes almost every business.

So perhaps it's no wonder that the list of fastest-growing global brands is increasingly dominated by platform businesses. In fact, in 2014, three of the world's five largest firms as measured by market capitalization—Apple, Google, and Microsoft—all run platform business models. One of these, Google, debuted as a public company in

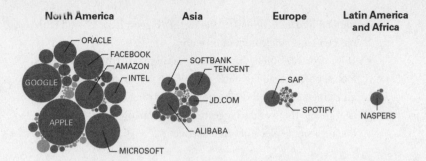

FIGURE 1.1. North America has more platform firms creating value, as measured by market capitalization, than any other region in the world. Platform firms in China, with its large, homogeneous market, are growing fast. Platform businesses in Europe, with its more fragmented market, have less than a quarter the value of such firms in North America, and the developing regions of Africa and Latin America are not far behind. Source: Peter Evans, Center for Global Enterprise.

2004. Another, Apple, nearly went bankrupt a few years earlier—when it still ran a closed business model rather than a platform. Now incumbent giants from Walmart and Nike to John Deere, GE, and Disney are all scrambling to adopt the platform approach to their businesses. To varying degrees, platform businesses are claiming a large and growing share of the economy in every region of the world (see Figure 1.1).

The disruptive power of platforms is also transforming the lives of individuals in ways that would have been impossible a few years ago:

- Joe Fairless was a New York advertising executive who dabbled in real estate investing on the side. Teaching a real estate class on Skillshare, an education platform, introduced Joe to hundreds of eager young investors and helped him hone his speaking skills—enabling him to raise over a million dollars to launch his own investment firm and quit the ad business.
- Taran Matharu was a twenty-two-year-old business student living in London when he decided to write a book during the

annual Novel Writing Month challenge. He posted excerpts on Wattpad, a story-sharing platform, and quickly attracted over five million readers. His first novel, *Summoner*, is being published in Britain and ten other countries, and Matharu is a full-time author.

- James Erwin was a software manual writer in Des Moines, Iowa, as well as a history buff. Browsing the community-based news platform Reddit one afternoon, he spotted a question about what would happen if a battalion of modern U.S. Marines took on the ancient Roman Empire. His typed response attracted eager followers and, within weeks, a movie deal. Erwin has now left his job to devote himself to screenwriting.

Teacher or lawyer, photographer or scientist, plumber or therapist—no matter what kind of work you do, the chances are good that a platform is poised to transform it, creating new opportunities and, in some cases, daunting new challenges.

The platform revolution is here—and the world it is ushering in is here to stay. But what exactly is a platform? What makes it unique? And what accounts for its remarkable transformative power? These are questions we'll begin to explore in the remainder of this chapter.

Let's start with a basic definition. A *platform* is a business based on enabling value-creating interactions between external producers and consumers. The platform provides an open, participative infrastructure for these interactions and sets governance conditions for them. The platform's overarching purpose: to consummate matches among users and facilitate the exchange of goods, services, or social currency, thereby enabling value creation for all participants.

Broken down in this way, the workings of platforms may seem simple enough. Yet today's platforms, empowered by digital technology that annihilates barriers of time and space, and employing smart, sophisticated software tools that connect producers and consumers more precisely, speedily, and easily than ever before, are producing results that are little short of miraculous.

THE PLATFORM REVOLUTION
AND THE SHAPE OF CHANGE

To understand the powerful forces that are being unleashed by the explosion of platform businesses, it helps to think about how value has long been created and transferred in most markets. The traditional system employed by most businesses is one we describe as a *pipeline*. By contrast with a platform, a pipeline is a business that employs a step-by-step arrangement for creating and transferring value, with producers at one end and consumers at the other. A firm first designs a product or service. Then the product is manufactured and offered for sale, or a system is put in place to deliver the service. Finally, a customer shows up and purchases the product or service. Because of its simple, single-track shape, we may also describe a pipeline business as a *linear value chain*.

In recent years, more and more businesses are shifting from the pipeline structure to the platform structure. In this shift, the simple pipeline arrangement is transformed into a complex relationship in which producers, consumers, and the platform itself enter into a variable set of relationships. In the world of platforms, different types of users—some of them producers, some of them consumers, and some of them people who may play both roles at various times—connect and conduct interactions with one another using the resources provided by the platform. In the process, they exchange, consume, and sometimes cocreate something of value. Rather than flowing in a straight line from producers to consumers, value may be created, changed, exchanged, and consumed in a variety of ways and places, all made possible by the connections that the platform facilitates.

Every platform operates differently, attracts different kinds of users, and creates different forms of value, but these same basic elements can be recognized in every platform business. In the mobile phone industry, for example, there are currently two major platforms—Apple's iOS and the Google-sponsored Android. Consumers who sign up for one of these platforms can consume value provided by the platform itself—for example, the image-making capability provided by the phone's built-in camera. But they can also consume value supplied by a set of developers who produce content for the platform to extend its functionality—for example, the value provided by an app that users access through Apple's iPhone. The result is an exchange of value that is made possible by the platform itself.

In itself, the shift from the traditional linear value chain to the complex value matrix of a platform may sound reasonably straightforward. But its implications are staggering. The spread of the platform model into one industry after another is causing a series of revolutionary changes in almost every aspect of business. Let's consider a few of these changes.

Platforms beat pipelines because platforms scale more efficiently by eliminating gatekeepers. Until recently, most businesses were built around products, which were designed and made at one end of the pipeline and delivered to consumers at the other end.* Today, plenty of pipeline-based businesses still exist—but when platform-based businesses enter the same marketplace, the platforms virtually always win.

One reason is that pipelines rely on inefficient gatekeepers to manage the flow of value from the producer to the consumer. In the traditional publishing industry, editors select a few books and authors from among the thousands offered to them and hope the ones they choose will prove to be popular. It's a time-consuming, labor-intensive process based mainly on instinct and guesswork. By contrast, Amazon's Kindle platform allows anyone to publish a book, relying on real-time consumer feedback to determine which books will succeed and which will fail. The platform system can grow to scale more rapidly and efficiently because the traditional gatekeepers—editors—are replaced by market signals provided automatically by the entire community of readers.

The elimination of gatekeepers also allows consumers greater freedom to select products that suit their needs. The traditional

* For simplicity's sake, we refer here to both products and services as "products." The main difference between the two is that products are tangible, physical objects, while services are intangible and delivered through activities. In traditional businesses, both are delivered through linear value chains—pipelines—which justifies our lumping them together in this discussion.

model of higher education forces students and their parents to pur-chase one-size-fits-all bundles that include administration, teaching, facilities, research, and much more. In their role as gatekeepers, uni-versities can require families to buy the entire package because it is the only way they can get the valuable certification that a degree offers. However, given the choice, many students would likely be selective in the services they consume. Once there is an alternate certification that employers are willing to accept, universities will find it increasingly challenging to maintain the bundle. Unsurpris-ingly, developing such an alternate certification is among the primary goals of platform education firms such as Coursera.

Consulting and law firms are also in the business of selling bundles. Firms might be willing to pay high prices for the services of experts. In order to gain access, they must also purchase the services of relatively junior staff at high markups. In the future, the most talented lawyers and consultants might work individually with firms and transact across a platform that can supply the back office and lower-level services once provided by a law or consult-ing firm. Platforms like Upwork are already making professional services available to prospective employers while eliminating the bundling effect imposed by traditional gatekeepers.

Platforms beat pipelines because platforms unlock new sources of value creation and supply. Consider how the hotel industry has tradi-tionally worked. Growth required hospitality firms like Hilton or Marriott to add additional rooms to sell through their existing brands using sophisticated back-office reservation and payments systems. This means continually scouting the real estate markets for promising territories, investing in existing properties or building new ones, and spending large sums to maintain, upgrade, expand, and improve them.

Upstart Airbnb is, in one sense, in the same business as Hilton or Marriott. Like the hotel giants, it uses refined pricing and booking systems designed to allow guests to find, reserve, and pay for rooms as they need them. But Airbnb applies the platform model to the hotel business: Airbnb *doesn't own any rooms.* Instead, it created and maintains the platform that allows individual participants to provide the rooms directly to consumers. In return, Airbnb takes a 9–15 percent (average 11 percent) transaction fee for every rental arranged through the platform.[1]

One implication is that growth can be much faster for Airbnb or any rival platform than for a traditional hotel company since growth is no longer constrained by the ability to deploy capital and manage physical assets. It may take years for a hotel chain to select and purchase a new piece of real estate, design and build a new resort, and hire and train staff. By contrast, Airbnb can increase its "inventory" of properties as quickly as it can sign up users with spare rooms to rent. As a result, in just a few years, Airbnb has achieved a scope and value that a traditional hotelier can hope to reach only after decades of often risky investment and hard work.

In platform markets, the nature of supply changes. Supply now unlocks spare capacity and harnesses contributions from the community which used to be only a source of demand. Whereas the leanest traditional businesses ran on just-in-time inventory, new organizational platforms run on not-even-mine inventory. If Hertz could deliver a car to an airport just as the plane arrived, it ran as well as could be expected. Now RelayRides borrows the car of a departing traveler in order to loan it to an arriving traveler. The person who used to pay to park an empty car now gets paid, complete with insurance, to let others use it. Everyone wins except Hertz and the other traditional car rental companies. TV stations built studios and hired staff to produce video. YouTube, operating a different business model, has more viewers than any station, and it uses content produced by the people who watch it. Everyone wins except the TV networks and movie studios that once had a near-monopoly on video production. Singapore-based Viki is challenging the traditional media value chain by using an open community of translators to add subtitles to Asian movies and soap operas. Viki then licenses the subtitled videos to distributors in other countries.

Thus, platforms disrupt the traditional competitive landscape by exposing new supply to the market. Hotels that must cover fixed costs find themselves competing with firms that have no fixed costs. This works for the new firms because there is spare capacity that can be brought to market through the assistance of the platform intermediary. The *sharing economy* is built on the idea that many items, such as automobiles, boats, and even lawnmowers, sit idle most of the time. Before the rise of the platform, it might have been possible to loan something to a family member, close friend, or neighbor, but much harder to loan to a stranger. This is because it would be difficult to trust that your home would be left in good shape (Airbnb), your car would be returned undamaged (RelayRides), or your lawnmower would come back (NeighborGoods).

The effort necessary to individually verify credit- and trustworthiness is an example of the high transaction costs that used to prevent exchange. By providing default insurance contracts and reputation systems to encourage good behavior, platforms dramatically lower transaction costs and create new markets as new producers start producing for the first time.

Platforms beat pipelines by using data-based tools to create community feedback loops. We've seen how the Kindle platform relies on reactions from the community of readers to determine which books will be widely read and which will not. Platforms of all kinds rely on similar feedback loops. Platforms like Airbnb and YouTube use such feedback loops to compete with traditional hotels and television channels. As these platforms gather community signals about the quality of content (in the case of YouTube) or the reputation of service providers (on Airbnb), subsequent market interactions become increasingly efficient. Feedback from other consumers makes it easy to find videos or rental properties that are likely to suit your needs. Products that receive overwhelmingly negative feedback usually disappear from the platform completely.

By contrast, traditional pipeline firms rely on mechanisms of control—editors, managers, supervisors—to ensure quality and shape market interactions. These control mechanisms are costly and inefficient to grow to scale.

Wikipedia's success demonstrates that platforms can leverage community feedback to replace a traditional supply chain. Reference works like the venerable *Encyclopaedia Britannica* were once created through costly, complex, difficult-to-manage centralized supply chains of academic experts, writers, and editors. Using the platform model, Wikipedia has built an information source comparable to *Britannica* in quality and scope by leveraging a community of external contributors to grow and police the content.

Platforms invert the firm. Because the bulk of a platform's value is created by its community of users, the platform business must shift its focus from internal activities to external activities. In the process, the firm *inverts*—it turns inside out, with functions from marketing to information technology to operations to strategy all increasingly centering on people, resources, and functions that exist *outside* the business, complementing or replacing those that exist inside a traditional business.

The language used to describe this process of inversion differs from one business function to another. In marketing, for example, Rob Cain, the CIO of Coca-Cola, notes that the key terms used to define systems of message delivery have shifted from *broadcast* to *segmentation*, and then to *virality* and *social influence*; from *push* to *pull*; and from *outbound* to *inbound.* All these terminological changes reflect the fact that marketing messages once disseminated by company employees and agents now spread via consumers themselves—a reflection of the inverted nature of communication in a world dominated by platforms.[2]

Similarly, information technology systems have evolved from back-office enterprise resource planning (ERP) systems to front-office consumer relationship management (CRM) systems and, most recently, to out-of-the-office experiments using social media and big data—another shift from inward focus to outward focus. Finance is shifting its focus from shareholder value and discounted cash flows of assets owned by the firm to stakeholder value and the role of interactions that take place outside the firm.

Operations management has likewise shifted from optimizing the firm's inventory and supply chain systems to managing external assets the firm doesn't directly control. Tom Goodwin, senior vice president of strategy for Havas Media, describes this change succinctly: "Uber, the world's largest taxi company, owns no vehicles. Facebook, the world's most popular media owner, creates no content. Alibaba, the most valuable retailer, has no inventory. And Airbnb, the world's largest accommodation provider, owns no real estate."[3] The community provides these resources.

Strategy has moved from controlling unique internal resources and erecting competitive barriers to orchestrating external resources and engaging vibrant communities. And innovation is no longer the province of in-house experts and research and development labs, but is produced through crowdsourcing and the contribution of ideas by independent participants in the platform.

External resources don't completely replace internal resources—more often they serve as a complement. But platform firms emphasize ecosystem governance more than product optimization, and persuasion of outside partners more than control of internal employees.

THE PLATFORM REVOLUTION: HOW WILL YOU RESPOND?

As you'll see in this book, the rise of the platform is driving transformations in almost every corner of the economy and of society as a whole, from education, media, and the professions to health care, energy, and government. Figure 1.2 is a necessarily incomplete table of some notable current arenas of platform activity, along with examples of some of the platform enterprises at work in those industry sectors. Note that platforms are continually evolving, that many platforms serve more than one purpose, and that new platform companies are appearing every day. Many of the businesses listed here are likely to be familiar to you; some may not be. The stories behind a number of them will be recounted in this book. Our goal here is to provide not a comprehensive or systematic overview but simply a sketch which we hope will convey the growing scope and importance of platform companies on the world stage.

INDUSTRY	EXAMPLES
Agriculture	John Deere, Intuit Fasal
Communication and Networking	LinkedIn, Facebook, Twitter, Tinder, Instagram, Snapchat, WeChat
Consumer Goods	Philips, McCormick Foods FlavorPrint
Education	Udemy, Skillshare, Coursera, edX, Duolingo
Energy and Heavy Industry	Nest, Tesla Powerwall, General Electric, EnerNOC
Finance	Bitcoin, Lending Club, Kickstarter
Health Care	Cohealo, SimplyInsured, Kaiser Permanente
Gaming	Xbox, Nintendo, PlayStation
Labor and Professional Services	Upwork, Fiverr, 99designs, Sittercity, LegalZoom
Local Services	Yelp, Foursquare, Groupon, Angie's List
Logistics and Delivery	Munchery, Foodpanda, Haier Group
Media	Medium, Viki, YouTube, Wikipedia, Huffington Post, Kindle Publishing
Operating Systems	iOS, Android, MacOS, Microsoft Windows
Retail	Amazon, Alibaba, Walgreens, Burberry, Shopkick
Transportation	Uber, Waze, BlaBlaCar, GrabTaxi, Ola Cabs
Travel	Airbnb, TripAdvisor

FIGURE 1.2. Some of the industry sectors currently being transformed by platform businesses, along with examples of platform companies working in those arenas.

Figure 1.2 also suggests the remarkable diversity of platform businesses. At a glance, there doesn't seem to be much that companies like Twitter and General Electric, Xbox and TripAdvisor, Instagram and John Deere all have in common. Yet all are operating businesses that share the fundamental platform DNA—they all exist to create matches and facilitate interactions among producers and consumers, whatever the goods being exchanged may be.

As a result of the rise of the platform, almost all the traditional business management practices—including strategy, operations, marketing, production, research and development, and human resources—are in a state of upheaval. We are in a disequilibrium time that affects every company and individual business leader. The coming of the world of platforms is a major reason why.

Consequently, platform expertise has now become an essential attribute for business leadership. Yet most people—including many business leaders—are still struggling to come to grips with the rise of the platform.

In the chapters that follow, we'll provide a comprehensive guide to the platform business model and its growing impact on practically every sector of the economy. The insights we'll share are based on extensive research as well as our experience as consultants working with platform businesses large and small, in a wide range of industries and nonprofit arenas in countries around the world.

You'll learn precisely how platforms work, the varying structures they assume, the numerous forms of value they create, and the almost limitless range of users they serve. If you're interested in starting your own platform business—or in modifying an existing organization to take advantage of the power of the platform—this book will serve as a manual to help you navigate the complexities of designing, launching, managing, governing, and growing a successful platform. And if running a platform business isn't for you, you'll learn how the growing impact of platforms is likely to affect you as a businessperson, a professional, a consumer, and a citizen—and how you can participate happily (and profitably) in an economy increasingly dominated by platforms of every type.

No matter what role you play in today's rapidly changing economy, now is the time for you to master the principles of the world of platforms. Turn the page, and we'll help you do just that.

TAKEAWAYS FROM CHAPTER ONE

❑ A platform's overarching purpose is to consummate matches among users and facilitate the exchange of goods, services, or social currency, thereby enabling *value creation* for all participants.

❑ Because platform businesses create value using resources they don't own or control, they can grow much faster than traditional businesses.

❑ Platforms derive much of their value from the communities they serve.

❑ Platforms invert companies, blurring business boundaries and transforming firms' traditional inward focus into an outward focus.

❑ The rise of the platform has already transformed many major industries—and more, equally important transformations are on the way.

2

NETWORK EFFECTS
The Power of the Platform

For several weeks in June 2014, a very public debate over a seemingly arcane topic raged between a famous finance professor at New York University and a renowned venture capitalist in Silicon Valley.

Aswath Damodaran—a chaired professor at NYU, author of textbooks on corporate finance and valuation, and the 2013 recipient of the prestigious Herbert Simon Award—launched the debate when he published an article estimating the value of Uber, the platform company whose smartphone app connects riders with drivers. Earlier that month, investors had ponied up $1.2 billion in financial capital for Uber, receiving in return a share of the company that suggested the overall value of the business was around $17 billion. Damodaran called this "a mind-boggling sum for a young company with only a few hundred million in revenue."[1] He implied that the idea that Uber was worth this much—or even more, as some were claiming—was yet another mark of Silicon Valley hubris.

Damodaran's judgment was based on the classic tools of finance. He estimated the size of the global taxi market, Uber's prospective market share, and the revenues this was likely to yield. Then he used risk-adjusted cash flows to come up with a company valuation of $5.9 billion. With admirable forthrightness, he even posted his spreadsheet online so others could examine and test his assumptions.

Bill Gurley, a partner at Benchmark Capital and one of Uber's Silicon Valley investors, took up the challenge. A venture capitalist famous for having been among the first to spot such technology skyrockets as OpenTable, Zillow, and eBay, Gurley argued that the $17 billion valuation was likely an *underestimate*, and that Damodaran's figure could be short by a factor of 25.[2] Gurley questioned Damodaran's assumptions about both the total market size and Uber's potential market share, basing his calculations on economist W. Brian Arthur's analysis of network effects.[3]

In classic platform style, Uber performs a matching service. It helps riders find drivers, and vice versa. As drivers sign on and coverage density rises within a city, a number of striking growth dynamics are set in motion. Riders tell their friends about the service; some even start driving themselves in their spare time. Wait time falls for riders, and downtime falls for drivers. Less downtime means that a driver can make the same amount of money even if fares are lower, because he has more riders during the same number of working hours. Thus, less downtime means that Uber can cut fares and stimulate even more demand, which creates a virtuous cycle that increases coverage density still further.

In his article, Gurley reproduced a graphic from another investor that illustrates how this virtuous cycle works—a napkin sketch created by David Sacks, co-founder of Yammer and veteran of PayPal (Figure 2.1).

Sacks's napkin sketch captures a classic example of *network effects*. It shows how the value of Uber to each of its participants grows the more people use it—which attracts still more users, thereby increasing the value of the service even more.

Network effects refers to the impact that the number of users of a platform has on the value created for each user. *Positive network effects* refers to the ability of a large, well-managed platform community to produce significant value for each user of the platform. *Negative network effects* refers to the possibility that the growth in numbers of a poorly-managed platform community can *reduce* the value produced for each user.

As we'll see, positive network effects are the main source of value creation and competitive advantage in a platform business. However, network effects can also be negative, and in this chapter we'll explain how and why negative network effects arise and what

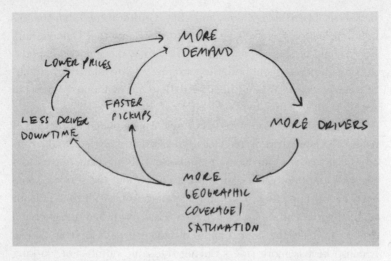

FIGURE 2.1. David Sacks's napkin sketch of Uber's virtuous cycle. Reprinted by permission.

platform business managers can do about them. But understanding value creation via positive network effects is the essential first step.

Gurley's data showed that, by mid-2014, network effects were already beginning to drive Uber's growth. When Travis Kalanick, CEO of Uber, sought seed funding in 2009, the size of the taxi and limousine market in Uber's hometown of San Francisco was $120 million. Based on Uber's own data, the market in 2014 appeared already to be three times as large and still growing. This threefold multiple would, all by itself, justify increasing Damodaran's $5.9 billion valuation to the $17 billion value imputed by investors. Unaware of this insider information, Damodaran hadn't adjusted his equations for network effects—as he graciously conceded in an elegant and well-reasoned response.

DEMAND ECONOMIES OF SCALE

The network effect represents a new economic phenomenon, driven by technological innovation. In the twentieth-century industrial era, giant monopolies were created based on *supply economies of scale*. These are driven by production efficiencies, which reduce the unit cost of creating a product or service as the quantities produced increase. These supply economies of scale can give the largest company in an industrial economy a cost advantage that is extremely difficult for competitors to overcome.

Consider some of the giant businesses that grew up during the industrial era. In steel production, the British Bessemer process of blowing air through molten slag removed impurities and cut costs of production from £40 to £7 per ton. Operating eighteen five-ton Bessemer blast furnaces, Barrow Hematite Steel Company became the largest steel mill in the world at the turn of the twentieth century. Similarly, the German Haber-Bosch process of producing fertilizer from nitrogen in air, which is used in the production of half of all foodstuffs consumed today, was one factor contributing to rise of giant BASF, which is still the world's largest chemical company. And American Thomas Edison's inventions in lighting and cheap power generation gave rise to General Electric, while Henry Ford's use of mass production accelerated the rise of Ford Motor Company. The bigger the business, the cheaper the costs of production, marketing, and distribution—a positive spiral that helped companies grow steadily larger and more profitable (until the process was derailed by government intervention or disruptive technological change that rendered the old economies obsolete).

In the twenty-first-century Internet era, comparable monopolies are being created by *demand economies of scale* (a term used by the two experts largely responsible for popularizing the concept of network effects, Hal Varian, the chief economist at Google, and business professor Carl Shapiro).[4] By contrast with supply economies of scale, demand economies of scale take advantage of technological improvements on the demand side—the other half of the profit equation from the production side. Demand economies of scale are driven by efficiencies in social networks, demand aggregation, app development, and other phenomena that make bigger networks more valuable to their users. They can give the largest company in a platform market a network effect advantage that is extremely difficult for competitors to overcome.

Demand economies of scale are the fundamental source of positive network effects, and thus the chief drivers of economic value in today's world. This is not to say that supply economies of scale no longer matter; of course they do. But demand economies of scale, in the form of network effects, have become the most important differentiating factor.

Metcalfe's law is a useful way of encapsulating how network effects create value for those who participate in a network as well as for those who own or manage the network. Robert Metcalfe, co-inventor of Ethernet and founder of 3Com, pointed out that the value of a telephone network grows nonlinearly as the number of subscribers to the network increases, making more connections among subscribers possible.

When there's only one node in a network, no connections are possible. An MIT professor we know likes to joke that the prize for "greatest salesperson in history" should go to whoever sold the *first* telephone. Arguably, it had zero value, because when there's only one telephone in the world, you can't call anyone. But as more people buy telephones, the value grows. With two telephones, one connection is possible. With four telephones, six. With twelve, sixty-six. And with 100 telephones, there are 4,950 connections. This is known as *nonlinear* or *convex growth,* and it is precisely the characteristic growth pattern seen in companies like Microsoft in the 1990s, Apple and Facebook today, and Uber tomorrow. (Working in reverse, it explains the *convex collapse* of Blackberry in the 2000s: as users began to flee the Blackberry platform, the loss of network nodes caused the value of the network itself to plummet, encouraging still more people to abandon Blackberry for other devices.)

Major economic consequences follow from this pattern. Growth via network effects leads to market expansion. New buyers enter the market, attracted by the growing number of friends who are part of the network. If prices also fall—as they often do when technology matures and production quantities increase—then network effects work together with more attractive pricing to drive massive market adoption.

TWO-SIDED NETWORK EFFECTS

David Sacks's napkin sketch suggests a second dynamic at work in the growth of Uber, one we refer to as a *two-sided network effect*.[5] In Metcalfe's telephone example, phone users attract more phone users. But in the case of Uber, two sides of the market are involved: riders attract drivers, and drivers attract riders. A similar dynamic can be seen in many other platform businesses. In the case of Google's Android, app developers attract consumers, and consumers attract app developers. On Upwork (formerly known as Elance-oDesk), job listings attract freelancers, and freelancers attract job listings. On PayPal, sellers attract buyers, and buyers attract sellers. And on Airbnb, hosts attract guests, and guests attract hosts. All of these businesses attract two-sided network effects with *positive feedback*.

The importance of these effects for stimulating network growth is so great that platform businesses will often spend money to attract participants to one side of the market. They know that, if they can get one side to join the platform, the other side will follow. Two-sided network effects with positive feedback explain how Uber can afford to use millions of dollars of money from Bill Gurley and other investors to give away free rides worth $30 each. Uber's coupons buy market share in a way that attracts a virtuous cycle of drivers and riders who will later pay full price to participate in the network.

A familiar (non-tech) example is a local bar that holds a weekly Ladies' Night, when discounted drinks are offered to female customers. When the women show up, the men appear— and they're happy to buy their own drinks at full price. Thus, in a two-sided market, it can sometimes make economic sense to accept financial losses—not just temporarily, but permanently!—in Market A if growing that market enables growth in a related Market B. The only proviso is that the profits to be earned in Market B must outweigh the losses incurred in Market A.

NETWORK EFFECTS VERSUS
OTHER GROWTH-BUILDING TOOLS

It's important to distinguish network effects from other familiar market-building tools, such as *price effects* and *brand effects*. Misunderstanding of these distinctions is a source of the current confusion over how to value platform business models, and contributed to the dot-com boom and bust of 1997–2000.

During the dot-com boom, investors in startups like eToys, Webvan, and FreePC regarded market share as practically the only significant metric of business success. Captivated by slogans like "Get big fast" and "Get large or get lost," they urged companies to spend lavishly to lure customers in hopes of achieving an insurmountable market share advantage. The companies responded: for example, via discounting and couponing, they created price effects. Attracting customers through extraordinarily low pricing—as low as zero in some cases—is a foolproof way of buying market share, at least temporarily. Books like the bestselling *Free: The Future of a Radical Price*, published in 2009 by Chris Anderson, then the editor-in-chief of *Wired* magazine, preached the gospel of the giveaway, positing a steady climb from "free" to "premium" to "freemium" (free + premium) pricing of the product or service.

The problem is that price effects are evanescent. They disappear the moment the discounts end or another firm offers a better price. Typically, only 1–2 percent of customers convert from free to paying. Thus, as David Cohen, CEO and founder of the venture incubator Techstars, says, you need to reach millions of customers before the giveaway model becomes profitable.[6] Freemium models also create freeloaders than can be hard to monetize (that is, to profit from), as FreePC discovered in 1999 when it gave away free Pentium PCs in exchange for viewing ads and the prospect of online sales.[7]

Brand effects are stickier. They arise when people come to associate a particular brand with quality. But brand effects, like price effects, are often difficult to sustain. They can also be extremely expensive. EToys spent millions to establish a brand in hopes of competing with Amazon and Toys"R"Us. Kozmo, an online company that promised free one-hour delivery of food, books, coffee, and other basic goods in major U.S. cities, hired actress Whoopi Goldberg as a spokesperson and paid her in stock, only to have the business collapse soon thereafter. In January 2000—the peak before the dot-com crash—nineteen startups bought Super Bowl ads, spending over $2 million each in order to build brand recognition. A decade or so later, eight of them no longer existed.[8]

Price effects and brand effects have their place in a startup's growth strategy. But only network effects create the virtuous cycle we described above, which leads to the building of a longlasting network of users—a phenomenon we called *lock-in*.

Another growth-building tool that's easy to confuse with network effects is *virality*. Derived from the expression "going viral," virality is the tendency of an idea or brand to be circulated rapidly and widely from one Internet user to another.

Virality can attract people to a network—for example, when fans of an irresistibly cute, funny, or startling video persuade their friends to visit YouTube. But network effects keep them there. Virality is about attracting people who are off the platform and enticing them to join it, while network effects are about increasing value among people on-platform.

When the dot-com boom turned to bust in 2000, two of the authors of this book (Geoff Parker and Marshall Van Alstyne) were recent PhD graduates from MIT. We watched the cycle with fascination, observing as smart investment firms like Benchmark and Sequoia made both lucrative hits and expensive misses. (Benchmark Capital, the venture capital firm that is now getting it right in the case of Uber, invested in Webvan, which was listed by CNET as one of the biggest dot-com disasters in history,[9] as did Sequoia Capital, which nonetheless got it right with Apple, Google, and PayPal.)

Curious about what separated the successful companies from those that failed, we examined dozens of cases and found that the failures mostly relied on price or brand effects. By contrast, the successes hit on an idea that really worked—driving traffic from one user group in order to drive profits from another user group. We described our findings in a paper that analyzed the mathematics of two-sided network effects.[10] Today, such successful platform businesses as eBay, Uber, Airbnb, Upwork, PayPal, and Google exhibit this model extensively.[11]

SCALING NETWORK EFFECTS: FRICTIONLESS ENTRY AND OTHER SCALABILITY TOOLS

As you can see, network effects depend on the size of the network.[12] So one important corollary is that *effective platforms are able to expand in size quickly and easily, thereby scaling the value that derives from network effects.*

It's hard to remember now, but there was a time when Yahoo was a more popular portal to the Internet than Google. The story of how Google overtook Yahoo—despite the latter's four-year head start—vividly illustrates the importance of being able to scale both sides of a network.

Yahoo started out as a human-edited database. It classified web pages using a tree structure of subcategories within categories the same way librarians organize books or biologists organize plant and animal species. This worked well for a time. But during the 1990s and early 2000s, growth in Internet users and web page producers increased exponentially—and it soon became apparent that employee-edited hierarchical databases do not scale well.[13] One of the authors recalls submitting web pages to Yahoo, then waiting days and weeks until the results showed up in master lists. (No wonder frustrated users began claiming that Yahoo stood for "Yet Another Hierarchical Officious Oracle!")

By contrast, Google found a way to serve web page searchers by harnessing the work of web page producers. Google's page rank algorithm considers the extent to which web pages link to one another. To attract page viewers, page producers already consider what viewers want. More links from more important pages mean higher-priority search results. Therefore, Google's algorithm effectively matches both sides of the network. Not only do algorithms scale better than employees, but using web links as the key sorting tool shifted the focus from inside the firm to outside the firm, where the choices of the crowd could control the action—a far more scalable model than Yahoo's.

As the story of Google suggests, networks that permit *frictionless entry* are able to grow organically almost without bound. Frictionless entry is the ability of users to quickly and easily join a platform and begin participating in the value creation that the platform facilitates. Frictionless entry is a key factor in enabling a platform to grow rapidly.

Threadless is a T-shirt company founded by people with expertise in information technology services, web design, and consulting. Their business model involves holding weekly design contests open to outside participants, printing only T-shirts with the most popular designs, and selling them to their large and growing customer base. Threadless doesn't need to hire artistic talent, since skilled designers compete for prizes and prestige. It doesn't need to do marketing, since eager designers contact their friends to solicit votes and sales. It doesn't need to forecast sales, since voting customers have already announced what numbers they will buy. By outsourcing production, Threadless can also minimize its handling and inventory costs. Thanks to this almost frictionless model, Threadless can scale rapidly and easily, with minimal structural restrictions.

Threadless's business model arose by accident. The founders originally thought they were in the web services business, selling consulting to firms who needed websites. But selling web consulting didn't scale: each project had to be negotiated individually, each project required dedicated staff, and after completion, no project could be resold without modification. The company founders launched the T-shirt contest website as a side project to illustrate their capabilities. It was simply an online copy of an offline contest that one of the founders had entered. When this side venture exploded in popularity, its enormous scalability advantages became obvious.

Scaling a network requires that both sides of the market grow proportionally. For example, one Uber driver can serve an average of about three Uber riders an hour. It would make no sense for Uber to have one rider and 1,000 drivers—nor 1,000 riders and one driver. Airbnb faces a parallel issue in scaling both hosts and guests. If one side becomes disproportionally large, coupons or discounting to attract more participants to the other side becomes good business.

In some cases, the growth of a platform can be facilitated by an effect we call *side switching*. This occurs when users of one side of the platform join the opposite side—for example, when those who consume goods or services begin to produce goods and services for others to consume. On some platforms, users engage in side switching easily and repeatedly.

Uber, for example, recruits new drivers from among its rider pool, just as Airbnb recruits new hosts from among its guest pool. A scalable business model, frictionless entry, and side switching all serve to lubricate network effects.

NEGATIVE NETWORK EFFECTS: THEIR CAUSE AND CURE

So far, we've been focusing on positive network effects. But the very qualities that lead platform networks to grow so quickly may also lead them to fail quickly. The growth of a network can produce negative network effects that drive away participants, even leading to the death of a platform business.

One negative network effect occurs when the growth in numbers that enables more matches between producers and consumers also leads to increasing difficulty, or impossibility, in finding the best match. To avoid this dilemma, frictionless entry must be balanced through effective *curation*. This is the process by which a platform filters, controls, and limits the access of users to the platform, the activities they participate in, and the connections they form with other users. When the quality of a platform is effectively curated, users find it easy to make matches that produce significant value for them; when curation is nonexistent or poorly handled, users find it difficult to identify potentially valuable matches amid a flood of worthless matches.

Dating platform OkCupid discovered that scale can cause network collapse if not carefully managed. According to CEO Christian

Rudder, when you get lots of users on a dating website, the natural tendency of men on the platform is to approach the most beautiful women. Scaling male behavior creates the problem that most of the men who approach a highly attractive woman will be markedly *less* attractive—she is "out of their league," as the saying goes. When these B-level males (our description, not Rudder's!) bombard the A-level females with requests for a date, no one is happy. The beautiful females are unhappy and likely to abandon the site because of all the unfiltered attention, while the B-level males are unhappy because the women of their choice never respond. And the few highly attractive men who might have been a good match for the most attractive women are unhappy because the women they want have left the platform.[14]

Once this happens, the men at all attractiveness levels converge on the women in the second most beautiful tier, and the whole process repeats. Network effects reverse, and the business model breaks down.

To solve this problem, OkCupid implemented a curation strategy involving multiple levels of network matching. The first level addresses the obvious issue of matching compatible interests. Do both parties smoke? Do both parties like tattoos and horror movies? Do both parties believe in dinosaurs? This level eliminates many clearly unsuitable matches and reduces the number of participants in the process.

The second matching level addresses the question of comparative attractiveness—the "in her league" question. If OkCupid's algorithm determines, based on reactions by other users, that Joe is significantly less attractive than Mary (for example), then Joe's routine search for matches will not turn up Mary's picture. (She might show up in a highly targeted search, but not otherwise.) Instead, Joe will be presented with a selection of women thought to be comparable to him in attractiveness. The result is win-win. Mary is happier because the platform helps her find what she's looking for while protecting her from an onslaught. And Joe is happier, too, because women are returning his messages when previously he got the cold shoulder.

Of course, the use of this algorithm means that, if a guy only sees pictures of average-looking women when conducting an OkCupid search, he probably doesn't have the movie-star good looks he thought he had. But his chances for a successful match have greatly increased, which should lead in the long run to a higher level of satisfaction.

Skillful curation like that practiced by OkCupid greatly reduces negative network effects. At the same time, it increases and leverages the benefits of positive network effects. As the number of participants in the network grows, the volume of information about them increases. As any statistician will tell you, having more data to work with generally increases the accuracy and value of the inferences you can draw from the data. Thus, the larger your network grows, the better your curation can become—a phenomenon we refer to as *data-driven network effects*. Of course, this is dependent on having well-designed curation tools that are continually tested, updated, and improved.

By contrast, poor curation leads to greater noise, which makes the platform less useful and may even cause it to unravel. Such a negative feedback loop following the exponential growth of Chatroulette quickly led to an equally dramatic collapse.

Chatroulette pairs random people from around the world for webcam conversations. People can leave a conversation at any time by initiating a new connection or simply by quitting. The strangely addictive site grew from twenty people at launch in late 2009 to more than 1.5 million users six months later.

Initially, Chatroulette had no registration requirement and no controls of any kind, leading to what became known as the Naked Hairy Men problem. As the network grew without policing, a growing number of naked hairy men showed up to chat, leading many of the non-naked, non-hairy others to abandon the network. As legitimate users fled, the noise level on the platform increased, setting a negative feedback loop in motion.

Chatroulette realized it needed to curate access in a way that scales with platform growth. The platform now lets users filter other users in addition to using algorithms to screen callers with undesirable images, and it is growing again—though more slowly than during its initial phase.

Every successful platform faces the problem of matching content and connections at scale—which means that, at some point in its growth, every successful platform must address the challenge of effective curation. We'll return to the issue of curation in later chapters.

FOUR KINDS OF NETWORK EFFECTS

A two-sided network (i.e., one with both producers and consumers) has four kinds of network effects. It's important to understand and consider all four when designing and managing a platform.

In a two-sided market, *same-side effects* are network effects created by the impact of users from one side of the market on other users from the same side of the market—the effects that consumers have on other consumers and those that producers have on other producers. By contrast, *cross-side effects* are network effects created by the impact of users from one side of the market on users from the other side of the market—the effects that consumers have on producers and those that producers have on consumers. Both same-side effects and cross-side effects can be positive or negative, depending on the design of the system and the rules put in place. Here's how these four types of network effects work.

The first category, *positive same-side effects*, includes the positive benefits received by users when the number of users of the same kind increases—for example, the effect that arose as the number of subscribers to the Bell Telephone network grew. The more of your friends and neighbors who were accessible on "the Bell," the greater the value you received from your Bell membership. Today, a comparable positive effect on the consumer-to-consumer side can be seen with a gaming platform like the Xbox MMOG: the more fellow gamers you encounter on the platform, the greater the fun you experience when using it.

Positive same-side effects can also be found on the producer side. For example, consider Adobe's all-but-universal image production and sharing platform. The more people who are creating and sharing images using the PDF platform, the greater the benefit you get from using the same platform for your own image production needs.

However, not all same-side effects are positive. Sometimes there is a downside to the numbers growth on one side of a platform. This is called a *negative same-side effect*. For example, consider the information technology platform Covisint, which connects businesses that are interested in developing cloud-based networking tools with service providers. As the number of competing suppliers on the Covisint platform grows, customers are attracted to the platform, which makes the suppliers happy. But when the list of suppliers grows too great, it becomes more difficult for appropriate providers and customers to find one another.

Cross-side effects arise when either consumers or producers gain or lose based on the number of users on the *opposite* side of the platform. *Positive cross-side effects* occur when users benefit from an increase in the number of participants on the other side of the market. Think about a payment mechanism like Visa: when more merchants (producers) agree to accept the Visa card, the flexibility and convenience of the shopping experience increases for shoppers (consumers), creating a positive cross-side effect. The same effect works in the opposite direction, of course; more Visa cardholders lead to more potential customers for merchants. In a similar way, when the number of app developers for Windows grows, the versatility and power of the operating system increases for users; and when the number of Windows users grows, so do the potential benefits (financial and otherwise) for app developers. Positive cross-side effects produce win-win results.

Of course, cross-side effects are not necessarily symmetrical. On OkCupid, women attract men more than men attract women. On Uber, a single driver is more critical to growth than a single rider. On Android, a single developer's app attracts users more than a single user attracts developer apps. On Twitter, the vast majority of people read, while a minority tweet. On question-and-answer networks like Quora, the vast majority asks questions, while a minority answers them.[15]

Again, however, there is the dark side to consider—the situation in which *negative cross-side effects* arise. Think about a platform that facilitates the sharing of digital media—music, text, images, videos, and the like. In most circumstances, a growing number of producers (music companies, for example) leads to positive benefits for consumers, but it can also lead to growing complexity and expense—for example, too many varying digital rights management forms to read and accept. When this happens, the cross-side effects flip from positive to negative, leading consumers to abandon the platform or at least reduce their usage. In a similar way, when the proliferation of messages from competing merchants on a platform site leads to unpleasant advertising clutter, the positive impact of expanding producer choice may be transformed into a negative cross-side effect that turns off consumers and damages the platform's value.

We can foresee the arrival of growing pains at Uber as a result of increasing negative cross-side effects. If Uber attracts too many drivers relative to the number of riders, driver downtimes will go up; if Uber attracts too many riders relative to drivers, rider wait times will go up (see Figure 2.2, in which the resulting feedback loops have been inserted).

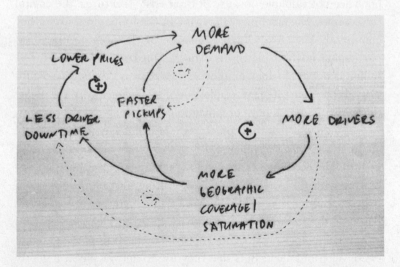

FIGURE 2.2. David Sacks's napkin sketch of Uber, with negative feedback loops inserted.

In fact, this is happening already. As Uber reaches saturation within a given market, too many drivers conflict with one another, increasing downtimes and causing some drivers to abandon the market. The more complete depiction of Uber's growth spiral in Figure 2.2 highlights the fact that a firm in a two-sided market must manage all four network effects. Good platform husbandry seeks to reinforce positive network effects, creating and strengthening as many positive feedback loops as possible. This is another topic we'll return to in later chapters, where we'll offer specific advice about how to manage these challenges effectively.

STRUCTURAL CHANGE: NETWORK EFFECTS TURN FIRMS INSIDE OUT

As we've seen, in the industrial era, giant companies relied on supply-side economies of scale. By contrast, most Internet era giants rely on demand-side economies of scale. Firms such as Airbnb, Uber, Dropbox, Threadless, Upwork, Google, and Facebook are not valuable because of their cost structures: the capital they employ, the machinery they run, or the human resources they command. They are valuable because of the communities that participate in their platforms. The reason Instagram sold for $1 billion is not its thirteen employees; the reason WhatsApp sold for $19 billion wasn't its fifty employees. The reasons were the same: the network effects both organizations had created.

Standard accounting practices might not factor the value of communities into the value of a firm, but stock markets do. Little by little, the accountants are catching up. A team of experts collaborating with the consulting and accounting firm of Deloitte published research that sorts companies into four broad categories based on their chief economic activity: asset builders, service providers, technology creators, and network orchestrators. Asset builders develop physical assets that they use to deliver physical goods; companies like Ford and Walmart are examples. Service providers employ workers who provide services to customers; companies like

UnitedHealthcare and Accenture are examples. Technology creators develop and sell forms of intellectual property, such as software and biotechnology; Microsoft and Amgen are examples. And network orchestrators develop networks in which people and companies create value together—in effect, platform businesses. The research suggests that, of the four, network orchestrators are by far the most efficient value creators. On average, they enjoy a market multiplier (based on the relationship between a firm's market valuation and its price-to-earnings ratio) of 8.2, as compared with 4.8 for technology creators, 2.6 for service providers, and 2.0 for asset builders.[16] It's only a slight simplification to say that that quantitative difference represents the value produced by network effects.

Furthermore, where network effects are present, industries operate by different rules.[17] One reason is that it is far easier to scale network effects outside a firm than inside it—since there are always many more people outside a firm than inside it. Thus, where network effects are present, the focus of organizational attention must shift from inside to outside. The firm inverts; it turns inside out. The management of human resources shifts from employees to crowds.[18] Innovation shifts from in-house R & D to open innovation.[19] The primary venue for activities in which value is created for participants shifts from an internal production department to a collection of external producers and consumers—which means that management of *externalities* becomes a key leadership skill. Growth comes not from horizontal integration and vertical integration but from functional integration and network orchestration. The focus on processes such as finance and accounting shifts from cash flows and assets you can own to communities and assets you can influence. And while platform businesses themselves are often extraordinarily profitable, the chief locus of wealth creation is now outside rather than inside the organization.

Network effects are creating the giants of the twenty-first century. Google and Facebook each touch more than one-seventh of the world's population. *In the world of network effects, ecosystems of users are the new source of competitive advantage and market dominance.*

TAKEAWAYS FROM CHAPTER TWO

❑ Whereas giant industrial-era firms were made possible by supply economies of scale, today's giants are made possible by demand economies of scale—expressed as network effects.

❑ Network effects are not the same as price effects, brand effects, or other familiar growth-building tools.

❑ Frictionless entry and other features of scalability maximize the value-building impact of network effects.

❑ A two-sided market (with both producers and consumers) gives rise to four kinds of network effects: same-side effects (positive and negative) and cross-side effects (positive and negative). A growing platform business must manage all four.

❑ The key to minimizing most negative network effects is quality curation, which increases the chances of a happy match between producer and consumer.

3

ARCHITECTURE

Principles for Designing
a Successful Platform

How do we build a platform that invites participation and creates significant value for all its users? How do we provide tools and services that make it easy for producers and consumers to interact in mutually rewarding ways? And how do we design a technological infrastructure that is capable of scaling rapidly, and encouraging positive network effects while minimizing negative ones?

These are daunting challenges. Platforms are complex, multi-sided systems that must support large networks of users who play different roles and interact in a wide variety of ways. An industry-wide platform—a platform for the health care industry, for example—may need to facilitate interactions among an enormous range of industry participants with motivations that vary widely and change frequently as economic, regulatory, and technological circumstances evolve.

Designers and builders of any complex system often find it difficult to identify a logical starting point. This problem is particularly acute with platform businesses, since they are less familiar and much more complicated than pipeline businesses, which generally feature a straightforward linear design. The natural tendency of those charged with creating a new platform business is to study similar implementations and imitate them. But because no two markets are identical, this strategy often fails. A poorly designed platform produces little or no value for users and generates weak network effects, or none at all.

So where do we start in designing a new platform? The best way is to focus on the fundamentals. What exactly does a platform do, and how does it work?

As we've seen, a platform connects producers with consumers and allows them to exchange value. Some platforms allow direct connection between users, as we see in the case of social networks. These connections then lead to the exchange of value between users. Other platforms do not facilitate direct connections between users but establish other mechanisms for value exchange. For example, on You-Tube, videos created by producers are delivered to consumers without a direct connection being made between them.

In this respect, interactions on a platform resemble any economic or social exchange, whether it occurs in the real world or in the virtual world of the Internet. In every such exchange, the producer and the consumer exchange three things: *information, goods or services*, and some form of *currency*.

Exchange of information. Whether it's the cattle auctioneer shouting out prices to an assembled crowd of ranchers or an eBay search results page displaying the goods available, every platform interaction starts with the exchange of information. This information enables the parties to decide whether, and how, to engage in any further exchange.

Thus, every platform business must be designed to facilitate the exchange of information. Some platforms have the exchange of information as their sole purpose—for example, a news forum like Reddit or a question-and-answer site like Quora. But even platforms whose primary goal is to enable the exchange of physical goods or services must enable the exchange of information. Uber provides information about driver availability and location in response to passenger requests; Yelp provides information about restaurants to enable users to choose a place to eat; and Upwork allows companies and freelancers to exchange information about themselves to facilitate hiring decisions.

Notice that, in every case, the exchange of information takes place through the platform itself. In fact, this is one of the fundamental characteristics of a platform business.

Exchange of goods or services. As a result of the information exchange, the platform participants may decide to exchange valuable goods or services as well. In some cases, the exchange of goods or services may also occur through the platform. On Facebook, photos, links, and posts with personal or other news are exchanged among users, while on YouTube videos are exchanged. Each item exchanged among platform users can be referred to as a *value unit*. In some cases, platforms feature sophisticated systems that make it easy and convenient for value units to be exchanged. Upwork, for example, provides clients with built-in tools to manage remote service delivery, so digital goods created by a freelancer, like slide decks and videos, can be exchanged directly through the platform itself.

In other cases, goods or services are exchanged outside of the platform (although information about the delivery may be tracked and exchanged on the platform). Transportation services requested via Uber are delivered on real city streets using actual cars; dinner reservations made via Yelp result in physical meals consumed around real tables in actual restaurants.

Exchange of currency. When goods or services are exchanged between platform participants, they are typically paid for using some form of currency. In many cases, this is traditional currency—money transmitted in one of a variety of ways, including credit card data, a PayPal transaction, a Bitcoin transfer, or (rarely) physical cash.

However, there are other forms of value, and therefore other ways in which consumers "pay" producers in the world of platforms. Video viewers on YouTube or followers on Twitter pay the producer with attention, which adds value to the producer in a variety of ways. (If the producer is a political pundit or business leader, for example, he gains value in the form of growing influence as a thought leader; if she is a singer, actor, or athlete, she gains value in the form of a growing fan base.) Community members on sites like TripAdvisor, Dribbble, and 500px pay by enhancing the reputation of producers whose work they like. Thus, attention, fame, influence, reputation, and other intangible forms of value can play the role of "currency" on a platform.

Sometimes the exchange of currency takes place through the platform itself. This is usually the case when the currency takes the form of attention or reputation. But monetary payment may also take place on the platform, even when the exchange of goods or services occurs elsewhere. Uber and Airbnb, for example, allow service delivery outside the platform, but they close the loop by ensuring that money is exchanged through the platform.

As we'll discuss in more detail in chapter 6, a platform's ability to monetize the value of the exchanges it facilitates is directly related to the types of currency exchange it can capture and internalize. A platform that can internalize the flow of money may be well placed to charge a transaction cut—for example, the fee of 10 percent of the sale price typically charged by eBay after a successful auction. A platform that can capture only attention may monetize its business by collecting payments from a third party that considers the attention valuable—for example, an advertiser willing to pay Facebook for "eyeballs" attracted by posts related to a particular topic.

The platform's goal, then, is to bring together producers and consumers and enable them to engage in these three forms of exchange: of information, of goods or services, and of currency. The platform provides an infrastructure that participants plug in to, which provides tools and rules to make exchanges easy and mutually rewarding.

THE CORE INTERACTION:
THE WHY OF PLATFORM DESIGN

Platforms are designed one interaction at a time. Thus, the design of every platform should start with the design of the *core interaction* that it enables between producers and consumers. The core interaction is the single most important form of activity that takes place on a platform—the exchange of value that attracts most users to the platform in the first place. The core interaction involves three key components: the *participants*, the *value unit*, and the *filter.* All three must be clearly identified and carefully designed to make the core interaction as easy, attractive, and valuable to users as possible. The fundamental purpose of the platform is to facilitate that core interaction.

This basic rule about the primacy of the core interaction applies despite the fact that many platforms involve a wide range of participants who may interact in a variety of ways. LinkedIn, for example, enables multiple interactions. Professionals exchange ideas about career and business strategy; recruiters exchange information about job listings with potential applicants; human resource managers exchange news about labor market conditions; and thought leaders offer their views about global trends. These various forms of interaction were built into the platform over time, each designed to meet a particular platform goal and to help users create a new form of value. The multisided LinkedIn platform we see today was first designed around a single core interaction: professionals connecting with other professionals.

So let's consider the three key components of the core interaction and how they connect to create value on the platform.

The participants. There are fundamentally two participants in any core interaction: the *producer*, who creates value, and the *consumer*, who consumes value. When defining the core interaction, both roles need to be explicitly described and understood.

One nuance of platform design is recognizing that the same user may play a different role in differing interactions. The same person may be both a host and a guest on Airbnb, although he or she will typically perform only one of those roles in a particular interaction. On YouTube, users may upload videos as well as view them. A well-designed platform makes it easy for users to move from role to role.

Conversely, many users, and many types of users, may perform the same role in an interaction. For example, one of the most common interactions on Facebook is a "status update"—a content posting that informs participants in the network about what a particular member is doing or thinking. The producer who drives a change of status on a particular Facebook page may be an individual, a business, a group of friends, or a nonprofit organization, but the fundamental role remains the same. Similarly, videos on YouTube are created by media companies as well as individuals. The incentives that encourage different parties to participate are different, but the roles remain consistent.

The value unit. As we've noted, every interaction starts with an exchange of information that has value to the participants. Thus, in virtually every case, the core interaction starts with the creation of a *value unit* by the producer.

Here are a few examples. On a marketplace like eBay or Airbnb, the product/service listing information is the value unit that is created by a seller and then served to buyers based on their search query or past interests. On a platform like Kickstarter, the project details constitute the value unit that enables potential backers to make a decision whether to fund it. Videos on YouTube, tweets on Twitter, profiles of professionals on LinkedIn, and listings of available cars on Uber are all value units. In each case, users are provided with a basis for deciding whether or not they want to proceed to some further exchange.

The filter. The value unit is delivered to selected consumers based on *filters*. A filter is an algorithmic, software-based tool used by the platform to enable the exchange of appropriate value units between users. A well-designed filter ensures that platform users receive only value units that are relevant and valuable to them; a poorly-designed filter (or no filter at all) means users may be flooded with units they find irrelevant and valueless, which may drive them to abandon the platform.

A search query is an example of a filter. Participants search for information of interest to them by specifying particular search terms: "hotels in and around Hana on the island of Maui" or "single straight males aged 18–25 in Austin TX," for example. Out of millions of value units previously created by producers (such as hotel proprietors and users in search of a mate), the platform employs the filter to select specific units that match the search terms and delivers them to the consumer.

In one way or another, every platform makes use of filters to manage the exchange of information. Uber's drivers announce their availability on the platform by sharing various parameters on location, occupancy, and so on—value units that enable them to be matched to the right consumers. When a consumer pulls out her phone and requests a car, she sets up a filter based on her location at the time of the request. Information about the drivers most relevant to the consumer is then exchanged.

Once this exchange of information happens, everything else clicks into action. The car turns up, the traveler is taken to her destination, the appropriate funds are transferred out of the traveler's account, and the driver is compensated. The core interaction is completed—value has been created and exchanged.

Some platforms have more complicated models, but the basic structure remains the same:

Participants + Value Unit + Filter → Core Interaction

Google's search engine acts in a fundamentally similar way. Google's crawlers search the web, creating web page indices (value units). A consumer types in a query. Google combines the query with other specified inputs, such as *social signals*—the volume of "likes," retweets, comments, and other responses received by a particular posting on the Internet. This combination of inputs constitutes the filter, which determines which value units are delivered to the consumer.

On Facebook, your entire network creates status updates, pictures, comments, links, and so on—all of them value units that are being added to the platform. Your news feed algorithm, based on signals you've given in the past through your interactions with previous content, acts as the filter that determines which units are delivered to you and which are not.

When designing a platform, your first and most important job is to decide what your core interaction will be, and then to define the participants, the value units, and the filters to make such core interactions possible.

As we see in cases like LinkedIn and Facebook, platforms often expand over time to embrace many kinds of interactions, each involving different participants, value units, and filters. But successful platforms begin with a single core interaction that consistently generates high value for users. A valuable core interaction that is easy, even enjoyable, to engage in attracts participants and makes the emergence of positive network effects possible.

The crucial role of the value unit. As this description of the core interaction shows, value units play a crucial role in the workings of any platform. Yet, in most cases, platforms don't create value units; instead, they are created by the producers who participate in the platform. Thus, platforms are "information factories" that have no control over inventory. They create the "factory floor" (that is, they build the platform infrastructure within which value units are produced). They can foster a culture of quality control (by taking steps to encourage producers to create value units that are accurate, useful, relevant, and interesting to consumers). They develop filters that are designed to deliver valuable units while blocking others. But they have no direct control over the production process itself—a striking difference from the traditional pipeline business.[1]

Fasal is an online system that connects farmers in rural India directly with market agents and other buyers. Via Fasal, farmers can quickly learn the price of goods at a number of nearby markets, choose the sales location most advantageous to them, and use the data to negotiate a better deal, a challenge that exists around the world.[2]

Sangeet Choudary, one of the authors of this book, led the commercialization and launch of the Fasal initiative. One of the challenges facing Choudary and his team was figuring out what kind of communications infrastructure they could use to enable producers and consumers to share value units. They realized that the big advantage working in their favor was cell phones. More than half of Indian farmers, even the poorest, own and use cell phones. In fact, as in much of the developing world, cell phone use in rural India has spread rapidly. Cellular telephony, with its instant communications capability, became the conduit for the market data the small farmers so desperately needed.

But creating the crucial value units needed to make exchanges possible between the farmers and the *mandis* (the local market-makers) would prove to be an even more significant challenge. "We needed information of various kinds," Choudary explains:

> Of course, we needed price data from the *mandis*—current market rates for various grades of commodities ranging from carrots and cauliflower to beans and tomatoes. This turned out to be fairly easy to gather. Some of the agents themselves would provide the information to us. And we supplemented this source by hiring local people to visit each of the *mandis* to gather price quotes firsthand and report them to us.
>
> The other side of the equation was more difficult. In order to create an electronic information resource that would be truly useful to the farmers, we needed data about the farmers themselves—the crops they were planting, the expected harvest cycle, the locations of the farms, their access to various *mandis*, and so on. All of these factors would influence the best deal they could make in the marketplace.
>
> But gathering this information from a widely scattered collection of farmers—most of them illiterate—was very tricky. We conducted a series of experiments. We tried relying on word of mouth to spread news about the service we were creating and to collect information for us. We tried using the local "head men"—the unofficial mayors of the villages—as conduits for the information. We tried arranging deals with local sellers of seeds, fertilizer, and SIM cards for cell phones, all of whom were frequently in touch with individual farmers. But none of these methods worked well—the people we tried to work with weren't interested, and the incentives simply weren't strong enough to produce a powerful flow of data.
>
> In the end, we had to build our own network of data gatherers— what Indians call a "feet on street" (FOS) sales force. The FOS team went door to door in each village, meeting with farmers and recording key information about their crops and their marketing plans on paper forms. Then they brought the data back to our offices, where we entered

it into our spreadsheets. Little by little, we built up the database we needed to begin making sense of the local markets.

As you can see, a focus on the value unit is extremely important if you're running a platform. Deciding who can create value units, how they are created and integrated into the platform, and what differentiates a high-quality unit from a low-quality one are all critical issues, and we'll explore these throughout this book.

PULL, FACILITATE, MATCH: THE HOW OF PLATFORM DESIGN

The core interaction is the why of platform design. The whole purpose of a platform is to make core interactions possible—indeed, to the extent possible, to make them inevitable by making them highly valuable to all participants. But how do you achieve this? What can the platform designer do to ensure that valuable core interactions begin to occur in significant numbers, thereby attracting more and more participants to the platform?

In the next few pages, we'll examine the how of platform design. Platforms must perform three key functions in order to encourage a high volume of valuable core interactions, which we summarize as *pull, facilitate,* and *match.* The platform must *pull* the producers and consumers to the platform, which enables interactions among them. It must *facilitate* their interactions by providing them with tools and rules that make it easy for them to connect and that encourage valuable exchanges (while discouraging others). And it must *match* producers and consumers effectively by using information about each to connect them in ways they will find mutually rewarding.

All three functions must be performed well if the platform is to succeed. A platform that fails to pull participants will be unable to create the network effects that make the platform valuable. A platform that fails to facilitate interactions—one with clunky technology or overly restrictive policies that make usage difficult—will eventually discourage and alienate participants. And a platform that fails to match participants accurately will waste their time and energy, soon driving participants away.

Let's examine each of these three crucial functions in a little more detail. Effective platform design is all about creating systems that perform these functions as powerfully as possible.

Pull. Attracting consumers to platforms presents challenges that pipeline companies don't face. Consequently, the approach to marketing such platforms is likely to seem counterintuitive, especially to business leaders who grew up in the old pipeline-dominated universe.

To begin with, platforms need to solve a chicken-or-egg problem that pipeline businesses don't suffer from: users won't come to a platform unless it has value, and a platform won't have value unless users use it. Most platforms fail simply because they never overcome this problem. It's such an important challenge that we'll devote all of chapter 5 to analyzing it and helping you solve it.

A second pull challenge revolves around keeping the interest of users who visit or sign up for the platform. The large social networks of our day have all faced this problem at some point. Facebook, for example, discovered that users found the platform valuable only after they had connected to a minimum number of other users. Until then, they were likely to stop using the network entirely. In response, Facebook shifted its marketing efforts away from recruiting new members to helping them form connections.

One powerful tool that encourages users to keep returning to the platform is the *feedback loop*. A feedback loop in a platform may take various forms, all of which serve to create a constant stream of self-reinforcing activity. In the typical feedback loop, a flow of value units is that generates a response from the user. If the units are relevant and interesting, the user will be drawn to the platform repeatedly, generating a further flow of value units and facilitating more interactions. Effective feedback loops help to swell the network, increase value creation, and enhance network effects.

One kind of feedback loop is the *single-user feedback loop*. This involves an algorithm built into the platform infrastructure that analyzes user activity, draws conclusions about the user's interests, preferences, and needs, and recommends new value units and connections that the user is likely to find valuable. When it is adroitly designed and programmed, the single-user feedback loop can be a powerful tool for increasing activity, since the more the participant uses the platform, the more the platform "learns" about him and the more accurate its recommendations become.

In a *multi-user feedback loop*, activity from a producer is delivered to relevant consumers, whose activity in turn is fed back to the producer. When effective, this creates a virtuous cycle, encouraging activity on both sides and ultimately strengthening network effects. Facebook's news feed is a classic multiuser feedback loop. Status updates from producers are served to consumers, whose likes and comments serve as feedback to the producers. The constant flow of value units stimulates still more activity, making the platform increasingly valuable to all participants.

Other factors strengthen or weaken a platform's ability to pull users. One is the value of the currency available for exchange on the platform. As we've discussed, some platform exchanges are paid for in intangible forms of currency: attention, popularity, influence, and so on. Thus, one form of network effect is the increased attractiveness of the currency available on a platform that is growing in size. Because Twitter has achieved such an enormous user base, a successful tweet is likely to attract far more currency in the form of attention than the same message disseminated on some other platform. So Twitter's huge size enlarges its pull, encouraging still more participant activity and making a competitive challenge to the platform increasingly unlikely.

Pull can also be increased by leveraging the *outside* networks of participants. Instagram and WhatsApp pulled in tens of millions of participants in a few years mainly by piggybacking on their users' Facebook networks. We'll examine these and other techniques for turbocharging pull in more detail in chapter 5, which focuses on the launch process.

Facilitate. Unlike traditional pipeline businesses, platforms don't control value creation. Instead, they create an infrastructure in which value can be created and exchanged, and lay out principles that govern these interactions. That's what the process of facilitating is all about.

One aspect of facilitating interactions is making it as easy as possible for producers to create and exchange valuable goods and services via the platform. This may involve providing creative tools for collaboration and sharing, as the Canadian photography platform 500px does with its infrastructure, which allows photographers to host their entire portfolios on the platform, or as invention platform Quirky does with its tools for letting users work together on creative ideas for innovative products and services.

Facilitating interactions may also involve reducing barriers to usage. Not long ago, a Facebook user who wanted to share photos with friends had to use a camera, transfer the images to a computer, use Photoshop or another software package to edit them, and finally upload them to Facebook. Instagram enabled users to snap, modify, and share pictures in three clicks on a single device. Lowering barriers to usage in this way encourages interactions and helps expand participation on the platform.

In some cases, increasing barriers has a positive effect on usage. Sittercity is platform that helps parents find babysitters. To inspire trust among its users (the parents), Sittercity has imposed a stringent set of rules that restrict those who can sign up as producers (the babysitters). In other cases, platforms must develop intrusive rules for curating value units and other producer-created content in order to encourage desirable interactions and discourage undesirable ones. Though relatively rare, misdeeds like the racist and sexist abuse spewed by trolls on Reddit, the murders of people found through Craigslist, and the trashing of apartments booked through Airbnb illustrate how undesirable interactions damage network effects.

Designing a platform to facilitate value-creating interactions is not a simple matter. We'll explore the challenges of platform curation and governance in more detail in chapters 7 and 8.

Match. A successful platform creates efficiencies by matching the right users with one another and ensuring that the most relevant goods and services are exchanged. It accomplishes this by using data about producers, consumers, the value units created, and the goods and services to be exchanged. The more data the platform has to work with—and the better designed the algorithms used to collect, organize, sort, parse, and interpret the data—the more accurate the filters, the more relevant and useful the information exchanged, and the more rewarding the ultimate match between producer and consumer.

The data required for optimal matching may be extremely diverse. They range from relatively static information such as identity, gender, and nationality to dynamic information such as location, relationship status, age, and point-in-time interest (as reflected in a search query). Sophisticated data models like the Facebook news feed may build a filter that considers all these factors as well as all of the participant's previous activities on the platform.

As part of the design process, platform companies need to develop an explicit data acquisition strategy. Users vary greatly in their willingness to share data and their readiness to respond to data-driven activity recommendations. Some platforms use incentives to encourage participants to provide data about themselves; others leverage game elements to gather data from users. LinkedIn famously used a progress bar to encourage users to progressively submit more information about themselves, thereby completing their personal data profiles. Data may also be acquired from third-party providers. Some mobile apps, such as the music streaming app Spotify, ask users to sign in using their Facebook identities, which helps the app pull in initial data to use in facilitating accurate matches. However, resistance from some users has led many app makers, including Spotify, to provide alternative ways to sign in that don't require a Facebook link.

Successful platforms create mutually rewarding matches on a consistent basis. As such, continual improvement of data acquisition and analysis methods is an important challenge for any organization seeking to build and maintain a platform.

Balancing the three functions. All three key functions—pull, facilitate, and match—are essential to a successful platform. But not all platforms are equally good at all three. It's possible for a platform to survive, at least for a time, thanks mainly to its strength at a particular function.

As of mid-2015, Craigslist continues to rule the classifieds space despite a poor interface, an utter lack of governance, and an unsophisticated data system. Craigslist's massive network keeps pulling users back. Thus, this platform's enormous advantage in pull has compensated for its weaknesses in facilitate and match—at least, so far.

Vimeo and YouTube coexist in the video sharing arena by focusing on different functions. YouTube employs a strong pull and deep understanding of the use of data in matching, while Vimeo differentiates itself through better hosting, bandwidth, and other tools for facilitating production and consumption.

BEYOND THE CORE INTERACTION

As we've seen, platform design begins with the core interaction. But over time, successful platforms tend to scale by layering new interactions on top of the core interaction.

In some cases, the gradual addition of new interactions is part of the long-term business plan that platform founders had in mind from the beginning. In early 2015, both Uber and Lyft began experimenting with a new ride-sharing service that complements their familiar call-a-taxi business model. The new services, known as UberPool and Lyft Line, allow two or more passengers traveling in the same direction to find one another and share a ride, thereby reducing their cost while increasing the revenues enjoyed by the driver. Lyft cofounder Logan Green says that ride-sharing was always part of the Lyft idea. The initial version of Lyft, he explains, was designed to attract an initial customer base "in every market." Having achieved that, he continues, "Now we get to play that next card and start matching up people to take rides."[3]

Uber isn't taking the competition lightly. To try to ensure that its ride-sharing service out-competes Lyft's, Uber has joined the bidding for Here, a digital mapping service owned by Nokia that is the chief alternative to Google Maps. Uber hopes to buy Here and use its mapping power to produce swift and accurate ride-sharing matches more effectively than any other service.[4]

In other cases, ideas for new interactions emerge from experience, observation, and necessity. In its search for new drivers, Uber discovered that many of its best prospects were recent immigrants to the U.S. who were eager to supplement their incomes by driving for Uber but who lacked the credit histories and financial qualifications needed to finance car purchases. Andrew Chapin of Uber's driver operations group came up with the idea of having Uber act as a middleman to guarantee car loans for its drivers, deducting repayments from driver revenue and sending them directly to the lenders. Finance companies like the program because loans backed by Uber's massive corporate cash flow are almost risk-free, and local auto dealers are happy with the additional inventory turnover.[5]

Another example: LinkedIn started by enabling professionals to network with one another. During its initial days, it focused exclusively on enabling its core interaction. Over time, the team at LinkedIn realized that the platform hadn't created the same high level of daily engagement that Facebook and a handful of other platforms had achieved. To address this issue, LinkedIn layered an additional interaction on top of its core interaction: It began allowing users to organize themselves into groups and start discussions.

This second form of interaction didn't achieve the popularity LinkedIn had hoped for either. Given the self-promotional behavior that a professional network encourages, the loudest users in the groups were often also the most obnoxious. So LinkedIn went on to add a further interaction, partly driven by the quest to monetize the platform: it allowed recruiters to use the site to target candidates, and advertisers to target ads to relevant professionals. Later still, LinkedIn created another interaction when it allowed thought leaders, and subsequently all users, to publish posts on LinkedIn for others to read, effectively turning the site into a publishing platform. This combination of many forms of interaction gives users more reasons to visit LinkedIn.

The evolution of Uber, Lyft, and LinkedIn illustrates several of the ways that new interactions may be layered on top of the core interaction in a given platform:

- By changing the value unit exchanged between existing users (as when LinkedIn shifted the basis of information exchange from user profiles to discussion posts)
- By introducing a new category of users as either producers or consumers (as when LinkedIn invited recruiters and advertisers to join the platform as producers)
- By allowing users to exchange new kinds of value units (as when Uber and Lyft made it possible for riders to share rides as well as arranging solo pickups)
- By curating members of an existing user group to create a new category of users (as when LinkedIn designated certain participants as "thought leaders" and invited them to become producers of informational posts)

Of course, not every new interaction is successful. Jake McKeon founded the social network Moodswing as a place where people could share their emotional states, from elation to gloom. Over time, he found that some users were turning to Moodswing in times of severe depression, and a few even used the site to threaten suicide. Distressed, McKeon decided to try to provide these users with the emotional support they needed. He concocted a plan to recruit psychology students who would volunteer to offer counseling and advice via chat lines to depressed Moodswing members. The volunteers would be tested and vetted in an effort to curate their quality This "amateur therapy" offering would represent a new form of value exchange facilitated by Moodswing.

It's an intriguing concept, but one that raises some obvious questions—in particular the potential danger in having untrained and unlicensed counselors offering psychological guidance to people whose lives are at risk. As of mid-2014, McKeon was in the process of seeking crowdfunding support for the project. It remains to be seen whether Moodswing's new interaction will be launched successfully and produce the user benefits McKeon hopes for.

APPLYING THE END-TO-END PRINCIPLE
TO PLATFORM DESIGN

As we've seen, adding new features and interactions to a platform can be a powerful way to increase its usefulness and attract more users. But innovation can easily lead to excessive complexity, which makes the platform more difficult for users to navigate. Needless complexity can also create enormous technical problems for the programmers, content developers, and managers who are charged with updating and maintaining the platform. The derisive term *bloatware* has been coined to describe software systems that have become complicated, slow, and inefficient through thoughtless accretion of features.

However, avoiding innovation altogether is no solution. A platform that fails to evolve by adding desirable new features is likely to be abandoned by users who discover a competing platform with more to offer. Instead, a way must be found to strike a balance, changing the core platform only slowly while allowing positive adaptations at the periphery.

This concept is the equivalent, for a platform business, of a long-established computer networking idea known as the *end-to-end principle*. Originally formulated in 1981 by J. H. Saltzer, D. P. Reed, and D. D. Clark, the end-to-end principle states that, in a general-purpose network, application-specific functions ought to reside in the end hosts of a network rather than in intermediary nodes.[6] In other words, activities that are not central to the workings of the network but valuable only to particular users should be located at the edges of the network rather than at its heart. In this way, secondary functions don't interfere with or draw resources away from the core activities of the network, nor do they complicate the task of maintaining or updating the network as a whole. Over time, the end-to-end principle has been expanded from network design to the design of many other complex computing environments.

One of the most storied examples of failure to heed the end-to-end principle concerns Microsoft's 2007 introduction of Vista, the latest version of its Windows operating system. CEO Steven Ballmer trumpeted Vista as "the biggest product launch in Microsoft's history" and backed the launch with a marketing budget of hundreds of millions of dollars.[7]

Yet Vista failed badly. The problem was that Microsoft's design team had sought to retain the software components needed to maintain backwards compatibility with older computer systems while adding features needed by next-generation systems—-all within the core platform. As a result, Vista was less stable and more complex than its predecessor, Windows XP, and outside app developers had difficulty writing code for it.[8]

Critics described Vista as worse than bloatware—in fact, they dubbed it *goatware* because it ate *all* a system's resources.[9] To this day, millions of Windows users have refused to adopt Vista, clinging to Windows XP despite repeated efforts by Microsoft to retire it. Ironically, while Microsoft stopped retail sales of XP in 2008 and of Vista in 2010, XP's market share in 2015 was above 12 percent, while that of Vista was below 2 percent.[10]

By contrast, when Steve Jobs returned to the leadership of Apple in 1997 after his years developing the ambitious but unsuccessful NeXT computer, he made a crucial decision that honored the end-to-end principle and helped lead to Apple's subsequent success. At NeXT, Jobs and his team had developed an elegant new operating system with a clean, layered architecture and a beautiful graphical interface. Now, planning a successor to Apple's Mac OS 9 operating system, Jobs faced a hard choice: he could merge the NeXT and Mac OS 9 software code, thereby producing an operating system that would be compatible with both systems, or he could jettison Mac OS 9 in favor of NeXT's clean architecture.

Jobs placed a dangerous bet on dumping the old code from OS 9. However, he made one concession: the design team developed a separate "Classic Environment" that would allow consumers to run their old OS 9 applications. This compartmentalized approach satisfied the end-to-end principle. The old code did not slow down or add complexity to the new applications, and new Mac buyers were unburdened by software written to accommodate apps they didn't own. Jobs's choice made innovation on the new Mac OS X easier and more efficient, which enabled Apple to develop new features that made Microsoft's operating systems look dated by comparison.[11]

The end-to-end concept can also be applied to the design of a platform. In this case, the principle states that application-specific features should reside in the layer of process at the edge or on top of the platform, rather than at the roots deep within the platform. Only the highest-volume, highest-value features that cut across apps should become part of the core platform.

There are two reasons for this rule. First, when specific new features are incorporated into the core platform rather than attached to the periphery, applications that do not use those features will appear slow and inefficient. By contrast, when application-specific features are run by the app itself rather than by the core platform, the user experience will be much cleaner.

Second, a platform ecosystem can evolve faster when the core platform is a clean, simple system rather than a tangle of numerous features. For this reason, C. Y. Baldwin and K. B. Clark of Harvard Business School describe a well-designed platform as consisting of a stable core layer that restricts variety, sitting underneath an evolving layer that enables variety.[12]

Today's best-designed platforms incorporate this structural principle. For example, Amazon Web Services (AWS), the most successful platform for providing cloud-based information storage and management, focuses on optimizing a handful of basic operations, including data storage, computation, and messaging.[13] Other services, which are used by just a fraction of AWS customers, are restricted to the periphery of the platform and provided through purpose-built apps.

THE POWER OF MODULARITY

There are advantages to an integral approach where the system is developed as quickly as possible to serve a single purpose, especially in the early days of a platform. However, in the long run, a successful platform must have a more modular approach. A full discussion of this trade-off is well beyond the scope of this chapter, but we will cover some of the important ideas. We begin with a definition provided by Baldwin and Clark (1996):

Modularity is a strategy for organizing complex products and processes efficiently. A modular system is composed of units (or modules) that are designed independently but still function as an integrated whole. Designers achieve modularity by partitioning information into visible design rules and hidden design parameters. Modularity is beneficial only if the partition is precise, unambiguous, and complete. The visible design rules (also called visible information) are decisions that affect subsequent design decisions. Ideally, the visible design rules are established early in a design process and communicated broadly to those involved.[14]

In a 2008 paper, Carliss Young Baldwin and C. Jason Woodard provided a useful and succinct definition of a stable system core:

We argue that the fundamental architecture behind all platforms is essentially the same: namely, the system is partitioned into a set of "core" components with low variety and a complementary set of "peripheral" components with high variety. The low-variety components constitute the platform. They are the long-lived elements of the system and thus implicitly or explicitly establish the system's interfaces, [and] the rules governing interactions among the different parts.[15]

A critical factor that makes modularity so effective is that when systems are cleanly partitioned into subsystems, they can work as a whole by connecting and communicating through well-defined interfaces. The implication is that subsystems can be designed independently so long as they adhere to overall design rules and connect to the rest of the system only through standard interfaces. Readers will likely have heard the term *application programming interfaces*, or APIs. These are the standard interfaces that systems such as Google Maps, the New York Stock Exchange, Salesforce, Thomson Reuters Eikon, Twitter, and many more use to facilitate access by external entities to core resources.[16]

Amazon has been especially effective at opening APIs to its modular services. Figure 3.1 compares the range of APIs made available by Amazon and by the leading traditional retailer, Walmart, which is making a strong effort to become a significant platform competitor. As you can see, Amazon has by far outstripped Walmart in the number and variety of APIs provided.

The power of modularity is one of the reasons that the personal computer industry grew so quickly in the 1990s. The key components of PC systems were central processing units (CPUs) that provided the computation, graphical processing units (GPUs) that created rich images on the screen, random access memory (RAM) that provided working storage, and a spinning hard drive (HD) that provided large amounts of long-term storage. Each of these subsystems communi-

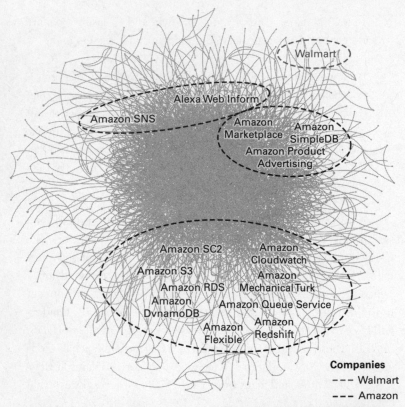

FIGURE 3.1. Amazon has far more remixes or "mashups" of APIs than Walmart. These span payments, e-commerce, cloud services, messaging, task allocation, and more. While Walmart optimizes logistics, Amazon also allows third parties to build value on its modular services. Source: Evans and Basole using ProgrammableWeb data.[17] Reprinted by permission.

cated with the others using well-defined interfaces that allowed for tremendous innovation, as firms such as Intel (CPUs), ATI and Nvidia (GPUs), Kingston (RAM), and Seagate (HD) all worked independently to improve the performance of their products.

The reason that most platforms launch with a tightly integrated architectural design is that there is significant work involved in carefully specifying subsystem interfaces—and even in simply documenting them. When firms are pursuing narrow market windows with limited engineering resources, they can easily be tempted to skip the hard work of decomposing systems into clean modules and instead proceed as quickly as possible to a viable solution. Over time, however, this approach makes it much more difficult to mobilize an external ecosystem of developers who can build on top of the core platform and extend its offerings into new markets.[18] Thus, a firm that has an integral architecture will likely have to invest in remaking its core technology.[19]

RE-ARCHITECTING THE PLATFORM

It is possible to pull off the trick of re-architecting a system toward a modular design. The first step is to analyze the degree of modularity the system has already achieved. Fortunately, a number of tools have been developed to accomplish this goal. Key among these are "design structure matrices" that allow a visual examination of the dependencies in complex systems.[20]

In a 2006 article in *Management Science*, Alan MacCormack and Carliss Baldwin document an example of a product that successfully evolved from an integral to a modular architecture.[21] When the software was put into the public domain as open source, the commercial firm that owned the copyright invested significant resources to make the transition. This was critical because the software could not have been maintained by distributed teams of volunteer developers if it had not been broken into smaller subsystems.

The need to re-architect a complex system is not unique to software. In the early 1990s, Intel faced a major challenge in growing its market. The performance of Intel's CPU chips was doubling every eighteen to twenty-four months.[22] Similar performance improvements were occurring in the other key PC subsystems: GPU, RAM, and hard drives. However, the information connections between the subsystems were still defined by an old standard called the Industry Standard Architecture (ISA). As a result, consumers saw little improvement in PC performance and thus had little reason to buy new machines. In a 2002 paper, Michael A. Cusumano and Annabelle Gawer document how Intel took the lead by investing in a new Peripheral Component Interconnect (PCI) to better connect the main subsystems, and the universal serial bus (USB) standard which fostered tremendous amounts of innovation in connected devices such as computer mice, cameras, microphones, keyboards, printers, scanners, external hard drives, and much more.[23]

ITERATIVE IMPROVEMENT: THE ANTI-DESIGN PRINCIPLE

When you're launching a new platform—or seeking to enhance and grow an existing platform—thoughtful attention to the principles of platform design will maximize your chances of value creation.[24] But as we've seen, platforms cannot be entirely planned; they also emerge. Remember that one of the key characteristics that distinguishes a platform from a traditional business is that most of the activity is controlled by users, not by the owners or managers of the platform. It's inevitable that participants will use the platform in ways you never anticipated or planned.

Twitter was never meant to have a discovery mechanism. It originated as simply a reverse-chronological stream of feeds. There was no way to seek out tweets on particular topics other than by scrolling through pages of unrelated and irrelevant content. Chris Messina, an engineer at Google, originally suggested the use of hashtags to annotate and discover similar tweets. Today, the hashtag has become a mainstay of Twitter.

Platform designers should always leave room for serendipitous discoveries, as users often lead the way to where the design should evolve. Close monitoring of user behavior on the platform is almost certain to reveal unexpected patterns—some of which may suggest fruitful new areas for value creation. The best platforms allow room for user quirks, and they are open enough to gradually incorporate such quirks into the design of the platform.

Smart design is essential to building and maintaining a successful platform. But sometimes the best design is anti-design, which makes space for the accidental, the spontaneous, and even the bizarre.[25]

TAKEAWAYS FROM CHAPTER THREE

❑ The design of a platform should begin with its core interaction—one kind of interaction that is at the heart of the platform's value-creation mission.

❑ Three key elements define the core interaction: the participants, the value unit, and the filter. Of these, the value unit is the most crucial, and often the most difficult to control.

❑ In order to make the core interaction easy and even inevitable, a platform must perform three crucial functions: pull, facilitate, and match. All three are essential, and each has its special challenges.

❑ As a platform grows, it often finds ways to expand beyond the core interaction. New kinds of interactions may be layered on top of the core interaction, often attracting new participants in the process.

❑ It's important to design a platform thoughtfully to make mutually satisfying interactions easy for large numbers of users. But it's also important to leave room for serendipity and the unexpected, since users themselves will find new ways to create value on the platform.

4

DISRUPTION

How Platforms Conquer and Transform Traditional Industries

The platform concept is fundamentally simple: create a place where producers and consumers can come together in interactions that create value for both parties. It's an idea that humans have been practicing for millennia. After all, what is the traditional open-air marketplace found in villages and cities from Africa to Europe if not a platform in which farmers and craftspeople sell their wares to local consumers? The same is true of the original stock markets that grew up in cities like London and New York, where buyers and sellers of company shares would gather in person to establish fair market prices through the open outcry auction system.

The main difference between these traditional platform businesses and the modern platforms featured in this book is, of course, the addition of digital technology, which enormously expands a platform's reach, speed, convenience, and efficiency. (There's a good reason why most stock trading has now migrated from physical exchange floors to electronic marketplaces accessible from anywhere in the world.) The Internet and its associated technologies give today's platform businesses a truly breathtaking ability to transform industries, often in unpredictable ways.

We've already looked at the way in which the car-service platform Uber has leveraged network effects to claim a huge and growing share of the rides-for-hire market from such traditional businesses as taxis and limousine services—and in the process has built an enormous corporate valuation in a startlingly short period of time. By the end of 2014, the five-year-old company was valued by investors at $40 billion (up from the $17 billion valuation of just six months earlier), making it more valuable, at least on paper, than such venerable commercial giants as Mitsubishi, Target, FedEx, General Dynamics, and Sony.[1] Uber, which now operates in more than 250 cities around the world, has scaled these heights by providing an exceedingly simple yet valuable service to both consumers and producers, bringing quick and inexpensive rides to passengers while enabling drivers to earn better incomes than most taxi drivers—and without having to shell out the enormous sums required for a traditional taxi license. At the height of the market, in mid-2013, a New York City taxi medallion was valued at over $1.2 million.

So the Uber platform, simply by providing an online location where riders and drivers can come together, has brought benefits to both consumers and producers while building vast wealth for its investors. It's a winning proposition for everyone—except for the hundreds of thousands of taxi drivers, car-service dispatchers, and limousine company employees whose jobs are suddenly in jeopardy. No wonder Barry Korengold, president of the cab drivers association in San Francisco (the city where Uber was launched back in the summer of 2010) describes the leaders of Uber as "robber barons": "They started off by operating illegally, without following any of the regulations and unfairly competing. And that's how they became big—they had enough money to ignore all the rules." The president of one San Francisco cab company predicted that the entire taxi industry would collapse before the end of 2015—a forecast echoed by taxi executives in cities around the world. As a result, the value of a New York City taxi medallion fell by almost $300,000 in one year—with no bottom in sight.[2]

In chapter 11, we'll return to the question of whether platform businesses like Uber are engaging in unfair competition, or whether traditional incumbent companies are simply angry about being outcompeted by digital interlopers. But for now, just let's marvel at how swiftly and seemingly effortlessly a platform business is revolutionizing a once-secure industry.

Even more remarkably, the changes that Uber has already brought are probably just the opening salvo in a barrage of further disruptions that may ultimately transform the entire transportation sector. Combining the platform model with another technology that is rapidly moving from the drawing board to the showroom—the self-driving car—will improve Uber's already stellar economic model and could lead to a series of cascading impacts that extend beyond the taxi industry. One futurist foresees a time when millions of people will eschew car ownership altogether, instead relying on an instantly deployable fleet of driverless Uber vehicles to take them wherever they want to go at a cost of around fifty cents per mile. Uber cofounder and CEO Travis Kalanick comments, "We want to get to the point that using Uber is cheaper than owning a car." The ultimate promise: "Transportation that's as reliable as running water."[3]

The implications are startling. The major automakers would be devastated by the shrinkage of their market. So would ancillary businesses such as auto insurance, car finance, and parking. On the other hand, the sudden decrease in demand for parking places (since driverless cars can be in virtually continual use) will free up tens of millions of square feet of real estate for development, liberate lanes on practically every city street, and drastically reduce the pollution and congestion caused by drivers cruising the streets in search of a parking spot. If this vision for the next phase of Uber's growth comes true, the landscape of America may well be rendered unrecognizable.[4]

And if all that is not enough, consider this observation by Kalanick: "If we can get you a car in five minutes, we can get you *anything* in five minutes."[5] Anything at all? One wonders what limits can be set on Uber's disruptive potential. Kalanick seems not to acknowledge any.

A CAPSULE HISTORY OF DIGITAL DISRUPTION

"Software is eating the world." The slogan was originally used by Netscape founder Marc Andreessen in the title of a 2011 op-ed article in the *Wall Street Journal* to encapsulate how technology—particularly the Internet—has transformed the world of business.[6]

The story of Internet-enabled disruption as we've witnessed it so far has occurred in two main stages.

In stage one, *efficient pipelines ate inefficient pipelines.* Most Internet applications during the 1990s involved the creation of highly efficient pipelines—online systems for distributing goods and services that outcompeted incumbent industries. Unlike traditional offline pipelines, online pipelines benefited from low marginal costs of distribution—sometimes as low as zero. This allowed them to target and serve large markets with much smaller investment.

Traditional media companies were the first to feel the pinch. Newspapers were upended by the Internet's ability to distribute news to a global audience without the traditional distribution costs (printing, shipping, retailing, delivery). An efficient pipeline had eaten an inefficient one. The unbundling of classifieds and other forms of advertising from editorial content then stripped the newspaper model of a crucial monetization mechanism, as the more efficient online method for delivering targeted advertising outcompeted the traditional ink-on-paper method. Again, an efficient pipeline ate an inefficient one.

Retail and mail order shopping soon felt the pain. Amazon's success in the book industry led to the fall of Borders and other bookstores. Blockbuster's bricks-and-mortar system for distributing DVDs failed to compete with Netflix's distribution economics, based initially on the online selection of DVDs that were delivered by mail, and later on streaming video. Music company revenues plummeted as sales of CDs collapsed, replaced by faster and cheaper file downloads, many of them pirated or shared illegally. Over time, many of the Internet distributors found ways to leverage granular data about consumer choice so as to serve their customers better than the traditional pipelines ever did.

Business revolutions such as these embodied Andreessen's vision of "software eating the world." Today, having attained the status of a cliché, his vision needs an update: "Platforms are eating the world." We've entered stage two of the disruption saga, in which *platforms eat pipelines.*

HOW PLATFORMS EAT PIPELINES

The evidence for this new stage of disruption is all around us. As we've seen, taxi companies—and regulators—have realized that Uber is on the march to global domination of local transportation. Once ridiculed by the hotel industry, Airbnb has rapidly scaled to become a global provider of accommodation, with more rooms booked every night than the largest global hotel chains. Upwork is gradually evolving from a marketplace for talent into an infrastructure that allows entire organizations to be built in the cloud, connecting freelance workers from remote locations without the need for a physical workspace and the costs associated with it. Amazon continues to expand its impact on traditional book publishing while making inroads into dozens of other retailing arenas. And while traditional pipeline giants Nokia and Blackberry have lost 90 percent of their market value in the last decade, platform giants Apple and Google have dominated the stock market.

How and why is this happening? Let's break it down.

In the world of platforms, the Internet no longer acts merely as a distribution channel (a pipeline). It also acts as a creation infrastructure and a coordination mechanism. Platforms are leveraging this new capability to create entirely new business models. In addition, the physical and the digital are rapidly converging, enabling the Internet to connect and coordinate objects in the real world—for example, through smartphone apps that allow you to control your home appliances at long distance. Simultaneously, organizational boundaries are being redefined as platform companies leverage external ecosystems to create value in new ways.[7]

In this new stage of disruption, platforms enjoy two significant economic advantages over pipelines.

One of these advantages is superior marginal economics of production and distribution. As we've noted, when hotel chains like Hilton and Sheraton want to expand, they build new rooms and employ thousands of staff. By contrast, Airbnb expands with near-zero marginal costs, since its cost for adding an additional room to its network listings is minimal.

A platform's ability to scale rapidly is further enhanced by network effects. When positive network effects kick in, higher production leads to higher consumption, and vice versa. More freelancers participating on Upwork make it more attractive to companies looking to hire, which in turn attracts more freelancers; a wider array of merchants on Etsy attracts more customers, who in turn attract more merchants. A virtuous feedback loop is set in motion, fueling the growth of the platform at minimal cost.

Leveraging network effects, platforms are able to build open electronic ecosystems embracing hundreds, thousands, or millions of remote participants. Such ecosystems can be larger than most pipeline-based organizations and can have access to more resources than a traditional pipeline company can command. As a result, the value created in such an ecosystem can be much larger than the value created in a comparable traditional organization. Therefore, firms that continue to compete on the basis of resources that are owned internally are increasingly finding it difficult to compete with platforms.

THE IMPACTS OF PLATFORM DISRUPTION ON VALUE CREATION, VALUE CONSUMPTION, AND QUALITY CONTROL

Platforms, then, have economic advantages that enable them to grow faster than similar pipeline businesses. This phenomenon alone would lead to significant disruption of traditional industries, as platform businesses displace pipeline businesses at the top of the Fortune 500 rankings. But the era of platforms-eat-pipelines is disrupting businesses in many other ways as well. In particular, the rise of the world of platforms is reconfiguring the familiar business processes of value creation, value consumption, and quality control.[8]

Reconfiguring value creation to tap new sources of supply. As self-serve systems, platforms grow and conquer markets when they minimize the barriers to usage for their users. In particular, every time a platform removes a hurdle that makes the participation of producers more difficult, value creation is reconfigured and new sources of supply are opened up.

Wikipedia became one of the first platforms to tap a new source of supply when it created a system that enabled volunteers to capture and organize the world's knowledge. Soon, YouTube was empowering any teenager with a video camera or a smartphone to compete with movie studios and television networks.

Today, we see the phenomenon of reconfigured value creation at work in many kinds of platform business. Singapore-based video-streaming platform Viki leveraged a global community of enthusiasts (rather than hiring employees) to add subtitles to Korean and Japanese dramas, which it then marketed in the U.S. After the resulting rapid burst of growth, Viki was sold to the Japanese company Rakuten for $200 million. Facebook used a similar approach to find translators for its website instead of relying on professionals.

To fuel the continued explosion of new sources of supply, platform businesses are steadily lowering barriers that might discourage producers. Twitter attracted millions of content creators with its new standard literary format—the message of 140 characters or fewer. By comparison with traditional blogging, which required more effort and time, the tweet is a quick and easy form of writing, which encouraged many more users to become content producers.

In similar fashion, Airbnb works to lower the hurdles for its member-hosts by regularly conducting events and programs designed to illustrate and teach its best practices. Uber works to remove economic barriers that might discourage would-be drivers by providing financial incentives like sign-up bonuses. Platforms like Dribbble, Threadless, and 99designs have built large ecosystems of designers, largely owing to the democratization of the tools of design and printing over the last several years—yet another case of barriers to entry being lowered, in part through the help of platform tools.

The proliferation of new production technologies further enables the emergence of new groups of producers. Just as the smartphone camera expanded the volume of content on platforms like Instagram and Vine, the spread of 3D printing is likely to lead to a new range of platforms for industry design. However, technology often needs the

support of innovative business design to produce massive reconfiguration of value creation. Software for word processing, typography, and graphic design has existed for decades, but not until Amazon's Kindle Publishing platform offered quick and easy access to a large readership did a whole new ecosystem of authors emerge.

Reconfiguring value consumption by enabling new forms of consumer behavior. The advent of the world of platforms is also disrupting traditional consumer behavior, inspiring millions of people to use products and services in ways that would have been unimaginable a few years ago. As journalist Jason Tanz puts it:

> We are hopping into strangers' cars (Lyft, Sidecar, Uber), welcoming them into our spare rooms (Airbnb), dropping our dogs off at their houses (DogVacay, Rover), and eating food in their dining rooms (Feastly). We are letting them rent our cars (RelayRides, Getaround), our boats (Boatbound), our houses (HomeAway), and our power tools (Zilok). We are entrusting complete strangers with our most valuable possessions, our personal experiences—and our very lives. In the process, we are entering a new era of Internet-enabled intimacy.[9]

Not so long ago, activities like these would have been viewed as weird, if not downright dangerous. Today, they are familiar to millions, thanks to the trust-building mechanisms established by platform businesses. A host of upstart platforms that bill themselves as "the Uber of X" are working to alter consumer behavior in other arenas.[10]

Reconfiguring quality control through community-driven curation. When new platforms such as YouTube, Airbnb, and Wikipedia are launched, they are often widely criticized, even ridiculed. This is because, in their early stages, they fail to offer the quality and reliability provided by their traditional competitors. YouTube's early content often bordered on pornography; much of it was pirated. Apartments listed on Airbnb would get raided by city inspectors responding to complaints about orgies. Wikipedia biographies declared many a living person deceased.

This is the problem with abundance. When platforms start unlocking new sources of supply, quality often nosedives—an example of the negative network effects we discussed in chapter 2.

These early days in the life of a platform can be difficult. However, over time, as the curation mechanism starts to work, the platform improves its ability to match consumers with relevant and high-quality content, goods, and services from producers. Strong curation encourages desirable behavior while discouraging and eventually weeding out undesirable behavior. As the platform nurtures quality, it develops the reliability needed to attract a wide array of customers. Mainstream competitors, often quite suddenly, find themselves competing with an unfamiliar upstart—one that is poised to grow much faster than they can.

Once platforms start scaling, they need to ensure that the curation mechanism doesn't break down. Platforms that successfully scale their curation efforts gather better data on their users and improve their matching algorithms over time. They also ensure that manual curation is gradually phased out in favor of automated curation mechanisms based on socially driven feedback loops. For example, Quora, the question-and-answer platform, started out with in-house editors curating its content. Once a critical mass of users started participating, curation was largely turned over to algorithms driven by community judgments.

The rise of the world of platforms, then, doesn't simply mean the emergence of new business entities competing with traditional incumbent firms. It also means the appearance of new forms of business activity, as these changes in the modes of value creation, value consumption, and quality control suggest.

STRUCTURAL IMPACTS OF PLATFORM DISRUPTION

The rise of platform businesses is transforming the structure of the business landscape in three specific ways that have largely gone unnoticed. We describe these three forms of platform-driven disrup-

tions as *de-linking assets from value, re-intermediation,* and *market aggregation.*

De-linking assets from value. The most familiar platform examples—Airbnb, Uber, Amazon—come from the business-to-consumer (B2C) arena. How do you convert a product to a platform in the business-to-business (B2B) arena? Many corporations own massive fixed assets like power generation plants, magnetic resonance imaging (MRI) machines, or tracts of farmland. How do you build platforms around those?

The answer: you de-link ownership of the physical asset from the value it creates. This allows the use of the asset to be independently traded and applied to its *best* use—that is, the use that creates the greatest economic value—rather than being restricted to uses specific to the owner. As a result, efficiency and value rise dramatically.

Two of this book's authors (Geoff Parker and Marshall Van Alstyne) used this approach in response to a request from the state of New York to help in designing a smart market to integrate the state's increasing number of distributed energy resources. These include solar rooftops, battery storage, and household generators, as well as the virtual storage that arises from a building's thermal inertia. Buildings can be preheated or cooled or can delay heating and cooling within a couple of degrees without affecting occupants' comfort. Together, these systems constitute resources that can be used to help the state's electric power system accommodate the swings in demand and supply that are part the natural daily and seasonal cycle—but only if there is a system in place to handle the coordination. Currently, price signals arise from the system-wide wholesale market and are aggregated, thereby obscuring the clearer signals that localized data would provide.

To solve this problem, we recommended a platform that separates the physical assets from the value they create—that is, the energy produced. Such a platform would allow small sellers to meet the demand by the larger buyers of power, who then deliver it to end consumers. To obviate the need for users of the platform to constantly check market prices, the system should create automated signals so that sellers' machines can be programmed to respond automatically to local relevant price and demand information distributed through the platform.

If the New York system is implemented, significant savings would be realized, since investments in new transmission, distribution, and generation capacity could be delayed or avoided entirely. In addition, the system, being highly flexible and responsive, could accommodate further deployments of renewable energy better than the current system can, as it relies on large power plants to respond to variability in supply and demand.

De-linking assets from value also allows expensive health care equipment such as MRI machines (each costing $3–5 million) to be used more efficiently. A single hospital may use just 40 to 50 percent of its own MRI capacity. Solution: time-slice the usage, and create a market for slices among other hospitals and small clinics that cannot afford their own machines. Separating the asset from the value it creates can drive the utilization rate to 70 or even 90 percent, producing incremental revenue for the machine's owner.

It's just one further step to turn a local market into a statewide or regional one. In fact, as of mid-2015, a Boston firm called Cohealo is taking that step, with the goal of becoming the Airbnb of expensive hospital equipment.

This concept of de-linking assets from value helped rescue Australian farmers from a drought more severe than that faced by California in 2015. Like California, Australia suffered from a patchwork system of water rights that limits the use of water to whatever an individual owner has in mind. The system was reformed beginning in 2003 by separating land ownership from water rights. With the help of a private company called Waterfind, Australia created a platform for water trading that greatly increased the economic efficiency of water use. A farmer with a low-value crop might stop farming and sell his water to a farmer with a high-value crop, or to a municipal water authority within transport distance. As a result, when Australia was hit by drought starting in 2006, its farmers suffered far less than those in California have. Now Waterfind is setting up a subsidiary based in Sacramento, hoping to apply the same platform-based solution to American agriculture.[11]

Re-intermediation. During the first stage of Internet-driven disruption, many business commentators predicted that the biggest impact of the new information and communication technologies would be widespread *disintermediation*—the elimination of middlemen, or intermediate layers, from industries, establishing direct connections between producers and consumers. Experts pointed to the decline of traditional businesses like travel agents and insurance brokers, as consumers learned to shop for airline tickets and insurance policies without intermediaries. The same process of disintermediation was expected to sweep many other industries over time.

The reality has proven to be somewhat different. Across numerous industries, platforms have repeatedly *re-intermediated* markets, introducing new kinds of middlemen rather than simply eliminating layers of market participants. Typically re-intermediation involves replacing non-scalable and inefficient agent intermediaries with online, often automated tools and systems that offer valuable new goods and services to participants on both sides of the platform.

Networked platforms serve as more efficient intermediaries owing to their ability to use market-mediating mechanisms that scale. While traditional intermediaries relied on manual efforts, platform intermediaries rely on algorithms and social feedback, both of which scale quickly and efficiently. Moreover, their ability to gather data over time and use it to make the system more intelligent allows platforms to scale their intermediation in the market in a manner that was impossible for traditional middlemen.

Intermediation by platform businesses is transforming industries, creating new venues where market participants are connected with greater power and efficiency than ever before. In the music industry, artist and repertoire (A & R) executives, who traditionally associated themselves with a large record label in order to attract talent, now operate as independent professionals, scouting for talent on platforms such as YouTube and SoundCloud. Literary agents search for new authors on content platforms such as Quora and Medium. Small businesses run advertising campaigns without using traditional ad agencies or media channels by relying on Google's AdWords platform. This, in turn, has led to the rise of an entire new range of intermediary agencies in Asia that manage AdWords campaigns for a fraction of the traditional price. Thus, while platforms displace large and inefficient intermediaries, they empower small and nimble service providers who leverage the platform to provide services to end users.

In another form of re-intermediation, platforms create a new layer of reputational information by leveraging social feedback about producers. Platforms like Yelp, Angie's List, and TripAdvisor have created an entirely new industry based on certifying the quality of product and service providers—in the process driving some traditional industry certifiers (such as travel guide and consumer magazine publishers) out of business.

The re-intermediation produced by platforms is also changing the economics of participation for producers and consumers, leading to both new winners and new losers. In the traditional book business, publishers absorb (and spend) the bulk of book revenues, generally paying author royalties that range between 10 and 15 percent. By contrast, authors on Amazon's self-publishing platform generally retain 70 percent of the revenues. Of course, Amazon authors must also defray many of the costs that a traditional publisher would cover, such as editing, design, publicity, and marketing—which makes the designation of "winners" and "losers" in this instance more complicated.

A similar economic shift in favor of app developers was set into motion with the emergence of the app ecosystem of the iPhone and Android. These new economics for participants are possible because of the superior marginal economics enjoyed by platforms.[12]

Market aggregation. Platforms are also creating new efficiencies by aggregating unorganized markets. *Market aggregation* is the process whereby platforms provide centralized markets to serve widely dispersed individuals and organizations. Market aggregation provides information and power to platform users who formerly engaged in interactions in a haphazard fashion, often without access to reliable or up-to-date market data.

Consider, for example, bus transportation in India. Different bus fleets operate on interstate, intrastate, and other routes. Many different types of bus exist, and pricing is extremely variable. Because the industry is so fragmented and unorganized, consumer search costs and decision overhead are high.[13] Now a platform business called red-Bus is aggregating information from all Indian bus operators in a central plug-and-play infrastructure. The result is quicker, easier, and cheaper decision-making for consumers, and, in the long run, a healthier transportation market for India.

Many successful platforms perform a similar market aggregation function. Amazon Marketplace, Alibaba, and Etsy provide online sites where vendors of thousands of kinds of products from around the world can offer their wares to consumers. Service platforms like Upwork bring thousands of skilled professionals under a single roof, making it easy for potential employers to evaluate, compare, and hire them.

THE INCUMBENTS FIGHT BACK: PIPELINES BECOMING PLATFORMS

Platform businesses, then, are disrupting the traditional business landscape in a number of ways—not only by displacing some of the world's biggest incumbent firms, but also by transforming familiar business processes like value creation and consumer behavior as well as altering the structure of major industries.

What can incumbents do to respond? Are entrenched companies that operate familiar pipeline businesses doomed to capitulate as platforms reshape and ultimately take over their industries?

Not necessarily. But if incumbents hope to fight the forces of platform disruption, they'll need to reevaluate their existing business models. For example, they'll need to scrutinize all their transaction costs—that is, the money they spend on processes such as marketing, sales, product delivery, and customer service—and imagine how those costs might be reduced or eliminated in a more seamlessly connected world. They'll also need to examine the entire universe of individuals and organizations they currently interact with and envision new ways of networking them so as to create new forms of value.[14] They'll need to ask questions such as:

- Which processes that we currently manage in-house can be delegated to outside partners, whether suppliers or customers?
- How can we empower outside partners to create products and services that will generate new forms of value for our existing customers?
- Are there ways we can network with current competitors to produce valuable new services for customers?
- How can the value of the goods and services we currently provide be enhanced through new data streams, interpersonal connections, and curation tools?

Nike has proven to be one of the most intelligent incumbent companies seeking new ways to survive and thrive in the world of platforms. Some of the competitive steps they've taken may seem obvious. They aren't.

Pipeline businesses like Nike have traditionally scaled in one of two ways. Some expand by owning and integrating a greater length of the value-creation-and-delivery pipeline—for example, by buying upstream suppliers or downstream distributors. This is referred to as *vertical integration.* Others expand by widening the pipeline to push more value through it. This is *horizontal integration.* When consumer goods companies grow by creating new products and brands, it's an example of horizontal integration.

In January 2012, Nike brought out a wearable technology device, the FuelBand, to track user fitness activities, including steps walked and calories burned. Like many other companies, Nike has also been developing apps—in this case, apps related to sports and fitness. On the surface, these might seem like traditional product-line extensions aiming at horizontal integration. But in reality, Nike is testing an approach that, if successful, will lead to a new form of growth—one pioneered by platform businesses like Apple.

Over the last decade, Apple has grown in part by connecting its products and services to one another in the cloud. The ability to sync contents and data over iTunes and iCloud makes the ownership of multiple Apple products particularly valuable, and much more useful than (say) the ownership of multiple products from Sony, Toshiba, or another electronics manufacturer. Data acts as an integration glue to make all these products and services perform in concert.

This leads to a new form of growth. When multiple products and services connect and interact using data, pipelines can start behaving like platforms, producing new forms of value and encouraging users to engage in more interactions.

Like a suite of Apple products, Nike's FuelBand-connected shoes and mobile apps are not simply separate products and services connected by a brand name. Instead, they constantly interact, providing users with information and advice about their athletic performance, their fitness regime, and their health goals. Unlike a traditional sporting goods company, Nike is building an ecosystem of users using the data it captures about them. Over time, it can leverage this data to create more relevant experiences for its users and connect them with one another to enable valuable interactions.

Nike is not the only company taking the first steps in transforming its traditional pipeline business into a platform business. Under Armour, a rival of Nike in the sports and casual wear market, has been moving quickly to build its own fitness ecosystem. In November 2013, it purchased MapMyFitness, a leading workout and exercise tracking platform. Then, in February 2015, it followed up by buying two more fitness platforms—MyFitnessPal, which focuses on nutrition, and Endomondo, a "trainer in your pocket" that mainly serves consumers in Europe. The total purchase price for the three companies: a hefty $710 million. "What's really astounding," one analyst commented, "is that none of the companies acquired make actual devices. Instead, everything is about platform and data. And—more importantly—users." In combination, the three acquisitions boast 130 million platform users.[15] Like Nike, Under Armour sees that the future of its industry is platform-based, and it is determined to be a disruptor.

Similar competitive moves are occurring in other sectors. Industrial giants including GE, Siemens, and Haier are connecting their machines to the nascent *Internet of things*.[16] These networked machines constantly stream data into a central platform that enables them to interact with and learn from one another.[17] Access to data from this network of devices helps each machine better utilize its resources and provide more reliable service.

Can any product or service become the basis of a platform business? Here's the test: if the firm can use either information or community to add value to what it sells, then there is potential for creating a viable platform. This creates huge opportunities for a lot of firms.

Consider McCormick Foods, a 126-year-old company that sells herbs, spices, and condiments. By 2010, the company's traditional growth strategies had run their course. McCormick had already expanded into a full range of food seasonings and established a foothold up and down its supply chain, including operations in farming and food preparation. The company was running out of growth options. CIO Jerry Wolfe heard about Nike's move into platform-building. Could McCormick do the same?

Wolfe reached out to Barry Wacksman, a partner at R/GA, a leading New York design firm that had helped Nike design its platform. Together, they hit on the idea of using recipes and taste profiles to build a food-based platform. Wolfe and Wacksman used McCormick's taste laboratories to distill three dozen flavor archetypes—such as minty, citrus, floral, garlicky, meaty—that can be used to describe almost any recipe. Based on personal preferences, the system can predict new recipes an individual is likely to savor. Members of the McCormick platform community can modify recipes and upload the new versions, creating ever-expanding flavor options and helping to identify new food trends, generating information that's useful not only to the platform's users but also to managers of grocery stores, food manufacturers, and restaurateurs.[18]

As these examples demonstrate, the ability to leverage platforms is no longer restricted to the Internet upstarts of Silicon Valley. Nor is the incumbent's response to the forces of disruption restricted to merely attempting to fight back against the rising tide of platform power—or trying, usually in vain, to hurriedly build a copycat platform after their industry has been colonized.

The leaders of incumbent companies who understand the new business model can begin building tomorrow's platforms in a way that not only leverages their existing assets but strengthens and reinforces them.

■ ■ ■

So platforms *are* eating the world. The disruption they are driving is reaching businesses one industry at a time and is likely to hit practically all information-intensive industries at some point. We've already seen it play out in the media and telecom industries. Retail, city transportation, and hospitality are currently under assault. We expect banking, education, and health care to start feeling the heat soon. These industries are highly information-intensive but have so far resisted platform-driven disruption thanks largely to protective regulatory regimes and the consumer conservatism driven by greater risk sensitivity. When YouTube shows a user a tasteless or pirated video, the damage is less serious than when a poorly curated platform connects a borrower to a loan shark, an education platform offers a college student inaccurate math or science information, or a medical platform matches a patient with an incompetent physician. Nonetheless, Lending Club, Udemy, and Jawbone are chipping away at these markets and making early inroads.

In the end, of course, bringing platform disruption to these and other industries is *not* primarily a technological challenge. The innovators who hope to create the great new platforms of the future need to focus on the core interactions in the marketplaces they hope to conquer, and analyze the barriers that limit them. Overcoming those barriers will enable the building of platform-based ecosystems in those markets. We'll explore this topic in greater detail in the final chapter of this book, where we'll share our vision of the future of the world of platforms.

TAKEAWAYS FROM CHAPTER FOUR

❑ Platforms are able to outcompete pipelines because of their superior marginal economics and because of the value produced by positive network effects. As a result, platforms are growing faster than pipelines and taking leading positions in industries once dominated by pipelines.

❑ The rise of platforms is also disrupting business in other ways. It is reconfiguring value creation to tap new sources of supply; reconfiguring value consumption by enabling new forms of consumer behavior; and reconfiguring quality control through community-driven curation.

❑ The rise of platforms is also causing structural changes in many industries—specifically, through the phenomena of re-intermediation, separation of ownership and control, and market aggregation.

❑ Incumbent companies can fight back against platform-driven disruption by studying their own industries through a platform lens and beginning to build their own value-creating ecosystems, as Nike and GE are doing.

5

LAUNCH

Chicken or Egg? Eight Ways
to Launch a Successful Platform

The fall of 1998 was a heady time in the world of business. Fueled by the astonishing growth of the Internet, technology-based businesses were being launched by the hundreds, and many were enjoying acclaim and soaring valuations out of all proportion to their actual revenues (often minimal) and profits (often nonexistent). Inspired by the early experiences of companies like AOL and Amazon, high-tech entrepreneurs and their cheerleaders in the media decided that the key to long-term success was growth at all costs—and many of them burned through millions of dollars in pursuit of that growth. Countless ambitious nerds in their twenties and early thirties were amassing giant fortunes—on paper, at least.

In this tumultuous atmosphere, a pair of young entrepreneurs entered the exploding Internet arena. Thirty-one-year-old Peter Thiel was born in Germany and raised in California, where he became one of the country's highest-ranked young chess players and went on to study philosophy and law at Stanford University. An avowed libertarian, Thiel helped found the *Stanford Review*, a conservative newspaper that challenged the university's dominant liberal culture.

Max Levchin, twenty-three years old, was born in Ukraine and granted political asylum when he moved to the U.S. with his family. Levchin grew up in Chicago and studied computer science at the University of Illinois at Champaign–Urbana, where he developed a passion for cryptography—the science of making and breaking codes.

By 1998, he was ready to apply his genius for crafting secure forms of computerized communications to the world of business.

Thiel and Levchin (along with a third partner, John Bernard Powers, who soon departed) launched Confinity, a startup aimed at enabling money transfers on Palm Pilots and other personal digital assistants (PDAs) equipped with infrared ports. At the time, the Palm Pilot was an exceptionally popular mobile device whose adoption rate was expected to grow, and launching a payment system on a mobile device that people carried with them everywhere made sense. The business logic behind Confinity seemed indisputable. The notion of a payment mechanism that could potentially liberate millions of people from reliance on government-sponsored currency also appealed to the idealistic Thiel's libertarian streak, much as another ambitious online payment platform—Bitcoin—would fire the imagination of libertarians a decade later.

Nonetheless, Confinity attracted few users. After two years, having gained only 10,000 signups, Levchin and Thiel shut Confinity down.

Along the way, however, they unlocked a much more promising business prospect. Back in October 1999, a Confinity engineer had cobbled together an online demo to accept payments via email. This side project represented a significant potential improvement in payments processing; unlike previous systems for online payments, it allowed anyone in the world to receive an online payment from anyone else without needing to use the unwieldy system for transferring funds from one bank account to another. Levchin and Thiel recognized that it might be possible to turn this new form of online payment into a significant business on its own—one that could serve millions of consumers and the online businesses they patronized.

They came up with a name for the service—PayPal—and set out to build a company around it. It was, at that point, an inauspicious moment in the business cycle to launch such a service; the possibility of a collapse of the so-called Internet bubble was looming over the high-tech industry, and within a few months a precipitous decline in the NASDAQ index would make the dot-com bust official. Adding to the pressure was the fact that Thiel and Levchin knew they would have to make PayPal successful *fast*—they were spending some $10 million per month on the business, a large amount in the platform world, where huge capital expenditures are normally not required.[1]

They also realized they would have to overcome one of the toughest challenges associated with creating a business designed to serve two sides of a market—the chicken-or-egg problem. When trying to build a two-sided market in which both sides are equally essential, which comes first? And how do you attract one without the other?

In the case of a new payments mechanism, the chicken-or-egg problem is particularly obvious and acute. Without sellers who are willing to accept the new form of payment, buyers won't adopt it. But if buyers don't adopt the new form of payment, sellers won't invest time, effort, and money in accepting it. So how do you launch a new payments platform from a base of zero, starting with neither sellers nor buyers—when neither group has a reason to join until the other side joins first?

In terms of simple logic, the chicken-or-egg problem might seem insoluble. PayPal solved the problem through a series of ingenious strategies.

To start with, PayPal reduced the friction involved in accepting online payments. All a user needed was an email address and a credit card. This simplicity was in stark contrast to previous online payment mechanisms, which demanded multiple rounds of verification before an account could be set up, thereby discouraging early users. PayPal's user-friendly, almost frictionless system attracted a significant initial base of consumers—though not enough, in itself, to make the platform attractive to the universe of online sellers.

In a lecture he later gave at Stanford, Peter Thiel explained what happened next:

> PayPal's big challenge was to get new customers. They tried advertising. It was too expensive. They tried BD [business development] deals with big banks. Bureaucratic hilarity ensued. . . . the PayPal team reached an important conclusion: BD didn't work. They needed organic, viral growth. They needed to give people money.
>
> So that's what they did. New customers got $10 for signing up, and

existing ones got $10 for referrals. Growth went exponential, and PayPal wound up paying $20 for each new customer. It felt like things were working and not working at the same time; 7 to 10 percent daily growth and 100 million users was good. No revenues and an exponentially growing cost structure were not. Things felt a little unstable. PayPal needed buzz so it could raise more capital and continue on. (Ultimately, this worked out. That does not mean it's the best way to run a company. Indeed, it probably isn't.)[2]

Thiel's account captures both the desperation of those early days and the almost random experimentation the company resorted to in an effort to get PayPal off the ground. But in the end, the strategy worked. PayPal dramatically increased its base of consumers by incentivizing new sign-ups.

Most important, the PayPal team realized that getting users to sign up wasn't enough; they needed them to try the payment service, recognize its value to them, and become regular users. In other words, *user commitment* was more important than *user acquisition*. So PayPal designed the incentives to tip new customers into the ranks of active users. Not only did the incentive payments make joining PayPal feel riskless and attractive, they also virtually guaranteed that new users would start participating in transactions—if only to spend the $10 they'd been gifted in their accounts.

PayPal's explosive growth triggered a number of positive feedback loops. Once users experienced the convenience of PayPal, they often insisted on paying by this method when shopping online, thereby encouraging sellers to sign up. New users spread the word further, recommending PayPal to their friends. Sellers, in turn, began displaying PayPal logos on their product pages to inform buyers that they were prepared to honor this method of online payment. The sight of those logos informed more buyers of PayPal's existence and encouraged them to sign up. PayPal also introduced a referral fee for sellers, incentivizing them to bring in still more sellers and buyers. Through these feedback loops, the PayPal network went to work on its own behalf—it served the needs of users (buyers and sellers) while spurring its own growth.

However, the company leaders didn't sit back and rely on the positive feedback loops to do all the growth work on their own. They looked for opportunities to jack up the growth rate still further.

In early 2000, they noted the growing popularity of PayPal on eBay, the most popular online auction site. It was a natural place for PayPal, since most of the sellers on eBay aren't full-time merchants but ordinary people without facilities for accepting credit cards or other forms of online payment.

PayPal's marketing team opportunistically refocused its efforts toward enabling payments on eBay. Among other techniques, they simulated consumer demand on eBay by creating a bot (an automated software tool) that bought goods on the site and then insisted on paying for these transactions using PayPal. Noting this apparent growth in demand, many eBay sellers signed up for the PayPal service—which in turn made PayPal even more visible and attractive to consumers. The sellers began posting PayPal icons on their sites, enabling buyers to access the payment system with just a single click of the mouse, reducing friction still further.[3]

Within three months, PayPal's user base grew from 100,000 to one million.

The leaders of eBay noticed how PayPal had built its own platform business partly on eBay's back. Concerned about the potential competitive threat posed by a company that was building an independent connection with eBay customers (and siphoning off a fraction of the revenues from eBay transactions to boot), eBay tried to fight back. It launched its own payment system, Billpoint, in partnership with Wells Fargo Bank. It promoted Billpoint aggressively, at one point requiring eBay merchants who accepted both Billpoint and PayPal to post *larger* icons for Billpoint on their sale pages. Despite these efforts, Billpoint failed to get traction among eBay users, partly because of its belated launch, partly because of ill-advised business moves by eBay—for example, the decision to squelch deals that would have promoted Billpoint's use by non-eBay merchants.

PayPal continued to grow. By the time Confinity shut down its Palm Pilot business in late 2000, its offspring PayPal had already garnered three million accounts—three hundred times the number achieved by its parent company. Not since the launch of the first credit card, Diners Club, has the world seen such rapid global adoption of a new payment instrument. In February 2002, PayPal went public.

In October 2002, eBay finally gave up on Billpoint and acquired PayPal in exchange for $1.4 billion in stock—a modest sum by today's standards but a significant one at the time. At the time of the sale, 70 percent of all eBay auctions accepted PayPal, and roughly 25 percent of closed auction purchases were transacted using the payment service. Today, PayPal produces a major portion of eBay's revenues and profits while enabling hundreds of thousands of small merchants to conduct business online more easily, efficiently, and profitably than ever before.

THE HEART OF PLATFORM MARKETING: DESIGNING FOR VIRAL GROWTH

As the PayPal story suggests, building a platform business differs from traditional product or pipeline marketing in a number of ways. For starters, in the world of platform marketing, *pull* strategies rather than *push* strategies are most effective and important.

The industrial world of pipelines relies heavily on push. Consumers are accessed through specific marketing and communication channels that the business owns or pays for. In a world of scarcity, options were limited, and getting heard often sufficed to get marketers and their messages in front of consumers. In this environment, the traditional advertising and public relations industries focused almost solely on awareness creation—the classic technique for "pushing" a product or service into the consciousness of a potential customer.

This model of marketing breaks down in the networked world, where access to marketing and communication channels is democratized—as illustrated, for example, by the viral global popularity of YouTube videos such as PSY's "Gangnam Style" and Rebecca Black's "Friday." In this world of abundance—where both products and the messages about them are virtually unlimited—people are more distracted, as an endless array of competing options is only a click or a swipe away. Thus, creating awareness alone doesn't drive adoption and usage, and pushing goods and services toward customers is no longer the key to success. Instead, those goods and services must be designed to be so attractive that they naturally pull customers into their orbit.

Furthermore, for a platform business, user commitment and active usage, not sign-ups or acquisitions, are the true indicators of customer adoption. That's why platforms must attract users by structuring incentives for participation—preferably incentives that are organically connected to the interactions made possible by the platform. Traditionally, the marketing function was divorced from the product. In network businesses, marketing needs to be baked into the platform.

This new way of thinking about marketing is reflected in the strategies that the leaders of PayPal used to make their platform successful. Rather than pushing PayPal into the consciousness of users through, for example, television commercials, print advertisements, or email blasts, they created incentives that gave the platform itself a pull appeal—including both the ultra-simplicity of PayPal's service and the payments that rewarded those who delivered new sign-ups. They pulled sellers onto the platform by both creating demand for PayPal's service among buyers and simulating demand through the eBay shopping bot. As more users signed up, PayPal's attractiveness continued to intensify. In the end, competing payment services were swept away—testament to the power of pull.

Traditional push strategies continue to be relevant in the world of platforms. For example, Instagram received tens of thousands of downloads on the day of its launch when it was featured as the number one app on Apple's iTunes store—the kind of push strategy that pipeline companies have used for decades. And, as we'll discuss later, Twitter achieved liftoff largely because of a massively successful public relations event—another push type of strategy.

But in the world of platforms, rapid, scalable, and sustainable user growth is most often achieved through pull processes.

THE INCUMBENTS' ADVANTAGE:
REALITY OR ILLUSION?

The chicken-or-egg problem and the difficulties of attracting a large user base may cause you to wonder: why shouldn't incumbent companies with huge existing customer bases take over the world of platforms? Perhaps it's just a matter of time before companies like Walmart, Samsung, and GE leverage their head starts to crush the competition.

Large enterprises do have some advantages when launching platform businesses. They have existing value chains, powerful alliances and partnerships with other companies, pools of talent to draw upon, and vast arsenals of resources—including loyal customer bases.

However, these advantages can create complacency. In the traditional business world dominated by products and pipelines, there is usually time to observe the rise of outside competition and to make adjustments. Most big companies have evolved metabolisms that reflect this relatively slow pace of change: their processes for strategic planning, goal-setting, self-evaluation, and course correction operate on leisurely schedules with annual or, at best, quarterly checkpoints. However, in the world of platforms, dominated by networks that interact rapidly and unpredictably, the market can change quickly and customer expectations can change even faster. Management systems need to change accordingly.

As incumbent companies reinvent themselves for the world of platforms, they will find themselves on the same playing field as lithe, fast-moving startup companies. In a world of democratized network access and pull marketing, the advantages once produced by size, experience, and resources have become less important.

So if you're an entrepreneur or a would-be entrepreneur, or if you help to run a small or midsized company that has its eye on a platform business opportunity, don't be intimidated by the prospect of a giant competitor encroaching on your space. The rules of the growth game have changed, and if you understand and master the new rules, you have as good a chance of surviving and thriving as anyone.

THERE ARE MANY WAYS
TO LAUNCH A PLATFORM

It's tempting to assume that the launch strategy that works for Platform A will work for Platform B. But history shows it isn't so. In fact, even platforms that are direct competitors may need to adopt different launch strategies in order to carve out powerful and unique positions in the marketplace. The stories of three competing online video platforms—YouTube, Megaupload, and Vimeo—illustrate this point vividly.

YouTube was the first democratic (anyone can upload) video hosting platform to gain mainstream traction. It did this by focusing entirely on content creators. During its initial days, YouTube conducted contests incentivizing content creators to upload videos. Additionally, it allowed content creators to embed their videos off-platform, which rapidly spread the word about YouTube. Certain potential users found the new venue highly attractive. For example, much of the engagement on the then-popular social network Myspace was built around indie bands. YouTube improved on Myspace by creating the Flash-based, one-click video experience, making it easy for bands to upload videos of their music. This created an initial corpus of content for YouTube and simultaneously leveraged producers to bring in consumers, some of whom eventually converted to producers as well. Strengthening its focus on producers, YouTube even elevated top content creators to a partner status that entitled them to a share of ad revenue.

YouTube's unrelenting focus on producers helped in four ways. First, it seeded the platform with content. Second, it created a curation dynamic on the platform to identify quality content by letting viewers vote up or down on the videos they watched. Third, it leveraged producers to bring in consumers. Fourth, and most important, it created a set of content creators who had an investment in the platform, had a user following, and would not be easily incentivized to invest in another one.

Megaupload was faced with the *late-mover problem*. By 2005, when Megaupload launched, most content creators were already active on YouTube, and there was no incentive for them to participate in a new platform with a smaller market of viewers. As the second mover, Megaupload couldn't compete head-on following the same user acquisition strategy as the market pioneer. So it employed an alternative launch strategy. It focused exclusively on consumers (viewers) by seeding the platform with content internally, specifically creating content in categories that were increasingly being policed on YouTube, including pirated videos and pornography. Megaupload gained significant traction by addressing these seemingly underserved needs. However, in the process it exposed itself to lawsuits and negative publicity.

Our third player, Vimeo, was another late entrant (it was launched in November 2004)—but it succeeded with a producer-first strategy that competed directly with YouTube. The key was creating a set of higher-quality tools that appealed to a particular set of users who felt neglected by YouTube.

In its initial days, YouTube's hosting and bandwidth infrastructure, coupled with its embeddable player, constituted a compelling value proposition to producers. However, as YouTube gained traction among producers, the focus of the platform moved from improving video hosting infrastructure (as a value proposition to producers) to improving matchmaking of videos with consumers (focusing on video search, and a video feed).

Vimeo responded to YouTube's shift by focusing its platform on the producers and providing them with superior infrastructure, including built-in support for high-definition video playback and a better embeddable player for installation on blogs. This enabled it to compete successfully with YouTube in pursuit of producers who would create a sustainable flow of videos.

As these varying examples illustrate, if you're launching a platform, knowing the value propositions offered by your competitors can help you structure your own, allowing you to claim a relatively untouched market niche—even if your basic value unit may appear similar on the surface.

EIGHT STRATEGIES FOR BEATING THE CHICKEN-OR-EGG DILEMMA

Understanding the importance of pull strategies in a platform market, as well as the need to analyze and respond to your rivals' business designs, are significant elements of launch strategy. But the dilemma we call the chicken-or-egg problem still looms for virtually all platform founders. How to begin building a user base for a two-sided market when each side of the market depends on the prior existence of the other side?

One way to address this conundrum is to avoid the chicken-or-egg problem altogether by building a platform business on the foundation of an existing pipeline or product business. This approach is known as:

1. The follow-the-rabbit strategy. Use a non-platform demonstration project to model success, thereby attracting both users and producers to a new platform erected on your project's proven infrastructure.

Consider Amazon. It never faced the chicken-or-egg problem because, as a successful online retailer, it operated an effective pipeline business that used online product listings to attract consumers. With a thriving consumer base, Amazon converted itself into a platform business simply by opening its system to external producers. The result is Amazon Marketplace, which enables thousands of merchants to sell their products to millions of consumers—with Amazon enjoying a small slice of revenue from every transaction.

In the B2B space, Intel faced the same challenge in demonstrating the value of wireless technology. No one wants a wireless laptop if no hosts provide wireless service; no hosts will spend on wireless routers if no users demand them. Intel partnered with the Japanese telecom company NTT to demonstrate that a market existed. Once NTT showed that money could be made by catering to this market, dozens of other firms followed suit. Intel, in fact, originated the term "follow the rabbit" to define this strategy.

It's not always possible to use the follow-the-rabbit strategy. Sometimes you have to start your platform from scratch, which means that finding a way to attract a base of users on both sides of your market is an unavoidable challenge.[4] There are a number of specific, effective strategies that have been developed and demonstrated for overcoming the chicken-or-egg problem. In general, these strategies involve three techniques:

1. **Staging value creation.** The platform managers arrange for the creation of value units that will attract one or more sets of users and demonstrate the potential benefits of participating in the platform.[5] Those initial users create more value units, attract still other users, and set up a positive feedback loop that leads to continuing growth.[6] The *Huffington Post* followed this strategy by hiring writers to create an initial array of high-quality blog posts for the site, thereby attracting readers. Some of these readers began contributing blog posts of their own, leading to the gradual development of a wider network of content creators and attracting even more readers.

2. **Designing the platform to attract one set of users.** The platform is designed to provide tools, products, services, or other benefits that will attract one set of users—either consumers or producers. The existence of a critical mass of users on one side of a marketplace attracts users on the other side, leading to a positive feedback loop. As we'll detail below, the restaurant reservation platform OpenTable used this strategy by creating useful electronic tools for restaurateurs. Once a large number of restaurants were on board, consumers began to discover the site and started using it to make their dining plans.

3. **Simultaneous on-boarding.** To start, the platform creates conditions such that value units can be created that are relevant to users even when the overall size of the network is small. It then strives to stimulate a burst of activity that will simultaneously attract consumers and producers in sufficient numbers to create larger numbers of value units and value-producing interactions, so that network effects can begin to kick in. Later in this chapter, we'll show how Facebook employed this strategy to make its fledgling social network attrac-

tive to users even when the universe of potential members was very small—limited, in fact, to students at a single university.

These three techniques can be used individually or together, and a variety of combinations can work effectively under the right circumstances. What follows are some of the specific variations that we've identified. If you're in the process of developing a new platform or hoping to launch one, you may find one of these an inspiring model for your own chicken-or-egg strategy.

2. The piggyback strategy. Connect with an existing user base from a different platform and stage the creation of value units in order to recruit those users to participate in your platform.

This is a classic strategy used in many successful platform launches. As we've seen, PayPal used this strategy when it piggybacked on eBay's online auction platform.

Justdial is India's largest local commerce marketplace, facilitating consumer transactions with more than four million small businesses. It seeded the initial database by borrowing listings from existing yellow pages as well as by employing feet-on-street soldiers who went door to door collecting business information. Using this data, Justdial was launched as a phone directory service. A consumer would call in looking for service providers—for example, caterers for a wedding banquet. Justdial would pass on the lead to the producers—in this case, appropriate caterers in the town where the consumer was located. Grateful for the lead, some of these service providers would become subscribers to Justdial. To encourage more active participation by local merchants, many of whom weren't previously listed anywhere online, Justdial made it easy for them to join the platform through human interfaces, telephone connections, and text messaging.

After a successful IPO in May 2013, Justdial continues to be the dominant platform in the local commerce space in India. Its humble origin was in a collection of business listings "borrowed" from an existing platform, the local telephone directory.

In the U.S., startups have used a similar strategy by piggybacking on Craigslist. The new platform starts by "scraping" Craigslist, using automated data-gathering software tools to obtain information about merchants and service providers. It then posts this information on its platform, giving consumers the impression that these merchants are actually participating on the platform. When a consumer requests a certain service provider, the platform passes on the lead while inviting the merchant to join the platform.

As described earlier in this chapter, another compelling example of the piggyback strategy is the way YouTube rode the Myspace growth wave by offering its powerful video tools to attract indie bands that were members of the social network. Once YouTube was exposed to millions of Myspace members, its adoption rate grew virally. By 2006, YouTube's reach outgrew Myspace's, and the adoption graphs have only diverged further since then.

3. The seeding strategy. Create value units that will be relevant to at least one set of potential users. When these users are attracted to the platform, other sets of users who want to engage in interactions with them will follow.

In many cases, the platform company takes the task of value creation upon itself by acting as the first producer. In addition to kickstarting the platform, this strategy allows the platform owner to define the kind and quality of value units they want to see on the platform, thereby encouraging a culture of high-quality contributions among subsequent producers.[7]

When Google launched its Android smartphone operating system to compete with Apple's, it seeded the market by offering $5 million in prizes to developers who came up with the best apps in each of ten categories, including gaming, productivity, social networking, and entertainment. Winners not only got the prize money but became market leaders in their categories, attracting large numbers of customers as a result.

In other cases, the value units may be "borrowed" from another source rather than created by the platform developer from scratch. Adobe launched its now-ubiquitous PDF document-reading tool in part by arranging to make all federal government tax forms available online. The size of this instant market was huge, encompassing any individual or business that might need to pay U.S. taxes. Adobe induced the IRS to cooperate by suggesting that millions of dollars in printing and postage costs could be saved. Taxpayers, in turn, got fast, convenient access to documents that everyone needs, at least once a year. Impressed by the value provided, many adopted Adobe as their document platform of choice.

In still other cases, seeding is done through simulated ("fake") value units. As we've seen, PayPal employed this strategy when it created bots that made purchases on eBay, thereby attracting sellers to the PayPal platform. This was especially clever, since a bot could then turn around and list for sale the item it had just bought, thereby covering both sides of the two-sided market—and precluding PayPal from ever having to warehouse and ship the item itself.

Dating services often simulate initial traction by creating fake profiles and conversations. Many skew their profiles to showcase attractive women, in a bid to attract men to the platform. Users who visit the site see the activity and are enticed to stay on.

Reddit is a highly popular link-sharing community that circulates vast amounts of Internet content. When it first launched, the site was seeded with fake profiles posting links to the kind of content the founders wanted to see on the site over time. It worked. The initial content attracted people who were interested in similar content and created a culture of high-quality contributions to the community. Over time, its members have learned to rely on one another for guidance as to what's worth scrutinizing and what is not. (The success of Reddit's launch and expansion have not shielded it from controversy, of course, as the 2015 battles over allegedly racist and bigoted content on the site made clear.)

Similarly, when Quora first started, the editors would ask questions and then answer the questions themselves, to simulate activity on the platform. Once users started asking questions, editors continued to answer them, thereby demonstrating how the platform was intended to work. Eventually, users themselves took over the process, and the "pump-priming" by Quora personnel could cease.

4. The marquee strategy. Provide incentives to attract members of a key user set onto your platform.

In many cases, there's a single group of users who are so important that their participation can make or break the success of the platform. It may, therefore, make sense for the platform manager to incentivize their participation, either through a cash payment or through other special benefits.

In the world of electronic gaming, companies like Microsoft (Xbox), Sony (PlayStation), and Nintendo (Wii) create devices that serve as platforms that connect consumers with content produced by game developers. The dominant sports game developer is Electronic Arts (EA), whose licensed games that simulate NFL football, NBA basketball, NHL hockey, and other sports (such as its Tiger Woods pro golf tour game) are annually updated and outsell all competitors. No producer of a gaming device can hope to survive without having an attractive array of games from EA available for its platform. Thus, Microsoft, Sony, and Nintendo have all been willing to provide especially sweet partnership deals to entice EA to develop or adapt games so as to be ready for release at the moment their new platforms are released.

In a variation on this strategy, a platform company may choose to purchase a marquee participant in order to obtain exclusive access to the seeds it produces. For a number of years, software producer Bungie specialized in games, like the popular Marathon, for use on Apple computers. In 2000, with the Xbox nearing launch, Microsoft bought out Bungie and repurposed a game then in development under the title Halo: Combat Evolved as an Xbox exclusive. Halo became the marquee app that sold hundreds of thousands of Xbox devices, as well as a billion-dollar franchise in its own right.

Sometimes, the marquee players whose participation is vital to platform success are consumers rather than producers. That was the case with PayPal, which is why the company gave cash incentives to entice shoppers to adopt their online payment mechanism.

In 2009, the Swiss postal service made the decision to transform itself into a digital message-delivery platform using scanning-

and-archiving technology provided by Seattle-based Earth Class Mail.[8] Swiss Post soon recognized the importance of capturing and converting thousands of customers who were more comfortable with traditional mail delivery. To attract those holdouts, Swiss Post gave away thousands of iPads to households in remote neighborhoods. In the process, it encouraged these rural Swiss families to switch from physical mail to electronic messaging, thus greatly reducing the resources it had to dedicate to hand-delivering the mail. It also, not so incidentally, positioned Swiss Post to become the country's largest retailer of Apple products—a significant secondary benefit for the company.[9]

5. The single-side strategy. Create a business around products or services that benefit a single set of users; later, convert the business into a platform business by attracting a second set of users who want to engage in interactions with the first set.

Launching a service booking platform like OpenTable, the restaurant reservation system, poses a classic chicken-or-egg problem. Without a large base of participating restaurants, why would patrons visit the OpenTable site? But without a large base of patrons, why would restaurants choose to participate? OpenTable solved the problem by first distributing booking management software that restaurants could use to manage their seating inventory. Once OpenTable had enough restaurants on board, they built out the consumer side, which allowed them to start booking tables and collecting a lead generation fee from the restaurants.

The Indian bus reservation platform redBus gained traction in a similar manner. It provided bus operators with a seating inventory management system, then opened the platform to consumers once bus operators had started using the software.

Delicious is a social networking site that allows users to share lists of web bookmarks—links to Internet content that individuals love and that they want to revisit again and again. Delicious gained initial traction by allowing early users to produce valuable content in stand-alone mode, using Delicious to store browser bookmark lists in the cloud for their personal consumption. Once the user base hit critical mass, the social bookmarking features started getting used, and the value of the network expanded rapidly as the number of users increased. Now Delicious has become a popular tool for spreading Internet memes and trends as people share their bookmark lists.

6. The producer evangelism strategy: Design your platform to attract producers, who can induce their customers to become users of the platform.

Platforms that provide businesses with tools for customer relationship management (CRM) can often solve the chicken-or-egg problem simply by attracting one set of users—producers—who then take on the task of bringing along the other set—consumers— from their own customer base. The platform helps the producers cater to their existing set of consumers, and over time, the producers benefit from data-driven cross-pollination as other consumers on the network become interested in their products and services.

Crowdfunding platforms such as Indiegogo and Kickstarter thrive by targeting creators who need funding and providing them with the infrastructure to host and manage the funding campaign, making it easier for them to connect effectively with their customer base. Education platforms such as Skillshare and Udemy also grow through producer evangelism. They sign up influential teachers, allowing them to easily host online courses and prompting them to get their students on board.

In a similar fashion, expert marketplaces can build their consumer base by starting with customer lists provided by their producer members. For example, Clarity, which bills itself as an online marketplace that provides expert advice for entrepreneurs, enables bloggers and other experts to monetize their following through a Clarity widget that lets readers book paid calls with them. With every call, the producer helps Clarity sign up a new consumer who can then be directed to other producers.

Mercateo, a German B2B platform for business and industrial supplies, employs a producer evangelism strategy with a novel twist. It shrewdly offers producers this invitation: "Bring us your customers, and you will have the last word in any bidding competition . . . but only for the customers you bring." Thus, suppliers are incentivized to invite their customers to join Mercateo, and to do so promptly, before a competing company can claim them and enjoy the advantage of final-offer bidding.

7. The big-bang adoption strategy. Use one or more traditional push marketing strategies to attract a high volume of interest and attention to your platform. This triggers a simultaneous on-boarding effect, creating an almost fully-developed network virtually instantaneously.

As we've noted, in today's crowded, networked, and ultra-competitive arena, push strategies have become increasingly ineffective at enabling companies to achieve rapid, large-scale growth. But there are occasional exceptions. Twitter's breakout moment occurred at the 2007 South by Southwest (SXSW) Interactive film, music, and tech festival. Twitter had launched nine months earlier, but wasn't getting heavy adoption. Jack Dorsey and Twitter's other founders needed a way to get a critical mass of users on the platform. Given the real-time nature of activity on Twitter, they realized they needed to build concentration in time as well as in space.

Twitter invested $11,000 to install a pair of giant flat-panel screens in the main hallways at SXSW. A user could text "Join sxsw" to Twitter's SMS shortcode number (40404) and find his or her tweets instantly appearing on the screens. Seeing the feedback on large screens in real time and watching as thousands of new users jumped into the fray created enormous excitement around Twitter and helped make it the hottest networking site in cyberspace. Twitter received the festival's Web Award for the year's best online innovation, and by the end of SXSW, Twitter usage had tripled, from 20,000 tweets per day to 60,000.

Other networks have modeled their breakout strategies on Twitter's. Two years later, blogging platform Foursquare achieved a comparable breakthrough at the 2009 SXSW festival. In 2012, Tinder, a location-based dating app, achieved its breakout by launching during a frat party at the University of Southern California—a hotbed of young men and women who were already looking for ways to hook up. Tinder made the task easier and, in the process, achieved critical mass during a live party in a small, contained location.

Not every platform can take advantage of the big bang strategy, as Twitter, Foursquare, and Tinder did. As South by Southwest has grown, the number of companies trying to use it as a platform launch vehicle has reached a point where there's virtually no way to be heard above the roar of the crowd.[10] And there isn't always a relevant opportunity for an explosion of real-time publicity interest that is capable of attracting thousands of potential users.

Nonetheless, when such an opportunity exists—as it did for Tinder—the smart platform manager will grab it.

8. The micromarket strategy. Start by targeting a tiny market that comprises members who are already engaging in interactions. This enables the platform to provide the effective matchmaking characteristic of a large market even in the earliest stages of growth.

The odds were heavily stacked against Facebook. Friendster had gathered more than three million users within a few months of its 2002 launch, and Myspace was growing fast. Of all platform businesses, social networks are probably the least forgiving of late market entrants. Users won't readily move to a new social network unless it offers something remarkably different. That's the power of the network effect.

What's more, because the value of a social network is so heavily based on network effects, achieving critical mass is especially important. If Facebook had launched worldwide and quickly achieved a few hundred signups—or even a few thousand—it wouldn't have taken off, since those widely dispersed, random users coming in wouldn't have interacted.

So Facebook's decision to launch in the closed community of Harvard University wasn't simply a matter of convenience. It was a masterstroke that enabled Facebook to solve the chicken-or-egg problem. Attracting an initial five hundred users in the geographically and socially concentrated community of Harvard University ensured the creation of an active community at launch. Facebook leveraged Harvard as an existing micromarket and gained traction by improving the quality of interactions among its members. Focusing on a micromarket reduces the critical mass required to start interactions and makes matchmaking much easier.

When it expanded beyond Harvard, Facebook had to build a user base in every new campus it opened up to, often competing with existing intra-campus networks. Initially, these campuses were unconnected nodes on the Facebook network. Growth took off when Facebook started allowing cross-campus friend connections. This eliminated the need to solve the chicken-or-egg problem afresh in every new campus. Users coming onto the network at a new campus had an existing list of connections across other campuses to keep them engaged while they waited for others from their own campus to join.

Geographic focus isn't the only way to define a micromarket. Stack Overflow started out as a question-and-answer community for programming topics (category focus). Later it expanded into a second category that users requested—cooking. Now Stack Overflow has a voting mechanism that allows the community to choose topics they are interested in.

VIRAL GROWTH:
THE USER-TO-USER LAUNCH MECHANISM

One of the most powerful ways to accelerate the growth of a platform is by achieving *viral growth*. The viral growth strategy complements any of the launch strategies we've discussed in this chapter.

Viral growth is a pull-based process based on encouraging users to spread the word about the platform to other potential users. When users themselves encourage others to join the network, the network becomes the driver of its own growth.

The term "viral growth," of course, contains a built-in metaphor: it analogizes the growth of the platform to the spread of an infectious disease. In nature, a disease spreads when four elements interact: a host, germs, a medium, and a recipient. An infected host sneezes or otherwise spreads germs that carry infection out into the environment. These germs are then spread through a medium, such as the atmosphere. Then, a recipient inhales, ingests, or otherwise absorbs the germs and becomes infected in turn. Now the recipient becomes the host, and the cycle repeats. If it happens often enough, an epidemic results.

Similarly, four key elements are necessary to begin the process of viral growth for a platform business—the *sender,* the *value unit,* the *external network,* and the *recipient.* Let's consider the viral growth of Instagram:

- **The sender.** A user on Instagram shares a picture that he has just created. This launches the cycle that will eventually bring in a new user.
- **The value unit.** On Instagram, the value unit is the picture that the user shares with friends.
- **The external network.** For Instagram, Facebook serves as a very effective external network, allowing value units (photos) to spread and be exposed to potential users.
- **The recipient.** Finally, a user from Facebook gets intrigued by the picture and visits Instagram. This user may create her own photo and start the cycle all over again. Now the recipient is acting as the sender.

Everyone has heard of Instagram's rapid growth—over 100 million active users in less than two years—which led to its billion-dollar acquisition in April 2012 by Facebook. What is less well known is that Instagram achieved this rapid growth *without employing a single traditional marketing manager.* It happened because the company's platform was carefully designed to make viral growth organic and practically inevitable.

Unlike its competitor Hipstamatic, Instagram didn't simply allow users to save, organize, and filter pictures. It encouraged them to share their photos on external networks like Facebook, converting a single-user activity into a social, multi-user activity. Every time users engaged the app, they shared their creations. Every point of app usage became an instance of app marketing. In essence, Instagram converted all its users into marketers.

The same cycle of viral growth—a form of growth impossible in the industrial economy of pipelines and products—helps to explain the success of many other platform startups. Airbnb encouraged users with rooms to rent (hosts) to list their offerings (value units) on Craigslist (external network). Those who saw the room listings (recipients) and were motivated to rent those rooms became Airbnb users— and many subsequently began renting out rooms of their own, fueling the growth of the platform. OpenTable similarly encourages diners (hosts) to share their dinner reservations (value units) over email or Facebook (external networks) with their friends and colleagues (recipients) who are joining them for dinner.

If you're a platform manager hoping to achieve the same kind of viral growth as Instagram, Airbnb, and OpenTable, you need to design rules and tools that will jumpstart the cycle. Your goal is to design an ecosystem where senders want to transfer value units through an external network to a large number of recipients, ultimately leading many of those recipients to become users of your platform.

Let's look at these four design elements in greater detail.

The sender. Getting senders to spread value units is *not* the same as word of mouth, which is a familiar tactic in traditional marketing. Word of mouth happens when users like your platform so much, they can't stop talking about it. When users become senders and spread value units, they aren't talking about your platform—they are spreading their own creations, and indirectly generating awareness of and interest in your platform.

In general, users spread self-created value units to get social feedback, which in turn may bring them fun, fame, fulfillment, or fortune—or some combination of these rewards. Channel owners on YouTube spread the word about their videos on multiple external networks in order to gain an audience; survey developers on SurveyMonkey spread their surveys via email, blogs, and social networks to get responses, which provide insight into the question the survey developers are trying to answer; creators seeking funding on Kickstarter spread their project page on their social networks in order to attract the money they need to complete their works as well as the audience they hope will appreciate the finished product.

These examples illustrate how well-designed platforms create natural incentives for users to share. As a rule, platform designers must avoid discouraging the spread of value units. The act of sending these units onto an external network like Facebook should not distract a creator from using the platform; instead, it should fit integrally into the workflow of the platform. The more closely this is aligned to the main use of the platform, the more likely the platform is to go viral.

A platform may also provide inorganic (artificial) incentives to encourage value-spreading behavior, but these need to be carefully structured. A monetary incentive, for example, can become a cash drain if the platform achieves viral growth. Dropbox, the popular cloud-based service for storing and sharing data files, does a good job of structuring inorganic incentives; it offers free storage space to the sender as well as the recipient when the recipient signs up to become a Dropbox user. Thus, the perk for spreading the word about Dropbox is not a cash payment that would only serve to empty the company's coffers, but rather an opportunity to use Dropbox's service even more, thereby stimulating further growth and encouraging users to make ever greater use of the Dropbox platform.

The value unit. This is the fundamental unit of virality—an embodiment of platform usage that can spread on an external network and demonstrate the platform's value. But not every value unit that exists on a platform is spreadable. For example, the users of a business platform designed to enable the exchange of proprietary documents among company partners will not want to spread their confidential information the way Instagram users share their snapshots. So designing *spreadable value units* is a crucial step toward virality.

A spreadable value unit may be one that helps to start an interaction on an external network, the way Instagram photos create conversations on Facebook among users intrigued by the images they've seen. Or it may create the opportunity to complete an incomplete interaction, the way an unanswered question on Quora demands social feedback in the form of an answer, or a fresh survey on Survey-Monkey invites responses. Making it easy for users to create and disseminate spreadable value units helps you build a platform that has high growth as well as high engagement.

Of course, as the example of a business platform for exchanging confidential documents indicates, not every value unit is spreadable. Platforms that don't lend themselves to the creation of spreadable value units are unlikely to go viral. Managers of such platforms will have to use other approaches to achieve growth.

The external network. Many platforms grow on top of other networks. Instagram, Twitter, Zynga, Slide, and other platforms have achieved viral growth by leveraging Facebook as an underlying network. Airbnb spread on Craigslist; OpenTable spreads on email.

However, leveraging an external network is not as simple as introducing a "Share on Facebook" button and waiting for users by the million to show up. External networks often introduce restrictions when more and more applications use them for growth—for example, Facebook has enforced limitations on the gaming apps that outside companies offer its users. In other cases, users overwhelmed by a constant flow of invitations sent by outside producers urging them to sample their goods or services become jaded over time and stop responding. To avoid this result, the managers of startup platforms need to be strategic about identifying the external networks they can use to build their growth and finding creative, value-adding ways to connect with their users.

When LinkedIn was launched in 2003, most social networks gained traction by integrating with a new user's Hotmail or Yahoo contact list and prompting him or her to send invites to the platform over email. Originally devised by Michael Birch (best known as cofounder of the short-lived social network Bebo), this simple hack helped generate growth for many early social networks. LinkedIn chose instead to engineer a more technologically challenging integration with Microsoft Outlook, the software that housed most of the business connections that LinkedIn wanted to access. The integration was time- and cost-intensive, but it helped LinkedIn establish itself as the premier social network for business.

The recipient. When the user of a platform sends a value unit to a friend or acquaintance, the recipient will respond if he or she finds the value unit relevant, interesting, useful, entertaining, or otherwise valuable. When the value units are intriguing enough, the recipients spread them further, sometimes giving rise to new interactions on another network. Media companies like Upworthy and BuzzFeed have grown almost entirely on the strength of consumer-initiated viral spread.

Unfortunately, since value units are created by users, managers of platforms have limited control over them. Instagram doesn't select photos or retouch them to make them more attractive, YouTube doesn't direct or edit user videos, and Facebook doesn't curate member posts to eliminate boring ones. However, sometimes a platform can nudge users in directions that will make seeds more attractive to recipients. For example, Instagram provides photo editing tools to help users enhance the attractiveness of the images they post, and it encourages users to label their photos with hashtags that are specific and relevant—#vwbus for a photo of a Volkswagen van rather than the more generic #van or (worse yet) the self-explanatory #photo.[11]

In addition, platform managers can connect the value unit to a call to action—a message that ensures the recipient recognizes the platform from which the value unit has been delivered and understands the opportunity to join. When the communications platform Hotmail first went viral, it affixed to the bottom of every email the message, "P.S. I love you. Get your FREE email at Hotmail." Free email for consumers was a new and compelling offer at the time, and this simple message attracted thousands of user adoptions.

Not every budding platform has an opportunity to achieve viral growth. But if it does, it can help turn slow but steady expansion into the kind of skyrocket growth that makes a platform into a national or global phenomenon with the potential to dominate its market for years to come.

TAKEAWAYS FROM CHAPTER FIVE

❑ One difference between platform businesses and traditional pipeline businesses is that, in the world of platforms, pull strategies designed to encourage virality are more important than the push strategies (such as advertising and public relations) used in conventional marketing.

❑ Successful platforms use one of eight proven strategies for solving the chicken-or-egg problem: the follow-the-rabbit strategy; the piggyback strategy; the seeding strategy; the marquee strategy; the single-side strategy; the producer evangelism strategy; the big bang adoption strategy; and the micromarket strategy.

❑ The speed of a platform's expansion can be accelerated through viral growth. This depends on four key elements: the sender, the value unit, the external network, and the recipient.

6

MONETIZATION
Capturing the Value
Created by Network Effects

Not long ago, one of the authors of this book—Marshall Van Alstyne—was approached by a pair of company founders on their way to a meeting with a group of venture capitalists. They'd created a new platform business that, for the purposes of this story, we'll give the fictitious name of Ad World. They were hoping to impress the assembled VCs with an astute business plan and thereby win a significant offer for funding.

"Here's the idea," one of the founders explained to Marshall. "Our new platform Ad World will provide a listing service for firms to find ad agencies. We'll make it easy for companies that are ready to begin new advertising campaigns to post requests for bids, and for ad agencies to post proposals and offers that companies can look at and respond to. It's just like 99designs, which lets graphic artists link up with consumers who want help with artistic projects, only in the B2B space instead of the B2C space."

"Okay," Marshall said. "I get the idea. What's your question?"

"Here's what we want to know," the founder replied. "We're pretty sure Ad World is going to provide value to our users and attract a fair amount of interest. But we're wondering how to generate revenues from it. Should we charge the ad agencies to join the platform and put up their profiles? Should we charge the firms that are seeking services? Or should we charge for individual project listings? Or maybe for all three?"

"And we need an answer fast," interjected his partner. "We need to figure out our strategy so we can run the numbers and make our business case to the VCs."

The aspiring platform moguls gazed at Marshall with such sincerity that he almost hated to burst their bubble. But he had to do it. As gently as he could, Marshall replied, "You've listed three possible ways to monetize Ad World, and you've asked me to pick one of them—or maybe all three. My answer is, none of the above."

The two founders in this story were smart, talented, thoughtful business leaders. They'd done a lot of homework on the nature of platform ecosystems. They did understand, in a general way, how platform businesses work and the challenges of attracting both sides of the market to make a robust set of interactions possible. But when it came to monetization, they were asking the wrong questions.

These founders shouldn't charge *either* side to be listed on their platform. Doing so would put terrible friction on entry into the ecosystem, discouraging many potential participants from becoming users. To charge for posting a deal simply means people post fewer deals. That's bad. It reduces potential interaction volume, not to mention realized interactions. As a result, it also reduces the volume of data available to the platform—data desperately needed to enable the platform to forge powerful matches between consumers and producers.

In fact, rather than *charging* users to join the platform, the founders should be *subsidizing* their participation—perhaps by providing tools and services to make it easy, fast, and effective for them to complete their profiles.

This wasn't a complete surprise to the founders. They had partly intuited this, as Marshall could tell by the fact that they'd used "scrapers"—automated software tools for collecting data from the Internet—to produce user profiles. They understood that building a base of users was their first and biggest challenge, and that creating friction around the process by charging money for it would be a serious mistake.

How, then, could the founders monetize their platform model? The answer: They *can* charge users for the value they accrue from the ecosystem, but the charge should be levied on *deal completion*, not at the time of listing. They would make it possible for firms to post a deal risk-free by charging a fee only once the firms get what they need. The fee becomes performance-based, and it feels negligible because it simply skims off a small fraction of a transaction that's occurring anyway.

What's more, the best strategy may be one the founders didn't even consider. Why not charge ad agencies for a service that helps them do a postmortem to discover why they *lost* a deal? Not only would this fee create no friction on a deal, but it would reflect the value of the feedback provided; it would be recurring revenue rather than one-time revenue; and it could help ad agencies improve the quality of their offerings, thereby encouraging a rise in the value of interactions over time.

The story of this fledgling platform and the strategic challenge its founders faced illustrates some of the complexity of platform businesses—as well as the creative thinking platform managers need to practice if they are going to realize the full value-creating potential of the ecosystems they are building. Monetization, in fact, is one of the most difficult—and fascinating—issues that any platform company must address.

VALUE CREATION AND THE CHALLENGE OF MONETIZING NETWORK EFFECTS

As we've explained, the inherent value of a platform business lies chiefly in the network effects it creates. But monetizing network effects poses a unique challenge. Network effects make a platform attractive by creating self-reinforcing feedback loops that grow the user base, often with minimal effort or investment by the platform manager. Higher value creation by producers on the platform attracts more consumers, who, in turn, attract more producers and further value creation.

Yet, ironically, this powerfully positive growth dynamic makes monetization very tricky. Any charge levied on users is likely to discourage them from participating on the platform. Charging for access may lead people to avoid the platform altogether; charging for usage may inhibit frequent participation; charging for production reduces value creation, making the platform less attractive to consumers; and charging for consumption reduces consumption, making the platform less attractive to producers. This was the precise dilemma that the founders of Ad World were grappling with.

How, then, do you monetize a platform without damaging or even destroying the network effects you've worked so hard to create?

Some students of platform businesses leap to the assumption that the collaborative nature of value creation on the Internet means that the natural price for goods and services distributed online must be free. But of course a business that charges nothing for the benefits it offers is unlikely to survive for very long, since it will not produce the resources needed to maintain or enhance it, and investors will have no incentive to provide the capital needed for its growth.

Some element of free pricing can be useful in building network effects for a platform business. But it's important to understand the different models in which *partially* free pricing can power growth. As every business student learns, the model behind the safety razor business that entrepreneur King Gillette founded in 1901 involved distributing the razors for free—or at a very low, subsidized cost— while charging for the blades.

As it happens, research by Randal C. Picker of the University of Chicago Law School has called into question the traditional story of Gillette and the razors-and-blades pricing strategy. Picker found that the timing of price changes for Gillette razors and blades, as well as the expiration date on the patent covering Gillette's unique razor design, seems to undermine the notion that the company was employing the razors-and-blades strategy as commonly understood.[1] Nonetheless, the familiar story remains a handy symbol for a strategy that has been used in a number of markets, including, for example, the printer market, where sales of high-priced toner cartridges generate profits that the relatively cheap printers themselves don't produce.

Another version of this strategy is the freemium model, in which a free layer of service attracts users who eventually pay for an enhanced version. Many online service platforms, including Dropbox and MailChimp, work this way. Both the razors-and-blades model and the freemium model monetize the same user base, or portions thereof.

Platforms may also offer free or subsidized pricing to one user base while charging full price to an entirely different user base. This makes the design of monetization models more complex, since the platform must ensure that the value it gives away to one side can be used to capture value on the other side. Significant scholarly work has been done in this area. Two of this book's authors (Geoff Parker and Marshall Van Alstyne) were among the first scholars to lay out the theory of two-sided market pricing.[2] And the theory was mentioned as part of the 2014 Nobel Prize awarded to one of the other originators of two-sided market economics, Jean Tirole.[3]

Achieving the right balance among the complex factors involved in two-sided market pricing isn't easy. Netscape, one of the pioneers of the Internet era, gave away browsers for free in hopes of selling web servers. Unfortunately, there was no proprietary connection between browsers and servers that Netscape could reliably control. Anyone could just as easily use Microsoft's web server or the free Apache web server, which meant that Netscape was never able to monetize the other side of its free browser business. As this example illustrates, platform businesses that intend to use free pricing as part of their strategy need to ensure that the value they create and hope to ultimately monetize is fully controlled by the platform.

Meeting the monetization challenge must begin with an analysis of the value created on the platform. Traditional non-platform businesses—pipelines—deliver value to their customers in the form of a product or service. They may charge for ownership of the product, as Whirlpool does when it sells a dishwasher, or for utilization of the product, as GE Aviation charges for installation and regular servicing of its aircraft engines.

Like Whirlpool and GE, platform companies are engaged in designing and building technology. But rather than putting the technology in the hands of customers in exchange for a fee, they invite users to join the platform—and then they seek to monetize the platform by charging for the value that the platform technology creates for those users. This value falls into four broad categories:

- **For consumers: Access to value created on the platform.** Video viewers find the videos on YouTube valuable; Android users find value in the various activities made possible by the apps; students on Skillshare find value in the courses made available through the site.
- **For producers or third-party providers: Access to a community or market.** Airbnb is valuable for hosts because it provides access to a global market of travelers. Company recruiters find LinkedIn valuable because it enables them to connect to potential job-seekers. Merchants find Alibaba valuable because it enables them to sell their products to customers around the world.
- **For both consumers and producers: Access to tools and services that facilitate interaction.** Platforms create value by reducing the friction and barriers that prevent producers and consumers from interacting. Kickstarter helps creative entrepreneurs raise money for new projects. eBay, combined with PayPal, allows anyone to start an online store that serves customers anywhere in the world. YouTube allows musicians to provide their fans with performance videos, without having to produce physical products (CDs or DVDs) and without having to sell through intermediary retailers.
- **For both consumers and producers: Access to curation mechanisms that enhance the quality of interactions.** Consumers value access to high-quality goods and services that address their specific needs and interests, while producers value access to consumers who want their offerings and are willing to pay a fair price for them. Well-run platforms build and maintain curation systems that connect the right consumers with the right producers quickly and easily.

These four forms of value wouldn't exist without the platform, and so they may be described as *sources of excess value* that the platform generates. Most well-designed platforms create far more value than they directly capture—which is why they attract large numbers of users, who are happy to enjoy the benefits of all the "free" value provided by the platform. A smart monetization strategy begins by considering all four forms of value, then determines which sources of excess value can be exploited by the platform without inhibiting the continued growth of network effects.

NUMBERS ARE NOT ENOUGH: FINDING THE VALUE IN NETWORK EFFECTS

Founded in 2005 by Ethan Stock, Zvents was originally an online guide to local events in the Bay Area. It grew rapidly, expanding beyond California and becoming the largest site of its kind, serving hundreds of markets and attracting over 14 million visitors every month. It was a hit with both producers—the local event organizers who posted their concerts, shows, fairs, festivals, and other activities on the site—and consumers, who logged on to Zvents to find something fun to do after work and on the weekend.

Stock seemed to be living the Silicon Valley dream. Having built a platform that millions of people had come to rely on, his only remaining challenge was to monetize it. But that proved to be far from simple.

"Once we reached critical mass," Stock recalls, "and it was clear we were becoming the market leader, we expected event organizers would start paying. . . . But there is a fatal flaw in some businesses that can hogtie their ability to make money—the expectation of completeness."

The problem was that consumers who visited Zvents expected to find a comprehensive listing of local events. If only a few of the available options were included, the interest of users would quickly evaporate. Which meant that Zvents didn't have much leverage over the event organizers they hoped to charge. If they'd threatened organizers with having their listings pulled, the threats would have no teeth, since the whole value of Zvents lay in the completeness of its listings. Charging producers for access to the platform wasn't going to work.

Zvents experimented with another monetization technique that we'll discuss later in this chapter—charging producers for enhanced access. They did manage to get a few organizers to pay for more prominent listings, but the value of the enhancements in terms of improved attendance or ticket sales proved small. Zvents ended up with a tiny trickle of revenue rather than the gusher they'd hoped for. In June 2013, with his hopes of building a lucrative platform empire to rival Google or Facebook dashed, Stock sold his company to eBay, which now uses Zvents as a bulletin board for arts and entertainment events in conjunction with its StubHub ticket resale platform.

The lesson? Network effects *as measured by numbers of visitors alone* don't necessarily reflect the monetary value of a platform. The interactions facilitated must generate a significant amount of excess value that can be captured by the platform without producing a negative impact on network effects. When that's not the case, monetization may not be possible.

The paradoxical relationship between network size and monetization potential doesn't stop there. In some cases, the ability to monetize a platform may actually *increase* dramatically when the number of users *declines*—reflecting the power of *negative* network effects to impact the value of a platform.

Meetup was launched in 2002 as a way for groups to organize offline meetings ("meetups") by connecting online. Its cofounder, Scott Heiferman, said he was inspired by the way people in New York came together as a community following the 9/11 terror attacks.

Meetup gained traction as a free platform, but the dot-com bust of the late 1990s served as a constant reminder to its managers of the need to develop a credible monetization model. They first tried to generate income by using lead generation, charging fees to offline venues such as restaurants and bars for the number of users that came in during a meetup. However, in a pre-smartphone world, this monetization model didn't work very well. The number of people who actually showed up for events was different from the number who signed up, and Meetup had no way of counting heads to determine an appropriate fee.

Meetup abandoned the lead generation model and experimented with other ways of monetizing its service. It tested advertising, but failed to attract significant numbers of advertisers. It tried offering a premium product called Meetup Plus, but the additional value provided generated little interest. (Perhaps understandably: years later, when asked in an interview to explain the extra service included with Meetup Plus, Heiferman responded with a laugh, "God, I don't even remember what it got you. It got you some kind of features where you would be able to . . . I don't know. I can't remember.") Meetup even tested charging fees to political organizations, which were a growing portion of the platform's user base, but this, too, produced only modest revenue. Meetup's options were running out.

Meanwhile, Meetup found itself confronted with another problem—one that, paradoxically, would help save the company. This was the growth of negative network effects. As the platform grew, with low barriers to planning a meetup, many meetups were being started without a clear purpose or adequate planning. There was a lot of noise on the platform, leading to disappointing experiences for users, who would sign up for a meetup only to discover that attendance was small and activity minimal.

Meetup's leaders made a risky decision. They decided to start charging meetup organizers, despite the potential for drastically diminishing the scale of the platform and weakening its network effects. They reasoned that charging organizers would help them solve their monetization problem while weeding out organizers who weren't serious about their goals. A letter went out to all organizers informing them that they would henceforth be asked to pay $19 per month for the right to keep using Meetup's service.

The backlash was huge. After *Businessweek* ran an article on Meetup's new strategy, the magazine received emails from countless platform users predicting the service's demise. One user from London wrote, "I think it's fair to say most organisers were shocked, and most of the ones I've spoken to will simply cease organising for their groups . . . There isn't anything Meetup is doing these days that users can't simply do on their own and more effectively, and there's plenty of open source software to make use of and create your own website."[4]

But despite the backlash, the strategy worked. The number of meetups promoted on the site fell drastically, but their quality, and therefore the quality of the interactions generated, improved significantly. As Heiferman explained in an interview five years later, "The big headline, by the way, in going from free to fee for us is: Yeah, we lost 95% of our activity but now we have much, much, more going on than we ever did before and half the Meetups are successful, as opposed to 1–2% being successful."[5]

As we've discussed, a platform's goal is not simply to pump up the numbers of participants and interactions. It must also take steps to encourage desirable interactions and discourage undesirable ones. Meetup's monetization model helped it achieve exactly that. By discouraging organizers who weren't serious about their objectives, the pricing mechanism created a culture of quality on the platform.

It's a mistake to assume that network effects can always be optimized by simply refraining from charging users. A better approach to analyzing the monetization challenge is to ask these questions: How can we generate revenues without reducing our positive network effects? Can we devise a pricing strategy that strengthens our positive network effects while reducing our negative network effects? Can we create a strategy that encourages desirable interactions and discourages undesirable ones?

WAYS TO MONETIZE (1):
CHARGING A TRANSACTION FEE

To begin exploring some of the ways that an effective monetization strategy can be developed, let's look back at the four forms of excess value created by platforms—access to value creation, access to the market, access to tools, and curation. All four culminate in some kind of interaction. In many cases, this interaction involves an exchange of money, as when an Uber customer pays a driver for a ride, an eBay buyer pays a seller for a product, or a company using Upwork pays a freelancer for a completed project. Platforms that facilitate such monetary transactions can monetize the value created by charging a transaction fee, which may be calculated as either a percentage of the transaction price or a fixed fee per transaction. The latter system, which is simpler to administer, is particularly appealing when a high frequency of transactions is expected without a significant variation in the transaction size.

Charging a transaction fee is a powerful way of monetizing the value created by the platform without hampering the growth of network effects. Because buyers and sellers are charged only when an actual transaction occurs, they are not discouraged from joining the platform and becoming part of the network. Of course, if the transaction fee is excessive, it may discourage transactions. Platform managers may need to experiment with various levels of fee to find the rate that captures a fair percentage of the value created without driving users away.

A more serious and persistent challenge is to capture on the platform itself all the interactions facilitated by the platform. Buyers and sellers who find each other on the platform are naturally incentivized to take the interaction off the platform if they can, in order to avoid paying the transaction fee.

This problem is especially rampant with platforms that connect service providers with service consumers. With the rise of the freelancer economy and the spread of the online sharing economy, platform businesses from Airbnb and Uber to TaskRabbit and Upwork have sprung up to facilitate service interactions. However, most of them are faced with the challenge of capturing the interaction on-platform. In most cases, the interaction can't occur until the producer (in this case, the service provider) and the consumer (the purchaser of the service) agree on the terms of the service, which usually requires the two to interact directly. Furthermore, the actual exchange of money often follows the delivery of the service, which also requires the two participants to interact directly. These direct interactions weaken the platform's ability to capture value by creating an opportunity for the parties to make a deal off-platform. As a result of avoiding the transaction fee, the consumer can obtain a discount on the service, while the provider gets to keep more of the total service charge. The only loser is the platform company itself.

Platforms like Fiverr, Groupon, and Airbnb solve this problem by temporarily preventing participants from connecting. These platforms try to provide all the information a consumer needs to make an interaction decision, without connecting the consumer directly with the producer. Groupon does this by featuring services that are largely standardized, while the less-standardized Airbnb and Fiverr provide rating mechanisms and other social metrics that indicate the reliability of a service provider, making direct contact between the parties less necessary.

Sometimes strategies like these are insufficient. This is especially the case with platforms that create a market for professional services, which often require discussions, exchanges, and workflow management before and during the provision of services. As a result, it may not be possible for the platform to retain control of all communications between the producer and the consumer, and charging the consumer ahead of the interaction may not be an option.

In cases like these, the platform must extend its role as an interaction facilitator to include more value-creating activities. For example, Upwork provides tools for monitoring the service provider remotely. This enables consumers of professional services to monitor projects and make payments based on actual delivery of work.

The Clarity platform for connecting advice seekers with experts retains control of the interaction through a similar mechanism. In the past, expert-matching platforms connected the two sides, charged a lead generation fee, and allowed the transaction to occur off-platform. Clarity provides additional call management and invoicing capabilities that serve to capture the interaction on the platform. To benefit producers, Clarity offers integrated payments and invoicing, making it simple for advice givers to generate income through small, one-off engagements. To benefit consumers, the call management software provides per-minute billing, which gives them the option to opt out of a call that isn't proving useful. Both sides receive enough additional value to keep them connected to Clarity, with minimal incentive to take their interaction off-platform.

As these examples illustrate, service provider platforms that want to capture and monetize interactions must create tools and services that benefit both parties by removing friction, mitigate risk, and otherwise facilitate interactions.

However, additional benefits like these may not be sufficient to enable all service provider platforms to thrive. Local service platforms that connect consumers with relatively simple services like plumbing and house painting continue to struggle with the challenge of owning the interaction. The risks involved in such interactions are lower than when hiring a professional freelancer: the two sides get to meet in person, the work is simpler, its quality is less variable, and, since the work itself happens off-platform, usually under the direct supervision of the consumer, the consumer can monitor the service provider without having to rely on software tools. Some of these local service platforms may need to move to the *enhanced access* monetization model, which we'll describe in a later section of this chapter.

WAYS TO MONETIZE (2):
CHARGING FOR ACCESS

In some cases, it's possible to monetize a platform by charging producers for access to a community of users who have joined the platform *not* in order to interact with producers but for other, unrelated reasons.

Dribbble has rapidly gained prominence in the design community as a high-quality platform for designers—artists, illustrators, logo creators, graphic designers, typographers, and others—to show off their work, thereby gaining exposure, credibility, and valuable feedback from their peers. Adapting the jargon of basketball, Dribbble users call new images "shots," image groups "buckets," and reposts of favorite images "rebounds." This unique lingo has helped foster a highly engaged community that includes many of today's best designers.

Dribbble's managers are eager to protect the long-term value of this specialized community. For this reason, they do not charge members for access to the platform, which could weaken network effects. They've also opted not to permit sponsored images that provide enhanced access to the community (for example, by popping up, uninvited, on users' home pages), since these could reduce the prestige of the site and its perceived value to its users. (We'll describe the enhanced access strategy in more detail a bit later in this chapter.) So to monetize the site, Dribbble has invited third parties to pay for access to the community. In this case, companies looking for designers are charged to post employment listings on the site's jobs board.

This form of monetization creates interactions that benefit both parties. Designers are motivated to put up their best work on Dribbble, since these may generate leads to new gigs, while companies get access to top-flight designers whose portfolios have already been curated by the creative community.

Dribbble's monetization method can be described by the simple shorthand term "advertising." But notice that, unlike most advertising, Dribbble's highly targeted job listings generate value for the community, enhance the core interaction, and strengthen network effects rather than adding noise and depleting value.

In a similar fashion, LinkedIn allows recruiters to present job opportunities to its members and offers companies the ability to compare and target professionals based on their résumés and professional brands. LinkedIn's power as a recruiting platform encourages users to update their profiles more often, thereby keeping the platform active and healthy.

As we've observed throughout this chapter, a monetization model is sustainable only when it strengthens network effects (rather than weakening them). Charging third-party producers for community access is effective if and only if the newly added contents—such as the job listings on Dribbble—enhance the value of the platform to its users.

WAYS TO MONETIZE (3): CHARGING FOR ENHANCED ACCESS

Sometimes a platform that facilitates a monetary transaction may be unable to own, and hence to monetize, the transaction. Such platforms may instead charge producers for enhanced access to consumers. This refers to the provision of tools that enable a producer to stand out above the crowd and be noticed on a two-sided platform, despite an abundance of rival producers and the resulting intense competition to attract consumer attention. Platforms that charge producers fees for better targeted messages, more attractive presentations, or interactions with particularly valuable users are using enhanced access as a monetization technique.

The system of monetizing enhanced access generally doesn't

harm network effects, since all producers and consumers are permitted to participate in the platform on an open, non-enhanced basis. But those for whom the additional value of enhanced access is particularly great can pay for that extra value—allowing a portion of that value to be captured by the platform business.

The traditional classified advertisement model, for example, supported local newspapers for decades through paid placement of commercial messages. Today, online platforms use a similar model, asking producers to pay for more prominent placement of their messages. Yelp, for example, offers restaurants enhanced visibility and better branding on its platform by charging for a premium listing in search results. Restaurants pay for this service, since it makes it easier for them to break through the noise and attract the attention of the most valuable potential consumers.

Google search may also be seen through a similar lens. Every website publisher can achieve higher placement for its site through search engine optimization, a self-managed website design and coding process that produces no revenue for Google. However, some publishers choose to buy premium placement through Google Adwords. In a similar fashion, Tumblr, a micro-blogging platform acquired by Yahoo in 2013, allows users to promote their posts to a larger audience for a fee. Twitter, too, promotes sponsored content at the top of its feed.

Another way of monetizing enhanced access is by charging users for lowering barriers that otherwise exist between users. Dating websites, for example, often allow men to see profiles of women without revealing identifying details. Users who pay a subscription fee are allowed access to additional information that enables them to connect directly with other users who interest them.

Monetizing enhanced access to users needs to be done with care. If not done right, it can increase the noise level on the platform and decrease the relevance of content for consumers, leading to negative network effects, as described in chapter 2.

One important principle is to ensure that consumers can easily distinguish between content that has been elevated or highlighted as part of a paid access program and content whose high ranking or prominence is organic. Premium listings on Yelp and ads associated with Google's search results look different from organic results, creating a sense of transparency that enhances user trust. Most search engines before Google that failed to follow this principle ended up confusing and annoying users and damaging the value of their platforms. So-called native advertising techniques, where paid content on the Internet is designed to resemble unpaid content, run the risk of appearing deceptive and alienating users.

Platform managers must also be careful not to allow monetization of enhanced access to create the impression that user access is being restricted. As the world's largest social network, Facebook creates tremendous value for brands that want to engage with current and potential customers. Some consumer brands have grown massive followings on Facebook. However, during 2014 and 2015, Facebook was widely criticized for making curation changes that limit the reach of brands on the platform—except for those that pay extra for access to a wider audience. The perception was that Facebook was reducing services available to platform participants in order to facilitate a revenue grab. Facebook's massive size and the powerful network effects it generates have enabled it to shrug off these complaints—at least, so far. But few other platforms would be able to get away with actions like these.

Finally, platform managers must ensure that their usual curation principles are applied rigorously to content from producers who pay for enhanced access. Facebook's value is based on the relevance of its news feed, and a torrent of sponsored posts that lack such relevance could eventually drive consumers away from the platform.

WAYS TO MONETIZE (4):
CHARGING FOR ENHANCED CURATION

When we think of network effects, we often assume that more is better. However, as we noted in chapters 2 and 3, positive network effects are driven not simply by quantity but also by quality. When the quantity of content on a platform becomes overwhelmingly great, consumers may find it increasingly difficult to find the high-quality content they want, thereby reducing the platform's value for them. When this happens, consumers may be willing to pay for access to guaranteed quality—in other words, for enhanced curation.

Sittercity, a platform we've mentioned elsewhere in this book, charges parents to access the platform. To ensure quality and choice, it performs rigorous curation and screening of the babysitters who get access to the platform—a source of significant additional value to parents who worry about the well-being of their children. This extra value allows Sittercity to charge a subscription fee to parents instead of the transaction fee usually associated with a service provider platform.

As an advisor at Skillshare, an education platform, Sangeet Choudary has helped the platform transition from a transaction-fee-only model to a model that provides enhanced value upon payment of a subscription charge. Skillshare allows students to pay separately for each course taken. But once the platform managers had curated a sizeable amount of high-quality courses, Skillshare began to allow students access to multiple courses via a monthly subscription fee. Teachers are paid "royalties" based on the number of subscription-paying students who sign up for their classes. The growing number of students who choose this model get better value per course consumed, while generating recurring revenues for the platform.

WHOM SHOULD YOU CHARGE?

A typical platform supports multiple types of users performing multiple roles. Given the differences among the users, their economic status, their motivations, their objectives, their incentives, and the differing forms and amounts of value they derive from the platform, decisions about whom you should charge and whom you should not can be complex—especially since every decision you make about one user category impacts others in ways that may not be obvious. However, the general goal of encouraging positive interactions that will create value for all participants—together with observations from the histories of successful platform businesses—enables us to develop a few useful heuristics about when particular pricing choices are appropriate and when they are not.

- **Charging all users.** As we've noted, platform businesses rarely charge all their users the way pipeline businesses generally do. Charging all users would, in most cases, discourage participation, thereby reducing or destroying network effects. However, in a few cases, charging all users actually enhances network effects. In the offline world, for instance, prestigious membership organizations like country clubs charge all members. High membership dues (along with vetting processes such as requiring recommendations from existing members) serve as curating techniques to guarantee member quality. Some online platforms use this model—for example, Carbon NYC, a platform for multimillionaire residents of New York City. However, in many social and business settings, "willingness to pay" and "quality" are far from synonymous, so this pricing system must be used very carefully and selectively.
- **Charging one side while subsidizing another.** Some platforms are able to charge members of one category of users (call them A) provided they allow members of another category of users (B) to participate for free—or even subsidize or incentivize them. This works when users from category A highly value the opportunity to make contact with users from category B—but the feeling is not equally reciprocated. As we've noted, bars and pubs in the offline world have long used this strategy by offering women free or discounted drinks on Ladies' Nights. Many online dating websites follow a similar strategy, incentivizing memberships for women as a way of attracting male members who will pay full freight.
- **Charging most users full price while subsidizing stars.** Certain platforms choose to subsidize or incentivize stars—super-users whose presence attracts large numbers of other users. In offline business, malls have been known to offer attractive lease terms to popular large retailers like Target, whose presence guarantees the cus-

tomer traffic that other mall occupants will readily pay a premium for. In a similar way, online platforms like Skillshare and Indiegogo go to great lengths to court celebrity teachers and campaign creators, whose star power attracts other producers as well as large numbers of curious consumers. Microsoft learned this lesson when creating its Xbox gaming platform. Its initial monetization strategy paid game developers (producers) a one-time purchase fee while channeling ongoing user fees to Microsoft. But superstar game developer Electronic Arts refused to work on these terms and threatened to develop for Sony instead. Microsoft eventually had to succumb and agree to special terms for EA, though the details have not been publicly disclosed.

- **Charging some users full price while subsidizing users who are price-sensitive.** The category of users that is most sensitive to pricing is more likely to abandon the platform when charged, killing the network effect. Thus, it generally makes sense to discount or subsidize users who are price-sensitive while charging others the full freight. Real-world experience shows that it can be difficult to predict which side of a platform market is likely to be more price-sensitive. During the 1990s, the Denver real estate market experienced a glut of properties, making property owners desperate for rentals. Real estate agents charged owners broker fees, while tenants paid nothing. By contrast, during the same period, Boston had a scarcity of available properties, making would-be renters desperate to find places to stay; real estate agents charged potential tenants, while allowing owners to list their properties without paying a fee.

As you can see, deciding whom to charge is a delicate balancing act. The need to monetize the platform must be carefully weighed against the friction invariably produced by imposing a cost. Deciding precisely where the system can afford to create some friction—and how much friction can be tolerated without crippling the growth of network effects—is no easy matter.

Sometimes, a less-than-optimal monetization strategy can be made workable through ingenuity. During its early years, Alibaba, the e-commerce platform company that has been called China's eBay and Amazon rolled into one, was unable to charge transaction fees simply because its primitive software had trouble tracking the flow of online deals. CEO Jack Ma was forced to charge membership fees instead—an option he would have preferred to avoid because of the entry friction it creates. Alibaba managed to overcome this problem by offering sizeable commissions to salespeople who convinced others to sign on to the platform. When word got around that some Alibaba sales agents were earning commissions in excess of a million Chinese yuan, equivalent to well over $100,000, the drive to enlist members shifted into high gear despite the friction caused by the entry fees. To this day, Alibaba charges no transaction fees, having managed to monetize the platform through advertising—as if a company that facilitated transactions, like Amazon and eBay, were to generate its profits by selling ads like Google.

FROM FREE TO FEE: HOW DESIGN DECISIONS IMPACT THE TRANSITION TO MONETIZATION

As many of the cases mentioned in this chapter suggest—and as plenty of familiar real-world examples illustrate—the imperative to create and grow network effects often leads platform founders to begin by offering their services for free. Creating value for users while asking nothing in return is often a great way to attract members and encourage participation. "Users first, monetization later," as the slogan goes. Or, in a variant that we heard from the executive in charge of platform strategy for Haier Group, a Chinese manufacturing company, "You never take first money." In other words, only after a value unit has been created and exchanged with results that are satisfactory to both the producer and the consumer should the platform business itself seek to capture a share of that value.

A number of highly promising platforms have foundered because they ignored this rule and instead rushed to monetize their offerings prematurely. Sean Percival, the former vice president of online mar-

keting for the failed social network Myspace, recalls the dire effect of
financial pressures following the acquisition of the platform by Rupert
Murdoch's News Corporation. The "last nail in the coffin," Percival
says, was when Murdoch promised stock analysts in an earnings call
that Myspace would generate a billion dollars in revenue that year—
at a time when the true revenue figure was a tenth of that. As a result,
Myspace managers began scrambling to sign up any program or service that someone was willing to sponsor—no matter how inane or
annoying it might be. This was one of the factors that ultimately led
users to abandon Myspace in favor of Facebook.[6]

As we've observed, there are a number of ways to shift later to a
monetization model that lets the platform business capture some
fraction of the value created. However, the transition is often fraught
with difficulty. These key principles of platform design help ensure
that the transition to monetization—from free to fee, as Meetup's
Heiferman put it—can be managed successfully.

- **If possible, avoid charging for value that users previously received for
  free.** People naturally resent being told that they have to pay for a
  good or service they've previously received for free—as we saw in
  the case of Meetup. And not all platform businesses have been as
  successful as Meetup at navigating such a transition. Some, like
  Zvents, either died or were forced to dramatically alter the nature
  of their offering.
- **Also, avoid reducing access to value that users have become accustomed
  to receiving.** As we noted, Facebook was offering tremendous value
  for free and actually needed to cut down on that organic value
  when it decided to provide premium content promotion to paying
  producers. This led to complaints from both producers and consumers. Facebook's enormous network effects enabled it to survive
  this course correction, but for many lesser platforms it might have
  been fatal.
- **Instead, when transitioning from free to fee, strive to create new, additional value that justifies the charge.** Of course, you must ensure that,
  if you charge for enhanced quality, you control for it and guarantee
  it. Critics have assailed Uber for charging a Safe Rides fee to pay

for drivers' background checks and other safety measures while apparently cutting corners on those same steps.

- **Consider potential monetization strategies when making your initial platform design choices.** From the time of launch, a platform should be architected in a manner that affords it control over possible sources of monetization. This directly impacts how open or closed the platform is. For example, if platform managers hope to monetize through a transaction fee, they need to ensure that the platform design makes it possible for them to capture control of transactions. If platform managers hope to monetize by charging for access to their user base, the platform should be designed to control the avenues through which content reaches the users as well as the flow of data about users.

As this chapter has shown, monetization is a complicated challenge—and a crucial one that may determine the ultimate viability of a platform. Those seeking to launch a successful platform can't afford to ignore the issues surrounding monetization or defer thinking about them until after network effects have been established. Instead, platform managers should be thinking about potential monetization strategies from day one, and plan their design decisions so as to keep as many monetization options as possible open for as long as possible.

TAKEAWAYS FROM CHAPTER SIX

❑ A well-managed platform can create excess value in four ways: access to value creation, access to the market, access to tools, and curation. Monetization is about capturing a portion of the excess value created.

❑ Techniques for monetizing a platform include charging a transaction fee, charging users for enhanced access, charging third-party producers for access to a community, and charging a subscription fee for enhanced curation.

❑ One of the most crucial monetization choices is deciding *whom* to charge, since the difference in roles played by various platform users means that charging them can have widely differing network effects.

❑ Given the complexity of the monetization challenge, platform managers should take potential monetization strategies into account in every decision they make regarding platform design.

7

OPENNESS
Defining What Platform Users and Partners Can and Cannot Do

Wikipedia is a marvel of the world of platforms—an open-sourced encyclopedia that, within a few years, eclipsed traditional purveyors of information to become the most popular reference site in the world. Millions of people have come to rely upon Wikipedia as a useful, universally accessible, virtually unlimited source of data that is generally highly reliable.

Except when it isn't. And when it isn't, the results can be horrific.

Many users of Wikipedia will be able to point to their own favorite tale of bizarre misinformation popping up on the site. Perhaps the most famous is the entry titled "Murder of Meredith Kercher"—better known by the names of the two people widely suspected of the crime, the American student Amanda Knox and her Italian boyfriend Raffaele Sollecito. Under Wikipedia's policy of largely open editing by any interested party, this entry has now been edited over 8,000 times by over 1,000 people—almost entirely by people who have been convinced of the guilt of Knox and Sollecito ever since the crime was committed back in 2007. Throughout their complicated legal ordeal, including one conviction, its overturning by a second court, and another conviction, these self-appointed editors continually revised the page to eliminate any potentially exculpating evidence and to emphasize the likelihood of guilt.

The controversy over the entry grew so intense that Wikipedia founder Jimmy Wales got involved. Wales studied the matter and issued a statement: "I just read the entire article from top to bottom, and I have concerns that most serious criticism of the trial from reliable sources has been excluded or presented in a negative fashion." Shortly thereafter, he wrote, "I am concerned that, since I raised the issue, even I have been attacked as being something like a 'conspiracy theorist.'" Perhaps most disturbing, some of the editors involved in slanting the Kercher page were found to be contributors to other websites dedicated to "hating" Amanda Knox, thereby shattering any illusion of objectivity.[1]

The problems Wikipedia faces in maintaining high quality while maximizing its accessibility to all the users who want to contribute to its content illustrate the challenges inherent in managing an open platform model. Yet the obvious solution—to close down the model and institute strict controls over participation—has a huge downside. Increasing the friction involved in actively using any platform inevitably reduces participation and can even destroy the value-creation potential of the platform altogether.

HOW OPEN? HOW CLOSED?:
WALKING THE TIGHTROPE

In one of the first discussions of platform openness back in 2009, two of the authors of this book (Geoffrey Parker and Marshall Van Alstyne, in collaboration with Thomas Eisenmann) provided a basic definition of openness:

> A platform is "open" to the extent that (1) no restrictions are placed on participation in its development, commercialization, or use; or (2) any restrictions—for example, requirements to conform with technical standards or pay licensing fees—are reasonable and non-discriminatory, that is, they are applied uniformly to all potential platform participants.[2]

Being closed isn't simply a matter of absolutely forbidding outside participants on the platform. It may also involve creating such onerous participation rules that would-be users are discouraged, or charging such excessive fees (or "rents") that the profit margins of potential participants are reduced below sustainable levels.[3] The choice between open and closed isn't a choice between black and white; there is a spectrum between the two extremes.

Calibrating the right level of openness is undoubtedly one of the most complex as well as one of the most critical decisions that a platform business must make.[4] The decision affects usage, developer participation, monetization, and regulation. It's a challenge that Steve Jobs struggled with throughout his career. In the 1980s, he got it wrong by choosing to keep the Apple Macintosh a closed system. Competitor Microsoft opened its less elegant operating system to outside developers and licensed it to a host of computer manufacturers. The resulting flood of innovation enabled Windows to claim a share of the personal computer market that dwarfed Apple's. In the 2000s, Jobs got the balance right: he opened the iPhone's operating system, made iTunes available on Windows, and captured the lion's share of the smartphone market from rivals like Nokia and Blackberry.[5]

Jobs liked to recast the open/closed dilemma as a choice between "fragmented" and "integrated," terms that subtly skewed the debate in favor of a closed, controlled system. He wasn't completely wrong: it's true that, the more open a system becomes, the more fragmented it becomes. An open system is also more difficult for its creator to monetize, and the intellectual property that defines it is more difficult to control. Yet openness also encourages innovation.

It's a difficult tradeoff to master. And the consequences of choosing the wrong level of openness in *either* direction can be severe, as the rise and fall of the social network Myspace suggests.

Although the history is now sometimes forgotten, Myspace was the dominant social network before Facebook was launched in 2004, and remained so until 2008. Even in its early days, it had much of the functionality that would be familiar to users of today's social networks. Its internal staff created a wide variety of features, such as instant messaging, classified ads, video playback, karaoke, "self-serve advertising" easily purchased through the use of simple online menus, and more.

However, because of limited engineering resources, these features were often buggy, leading to a poor user experience.[6] And an ill-considered decision to keep the site closed to outside developers made solving the problem practically impossible. Chris DeWolfe, cofounder of Myspace, recalled the company's flawed thinking in a 2011 interview: "We tried to create every feature in the world and said, 'O.K., we can do it, why should we [open up to] let a third party do it?' We should have picked 5 to 10 key features that we totally focused on and let other people innovate on everything else."

Facebook didn't make the same mistake. Like Myspace, it was initially closed to outside innovators. It opened to dot-com users in 2006. This helped Facebook begin a slow climb toward competitiveness with Myspace. The trend is reflected in Figure 7.1, which shows the average daily reach of the two platforms in terms of percentage of Internet users during 2006 and early 2007, when Myspace was still king.

When Facebook launched Facebook Platform to help developers create apps in May 2007, the big shift began. An ecosystem of partners willing to extend the capabilities of Facebook quickly took root.[7] By November 2007, there were 7,000 outside applications on the site.[8] Recognizing how this flood of new apps was enhancing its rival's appeal, Myspace responded by opening to developers in February 2008. But the tide had already turned, as

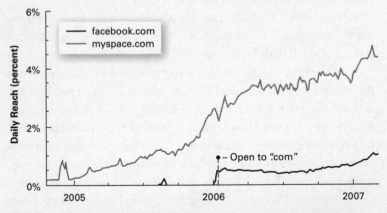

FIGURE 7.1. The market dominance of Myspace over Facebook during 2006 and early 2007. © 2015, Alexa Internet (www.alexa.com).

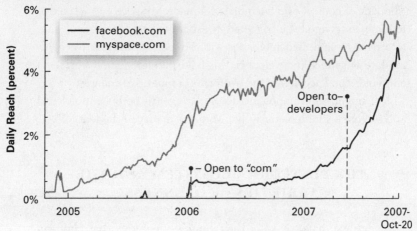

FIGURE 7.2. Facebook rapidly overtakes Myspace after opening its platform to developers in May 2007. © 2015, Alexa Internet (www.alexa.com).

shown in Figure 7.2. Facebook overtook Myspace in April 2008, and today it enjoys unquestioned supremacy in the social networking space.

Had Myspace opened itself earlier to contributions from a wider community of outside developers—especially those who had world-class technology for specific functions that Myspace wanted to build out, such as classified advertising, an effective spam filter, and user-friendly communication tools—they might have had a more robust product offering. Perhaps today Myspace and Facebook would still be competing on an almost equal footing.

At first glance, then, it would appear that Myspace's problems arose from precisely the opposite direction as Wikipedia's: the collaborative encyclopedia is struggling with the consequences of too much openness, while Myspace foundered as a result of too little. That's true to some extent—but the story is more complicated than that. Along some other important dimensions, Myspace was actually *too* open.

For example, Myspace's self-serve advertising feature created an all-too-accessible pathway for a significant amount of inappropriate content, including pornography available to platform users of any age.

The lack of control over such material made Myspace less attractive to many users and even triggered investigations by a number of state attorneys general. In combination with Myspace's slowness to accommodate outside app developers, this failure to adequately curate its content helped accelerate the platform's competitive collapse.

It might seem impossible for a platform to be both too closed and too open simultaneously, but Myspace managed the feat.

THE PLATFORM ECOSYSTEM AND THE VARIETIES OF OPENNESS

How can we make sense of the openness decisions that platform managers must make? It's helpful to start by recalling the key elements of a platform as discussed in chapter 3. As we explained there, a platform is fundamentally an infrastructure designed to facilitate interactions among producers and consumers of value. These two basic types of participants use the platform to connect with each other and to engage in exchanges—first, an exchange of information; then, if desired, an exchange of goods or services in return for some form of currency. These participants come together on the platform to engage in a core interaction that is at the heart of the platform's value-creating mission. In time, other kinds of interactions may be layered onto the platform, increasing its usefulness and attracting other participants.

Given this basic design, it's axiomatic that a vibrant and healthy platform is dependent on the value created by partners who are outside of the platform itself. If a platform is too closed, then partners cannot or will not contribute the value required to make mutually rewarding exchanges possible.[9]

Consider Google's YouTube. Because the system is highly open, it has become a viable outlet for commercial as well as amateur videos, delivering a wide array of content, ranging from the silly to the practical to the political and the inspirational. Without its vast array of user-supplied content, YouTube would be dependent on one or a few corporate sources of video material. Over time, it would likely evolve into more of a distribution system—similar to Hulu, for instance—than a true platform.

However, as we've noted, and as the examples of Wikipedia and Myspace illustrate, openness is not a black-or-white area. Decisions about degrees and kinds of openness are critical and often challenging.

There are three kinds of openness decisions that platform designers and managers need to grapple with. These are:

- Decisions regarding *manager and sponsor* participation
- Decisions regarding *developer* participation
- Decisions regarding *user* participation

Each type of decision has unique ramifications and implications. Let's consider them in turn.

MANAGER AND SPONSOR PARTICIPATION

Behind any platform, with responsibility for its structure and operation, are two entities: the firm that manages the platform and directly touches users, and the firm that sponsors the platform and retains legal control over the technology. In many cases, these two entities are one and the same. Companies like Facebook, Uber, eBay, Airbnb, Alibaba, and many others are both platform managers and platform sponsors. In this situation, control of the platform, including decisions about openness, rests completely with the manager/sponsor firm.

In other cases, however, the platform manager and the platform sponsor are not identical. In general terms, the platform manager organizes and controls producer/consumer interactions, while the platform sponsor controls the overall architecture of the platform, the intellectual property that underlies the platform (such as the software code that controls its operations), and the allocation of other rights. When the manager and the sponsor are separate, the manager is closest to the customer/producer relationship as well as to outside developers who may contribute to the platform. This gives the manager considerable influence over the daily operations of the platform. But, in general, the sponsor has greater legal and economic control over the platform and therefore a larger measure of power over its long-term strategy.

In some cases, both the platform manager and the platform sponsor can be either a single company or a group of companies—with further implications for issues of control and openness.[10]

Figure 7.3 illustrates four models for managing and sponsoring platforms. In some cases, a single firm both manages and sponsors the platform. We call this the *proprietary* model. For example, the hardware, software, and underlying technical standards for the Macintosh operating system and mobile iOS are all controlled by Apple.

Sometimes a group of firms manages the platform while one

		PLATFORM MANAGEMENT	
		ONE FIRM	**MANY FIRMS**
PLATFORM SPONSORSHIP	**ONE FIRM**	Proprietary Model *Examples:* Macintosh PlayStation Monster.com Federal Express Visa (after 2007)	Licensing Model *Examples:* Microsoft Windows Google Android Palm OS Amex-branded MBNA cards Scientific Atlanta set-tops Qualcomm radio transmission standards
	MANY FIRMS	Joint Venture Model *Examples:* CareerBuilder Orbitz Visa (prior to 2007)	Shared Model *Examples:* Android open source Linux DVD UPC bar code RFID inventory control standards

FIGURE 7.3. Four models for managing and sponsoring platforms. Adapted from "Opening Platforms: How, When and Why," by Thomas Eisenmann, Geoffrey Parker, and Marshall Van Alstyne.[11]

firm sponsors it. This is the *licensing* model. Google, for example, sponsors the "stock" Android operating system, but it encourages a number of hardware firms to supply devices that connect consumers to the platform. These device makers, including Samsung, Sony, LG, Motorola, Huawei, and Amazon, are licensed by Google to manage the interface between producers and consumers.

In still other cases, a single firm manages the platform while a group of firms sponsors it—the *joint venture* model. The Orbitz travel reservations platform was launched in 2001 as a joint venture sponsored by a collection of major airlines in order to compete with upstart Travelocity. Similarly, the job search platform CareerBuilder was created jointly in 1995 (under the original name of NetStart) by three newspaper groups as a platform for help-wanted advertising.

Finally, in some cases, a group of firms manages the platform while another group sponsors it—the *shared* model. For example, there are both many sponsors and many managers of the open source Linux operating system, which, like the Mac and iOS systems, serves as a platform connecting app developers and other producers to millions of consumers. Corporate sponsors of Linux include IBM, Intel, HP, Fujitsu, NEC, Oracle, Samsung, and many other companies, while the manager companies include dozens of device makers— TiVo, Roomba, Ubuntu, Qualcomm, and many others.

Sometimes, a particular platform may migrate from one model to another as business demands and the structure of the marketplace evolve. Consider, for example, the Visa credit card operation, which is a platform that permits merchants and consumers to engage in payment transactions with one another. It originated in 1958 as a proprietary platform under the name of BankAmericard, sponsored and managed by the Bank of America. In the 1970s, it took on the Visa brand name and morphed into a joint venture, independently managed while being sponsored by a number of banks. In 2007, Visa became a freestanding corporate entity and reverted to the proprietary model. It is now self-sponsoring rather than being supported by an outside institution.

As you can see, these four models of manager and sponsor participation are, in effect, variant patterns of openness. The proprietary model provides the greatest control and facilitates the most closed system of operation, as exemplified by Apple's management of the Mac operating system. The licensing and joint venture models are, in effect, open at one end and closed on the other, while the shared model, exemplified by Linux, leads to a platform that is open to both a wide array of sponsors and a wide array of managers.

Who wins? Who loses? Which of these four models is most advantageous to platform sponsors? Which works best for platform managers? Which model generates the greatest flow of predictable, controllable profits? It would be nice to offer definitive, one-size-fits-all answers to these questions—but, as is usually the case in business, the answer is, "It depends."

The proprietary model, used with enormous success by Apple, might seem to be every platform company's dream. After all, it allows you to capture an entire market and to realize all the profits it generates. The logical way to accomplish this is by developing a new technology standard and maintaining sole control of it. And this is not impossible—but in the real world, it doesn't always produce lasting economic returns.

A classic illustration is the so-called VCR war of the 1970s and 1980s, which pitted two technology platforms against each other: the Betamax videotape standard sponsored by Sony, and the VHS standard sponsored by JVC. Unlike most platforms of today, these standards from the pre-Internet era did not create an online venue in which producers and consumers could meet to conduct interactions together. However, they qualified as platforms because they established technology systems that would allow multiple producers (chiefly movie and TV studios) to sell products to consumers. Thus, they faced many of the same kinds of strategic challenges that today's Internet-based platforms must confront.

From a technical quality standpoint, the Betamax platform was slightly better, providing sharper images and longer recording times. But the outcome of the war was decided by the varying sponsorship/ management strategies chosen by the rivals.

Sony chose the proprietary platform model, retaining control of the Betamax standard on the theory that, in the long run, its better quality would win out in the marketplace. But that never happened. JVC followed the licensing model, enlisting many manufacturers to produce VHS recorders and players. As manufacturing volume increased, prices fell, making VHS devices more attractive to consumers. With more device makers supporting the VHS standard and with more consumers owning VHS players, movie studios and other content providers issued more products in VHS format than in Betamax. A feedback loop set in that gave VHS a large, steadily growing advantage over Betamax. By the mid-1980s, manufacturers that embraced the VHS standard came to dominate the VCR arena. Ironically, however, JVC itself enjoyed only modest profits from this victory; its development of the original VHS standard didn't lead to a large or lasting stream of income.

Years later, Sony became embroiled in a new format war with a different outcome—though one that proved to be no more satisfactory in the long run to the Japanese giant. In the mid-2000s, when videotape gave way to digital video discs (DVDs), Sony's Blu-ray high-definition video standard competed against the HD-DVD standard pioneered by Toshiba. Sony decided to pursue the same sole proprietorship model it had chosen for Betamax. In this case, Sony won the battle, thanks largely to its successful introduction of the PlayStation 3 gaming device, which included Blu-ray video and made it instantly available to millions of consumers.

Unfortunately for Sony, this victory proved short-lived. Today, a few years after the triumph of Blu-ray, the migration of consumers away from DVD to streaming video is well under way, making Blu-ray's dominance increasingly irrelevant. The lesson? If, like Sony, you choose to fight a standards battle in quest of proprietary control of a market, you'd better win it—and win it fast, before the next big thing supersedes the very technology you seek to dominate.

The story of Visa—another platform that originated in the pre-digital era—illustrates some of the other challenges faced by different management and sponsorship models. During its years of sponsorship by a consortium of big banks, Visa achieved significant success as a leading credit card company. But over time, this management model proved cumbersome. When a platform is sponsored—and therefore owned—by a number of companies, key decisions must be approved by a committee of owners with varying goals and preferences, which is an inherently inefficient management system. This is why Visa's owners ultimately agreed to spin off the business as a self-contained entity, granting it the capability to make competitive moves more nimbly.

The inherent awkwardness of multi-sponsor decision-making can affect the elegance, simplicity, and ease of use of technology. The long history of the personal computer wars between Apple's proprietary model and Microsoft's so-called Wintel standard clearly illustrates the fact that a standard controlled by a single company with a unified esthetic and technical vision can produce more attractive, intuitive tools and services than a collection of competing companies, each with its own design approach. Apple has also become far more profitable and valuable than any single company in the Wintel universe—despite the fact that its market share of computer sales has never approached that of the PC.

Similarly, Apple's iPhone is generally considered more elegant and user-friendly than any smartphone created using Google's less tightly controlled Android standard. This is particularly so today, with the Android Open Source Platform (AOSP) permitting experimentation and change by any interested company. AOSP is the platform used by Amazon in its Kindle Fire and by China's Xiaomi in its mobile phones.

This doesn't mean that Apple's proprietary iPhone strategy is necessarily "better" than Google's more open strategy. In fact, the story is a complicated one. Even though Apple's iPhone continues to be a more elegant device than competing Android phones, by 2014, open innovation by multiple phone manufacturers had earned Android about 80 percent of the smartphone market, as compared with just 15 percent for Apple.[12]

A big win for Google? Not really. The AOSP operating system doesn't automatically channel user traffic to Google's online services—which means that Google, despite being the progenitor of Android, receives no revenue or data flow from AOSP devices. In response, Google has reversed course and closed Android in an effort to reassert its control over the system.[13] (We'll return to this story later in the chapter.)

In the end, of course, the choice of a sponsorship/management model comes down to the purposes for which the platform is being developed and the goals of those designing it. The wireless radio frequency identification (RFID) technology is used to create smart tags that can be attached by the millions to products for inventory control. In effect, the RFID system is an inventory management platform that retailers can access to interact with the goods they distribute.

The RFID platform was sponsored by a huge consortium of retailers, and the tags themselves are now manufactured by many companies which compete on the basis of price as well as design. The shared model of sponsorship and management means that the RFID technology itself doesn't generate enormous profits for anyone—the tags sell for just a few cents apiece. But this suits the sponsors perfectly, since their goal all along was to make the technology as simple, accessible, and affordable as possible.

DEVELOPER PARTICIPATION

As you've seen, designing and building a platform generally starts with a core interaction. But over time, many platforms expand to include other kinds of interactions that create additional value for users and attract new kinds of participants. These new interactions are created by developers who may be afforded more or less open access to the platform and its infrastructure. We refer to the three kinds of developers as *core developers, extension developers,* and *data aggregators.*

Core developers create the core platform functions that provide value to platform participants. These developers are generally employed by the platform management company itself. Their main job is to get the platform into the hands of users and to deliver value through tools and rules that make the core interaction easy and mutually satisfying.

Core developers are responsible for basic platform capabilities.

Airbnb provides an infrastructure that allows guests and hosts to interact with each other using system resources, including the search capabilities and data services that allow guests to find attractive properties as well as the payment mechanisms necessary to conclude a transaction. In addition, Airbnb manages behind-the-scenes functions that reduce transaction costs for guests and hosts. For example, the platform provides default insurance contracts for both parties, protecting guests in the event of accident or crime and protecting hosts from negligent guest behavior (though, as we'll discuss in chapter 11, this insurance coverage is not without its shortcomings). It also verifies the identity of participants in order to make its reputation system a meaningful measure of user behavior. Designing, fine-tuning, maintaining, and continually improving systems like these are all elements of the work of Airbnb's core developers.

Extension developers add features and value to the platform and enhance its functionality. They are normally outside parties, not employed by the platform management firm, who find ways to extract a portion of the value they create and thereby profit from the benefits they offer. A familiar group of extension developers is the individuals and companies that produce apps sold via the iTunes store—games, information and productivity tools, activity enhancers, and so on. One of the crucial decisions a platform manager must make—and often reconsider as the market evolves—is the extent to which the platform will be open to extension developers.

A number of extension developers have enhanced the value of the Airbnb platform. For example, Airbnb's own research reveals that properties listed with professional-quality photographs are viewed by prospective renters twice as often as those with lower-quality images. In response, an extension developer now offers professional support under the rubric of "Airbnb photography service" to create compelling images that should make an Airbnb host more successful.

Extension developer Pillow (formerly known as Airenvy) supports hosts on the platform by providing tools to simplify property listing, guest checkin, and cleaning and linen delivery. Other developers, including Urban Bellhop and Guesthop, make travel arrangements for guests, such as dining reservations and babysitting services.

With the assistance of outside firms, an Airbnb host can offer a suite of services that compares to those provided by a full-service hotel.

In order to facilitate this extension of its platform's functionality, Airbnb must open its business to participation by these extension developers. But calibrating its degree of openness is a challenge for Airbnb. If the platform is too closed—if it is too onerous for extension developers to hawk their wares on the site—it will lose the opportunity to provide valuable extra services to platform users, perhaps alienating participants in the process. But if the platform is too open—if it is too easy for extension developers to appear on the site—then it's likely that poor-quality service providers will join the platform, tarnishing the reputation of the other developers as well as that of Airbnb itself. Furthermore, excessive openness may lead to too many providers of the same type of service, which will reduce the profit earned by any one provider and reduce the incentive to extension developers to customize services for Airbnb users.

Platforms that choose to encourage extension developers by granting a high degree of openness will usually create an *application programming interface*. This is one of the control points that a platform manager can use to manage open access to its system. An application programming interface (API) is a standardized set of routines, protocols, and tools for building software applications that makes it easy for an outside programmer to write code that will connect seamlessly with the platform infrastructure.

Currently, although Airbnb has developed an API, it is not generally available to all developers that wish to connect to the platform—an indication of the middle way the platform managers want to tread when it comes to developer participation.

Some companies erect steep barriers against extension developers not just to protect the quality of platform content but also in an effort to retain control of the revenue streams their platforms generate. We've already seen how this strategy backfired on Myspace. Today, a similar fate may be hitting Keurig, the popular maker of coffee machines—which, for this purpose, may be viewed as a platform dedicated to brewing hot beverages. We'll consider Keurig's story in chapter 8.

The *Guardian*, a British daily newspaper, has gone in the opposite direction. The paper's website enjoys significant international readership and has always been open to users, who are free to read its content, as written and edited by the newspaper's staff. However, the site was formerly closed to extension developers. Recognizing the value of the *Guardian's* vast trove of information and ideas, and the potential benefit to be derived from transforming the paper's website into an open platform, the company's management went through a months-long strategic exercise in which they discussed and analyzed the implications of such a shift. Having studied both the possible risks and the likely rewards, the *Guardian's* managers decided both to "open in" the website, by bringing in more data and applications from the outside, and to "open out" the site, by enabling partners to create products using *Guardian* content and services on other digital platforms.

To work toward the "open out" goal, the *Guardian* created a set of APIs that made its content easily available to external parties. These interfaces include three different levels of access. The lowest access tier, which the paper calls Keyless, allows anyone to use *Guardian* headlines, metadata, and information architecture (that is, the software and design elements that structure *Guardian* data and make it easier to access, analyze, and use) without requesting permission and without any requirement to share revenues that might be generated. The second access tier, Approved, allows registered developers to reprint entire *Guardian* articles, with certain time and usage restrictions. Advertising revenues are shared between the newspaper and the developers. The third and highest access tier, Bespoke, is a customized support package that provides unlimited use of *Guardian* content—for a fee.

Some of the first products released under the *Guardian's* new open platform model include a Content API, which provides access to over a million articles; a Politics API, which provides election results and candidate information; a Data Store, which provides access to data sets and visualizations, ranging from a table of country-by-country laws and practices regarding the death penalty to a colorful graph depicting all of the time-travel journeys of TV sci-fi hero Doctor Who; and an

App Framework, which facilitates app development, aimed at making the system easy to experiment with and build applications for. In response, over 2,000 extension developers signed up in the first twelve months.

The power of APIs to attract extension developers and the value they can create is enormous. Compare the financial results experienced by two major retailers: traditional giant Walmart and online platform Amazon. Amazon has some thirty-three open APIs as well as over 300 API "mashups" (i.e., combination tools that span two or more APIs), enabling e-commerce, cloud computing, messaging, search engine optimization, and payments. By contrast, Walmart has just one API, an e-commerce tool.[14] Partly as a result of this difference, Amazon's stock market capitalization exceeded that of Walmart for the first time in June 2015, reflecting Wall Street's bullish view of Amazon's future growth prospects.[15]

Other platform businesses have reaped similar benefits from their APIs. Cloud computing and computer services platform Salesforce generates 50 percent of its revenues through APIs, while for travel platform Expedia, the figure is 90 percent.[16]

The third category of developers who add value to the interactions on a platform are *data aggregators*. Data aggregators enhance the matching function of the platform by adding data from multiple sources. Under license from the platform manager, they "vacuum up" data about platform users and the interactions they engage in, which they generally resell to other companies for purposes such as advertising placement. The platform that is the source of the data shares a portion of the profits generated.

When the services provided by data aggregators are well designed, they can match platform users with producers whose goods and services are interesting and potentially valuable to them. For example, if a Facebook user has been posting information about plans for a vacation in France, a data aggregator might sell that data to an advertising agency that, in turn, would generate messages about Paris hotels, tour guides, discount airfares, and other topics likely to be of interest.

Data aggregation is now practiced by many kinds of businesses, both on and off digital platforms. When it works well, it produces results that consumers experience as seamless and even delightful: "How did they know I've been looking for kitchen tiles in exactly that shade of blue!" But when it is ham-fisted—as is too often the case—the results feel intrusive and sometimes creepy.

A story—possibly apocryphal—recounted by Charles Duhigg in the *New York Times* describes the angry father of a teenage girl marching into a Target store to ask why his daughter had been receiving coupons for baby products. "Are you trying to encourage her to get pregnant?" he demanded. The store manager apologized, but when he called the family to discuss the matter a few days later, the father was embarrassed and apologetic. "I had a talk with my daughter," he said. "She's due in August."

How did Target "know" about the girl's pregnancy before her family did? Duhigg describes Target's system for analyzing customer behaviors in an effort to anticipate future needs and purchasing activities. Thus, when a (hypothetical) female consumer visits her local Target store and buys cocoa butter lotion, a diaper bag–sized purse, zinc and magnesium supplements, and a bright blue rug, Target's algorithm calculates an 83 percent chance that she is pregnant. Cue the coupons for baby clothes.[17]

Perhaps for obvious reasons, data aggregation systems such as these are little discussed by the platform businesses that provide them access. Knowing the degree to which their personal behavior is being monitored makes many consumers queasy. Because data aggregation is a large and growing source of revenue for platform companies, managing it appropriately poses an enormous ethical, legal, and business challenge. We'll delve into this topic in more detail in chapters 8 and 11, which deal with platform governance and regulation.

WHAT TO OPEN AND WHAT TO OWN

As we've seen, innovations that are valuable to platform users can come from many sources. Some are created by core developers and therefore are owned and controlled by the platform company itself.

Others are created by extension developers and therefore are owned and controlled by outside businesses. This raises the question: when does the power of an outside developer threaten that of the platform itself? And when this happens, how should the platform manager respond?

The answer to these questions depends on the amount of value created by a particular extension app. If you are a platform manager, you don't want to let an outside firm control a primary source of user value on your platform. When this happens, you need to move to take control of the value-creating app—most often by buying the app or the company that created it. On the other hand, when an extension app adds a modest amount of additional value, then it's perfectly safe and generally very efficient to allow the outside developer to retain control of it.

Consider, for example, the ownership and control decisions Apple has made in regard to its mobile phone operating system. Apple has been careful to own most of the applications that come preloaded with the iPhone, such as music playing, photography, and voice recording. It bought SRI International, the company that developed the technology behind the iPhone's "virtual personal assistant," Siri.[18] All of these are all-high-value-adding features with significant impact on the market for the iPhone, which is why Apple is eager to own and control them.

By contrast, YouTube is content to own its video distribution and playing technology while leaving control of the millions of video clips available on the platform in the hands of the people and organizations that uploaded them. One might assume that globally popular videos like the Korean pop hit "Gangnam Style" generate significant value for YouTube consumers. But that value is ephemeral (this year's favorite video is quickly displaced by next year's) and represents just a tiny fraction of the total value of YouTube's video content. In a case like this, the platform owner has no need to own or control the individual element of value.

There are two other principles that platform managers should consider when weighing whether an extension app represents a threat to their economic power.

First, if a particular app has the potential to become a powerful platform in its own right, the manager of the platform that hosts the app should seek to own it—or to replace it with an app controlled by the platform itself.

In 2012, Google Maps had become the premier provider of mapping services and location data for mobile phone users. It was a popular feature on Apple's iPhone. However, with more consumer activity moving to mobile devices and becoming increasingly integrated with location data, Apple realized that Google Maps was becoming a significant threat to the long-term profitability of its mobile platform. There was a real possibility that Google could make its mapping technology into a separate platform, offering valuable customer connections and geographic data to merchants, and siphoning this potential revenue source away from Apple.

Apple's decision to create its own mapping app to compete with Google Maps made sound strategic sense—despite the fact that the initial service was so poorly designed that it caused Apple significant public embarrassment. The new app misclassified nurseries as airports and cities as hospitals, suggested driving routes that passed over open water (your car had better float!), and even stranded unwary travelers in an Australian desert a full seventy kilometers from the town they expected to find there. iPhone users erupted in howls of protest, the media had a field day lampooning Apple's misstep, and CEO Tim Cook had to issue a public apology.[19] Apple accepted the bad publicity, likely reasoning that it could quickly improve its mapping service to an acceptable quality level—and this is essentially what has happened. The iPhone platform is no longer dependent on Google for mapping technology, and Apple has control over the mapping application as a source of significant value.

Second, if particular functionality is reinvented by a number of extension developers and gains widespread acceptance by platform users, the manager of the platform should acquire the functionality and make it available through an open API. Widely useful functions such as video and audio playback, photo editing, text cutting-and-pasting, and voice commands have often been invented by extension developers. Recognizing their broad applicability, platform managers have moved to standardize these functions and incorporate them into APIs that all developers can use. This accelerates innovation and enables improvements in service for everyone who uses the platform.

USER PARTICIPATION

The third kind of openness that platform managers need to control is user participation—in particular, *producer openness,* which is the right to freely add content to the platform. Remember, many platforms are designed to facilitate side switching, which enables consumers to become producers, and vice versa; so the same individual users who consume value units on the platform can also create value units for others to consume. YouTube users can both view others' videos and upload videos of their own; Airbnb guests can become hosts; Etsy customers can sell their own craft products on the site.

The platform's objective in opening to these users is to facilitate the creation and provision of as much high-quality content as possible. Of course, this stipulation—that the objective is the development of *high-quality* content—is the reason most platforms reject absolute openness as a strategy for managing user participation.

When it was launched, Wikipedia aspired to a condition of complete openness. Maintenance of quality would be entrusted solely to the users of the platform, who would take it upon themselves to monitor the content of the site, fix errors, and challenge biases. This was a utopian vision that assumed good intentions on the part of all Wikipedia users; or, a trifle less idealistically, it assumed that the varying, sometimes conflicting motivations and attitudes of users would eventually balance one another, producing content that represented the combined wisdom of the entire community, much as, in capitalist theory, the "invisible hand" of the market is supposed to maximize the benefits for all through the interaction of countless self-interested participants.

However, reality teaches us that democracy—like free markets—can be messy, especially when intense passions and partisanship are involved. Hence the episode we recounted at the start of this chapter, in which the Wikipedia article about the death of Meredith Kercher was hijacked by "haters" of Amanda Knox who were determined to make sure the page should assert her guilt and were prepared to eradicate any signs of dissension.

The Kercher killing is not the only instance in which Wikipedia is embroiled in controversy—far from it. An article on the platform headed "Wikipedia: List of controversial issues" lists over 800 topics that "are constantly being re-edited in a circular manner, or are otherwise the focus of edit warring or article sanctions." Organized under headings that include "Politics and economics," "History," "Science, biology, and health," "Philosophy," and "Media and culture," they include everything from "Anarchism," "Genocide denial," "Occupy Wall Street," and "Apollo moon landing hoax accusations" to "Hare Krishna," "Chiropractic," "SeaWorld," and "Disco music."

Limiting openness through artful curation. How can Wikipedia establish high standards for the quality of the platform's content when some of its users are determined to manipulate it for their own purposes? That is not easy. Those who manage the platform try hard to rely primarily on community standards and social pressure. Guidelines are promulgated through articles like "Wikipedia: five pillars," which explains one of the platform's "fundamental principles" this way:

> Wikipedia is written from a neutral point of view: We strive for articles that document and explain the major points of view, giving due weight with respect to their prominence in an impartial tone. We avoid advocacy and we characterize information and issues rather than debate them. In some areas there may be just one well-recognized point of view; in others, we describe multiple points of view, presenting each accurately and in context rather than as "the truth" or "the best view". All articles must strive for verifiable accuracy, citing reliable, authoritative sources, especially when the topic is controversial or is on living persons. Editors' personal experiences, interpretations, or opinions do not belong.

Yet there are times when community pressure is not enough. When the quality of particular articles is repeatedly degraded by biased or dishonest content, other methods and tools for protecting Wikipedia's integrity kick in. These include VandalProof, a software program written especially for Wikipedia that highlights articles edited by users with a track record of unreliable work; tagging tools that draw attention to potentially problematic articles so that other editors can review and, if necessary, improve them; and a range of blocking and protection systems that can only be employed by users who have earned special privileges through the general consensus of the Wikipedia community.

This complex, largely self-organized set of interlocking systems for ensuring the quality of Wikipedia content is a form of curation— the crucial content protection process that must be fine-tuned to ensure the right degree and kind of producer openness.

Curation usually takes the form of *screening* and *feedback* at critical points of access to the platform. Screening decides who to let in, while feedback encourages desirable behavior on the part of those who have been granted entry. A user's reputation, as shaped by past behavior both on and off the platform, is usually a key factor in curation: users rated positively by the rest of the community are more likely to pass through the screening process and to receive favorable feedback than those with poor reputations.

Curation can be managed through human gatekeepers—moderators who personally screen users, edit content, and provide feedback designed to promote quality. Media platforms such as blogs and online magazines often use this kind of system. But employing moderators who are trained and paid by the platform company is time-consuming and costly. A better system—though one that can be challenging to design and implement—relies on users themselves to curate the platform, generally through software tools that quickly gather and aggregate feedback and apply it to curation decisions.

As we've seen, user-driven curation facilitated by software tools is the method Wikipedia employs. Similarly, Facebook relies on users to flag objectionable content such as hate speech, harassment, offensively graphic images, and threats of violence. Service platforms like

Uber and Airbnb incorporate user ratings into their software tools so consumers and producers can make informed choices about whom they choose to interact with.

No system of curation is foolproof. When curation tools err on the side of openness, potentially offensive or even dangerous content can slip through. When the tools are overly restrictive, valuable users and appropriate content may be screened out or discouraged—as when social networking algorithms intended to eliminate pornography end up blocking educational materials on topics like breast cancer awareness. Platform managers need to devote significant time and resources—including human eyeballs and informed judgment—to continually monitoring their platforms' boundaries between openness and closedness and ensuring they are set appropriately.

SIMILAR PLATFORMS CAN COMPETE THROUGH DIFFERING LEVELS OF OPENNESS

Platforms that operate in similar arenas may choose to differentiate themselves by adapting different levels and kinds of openness. These variant openness regimes will attract different kinds and numbers of participants, generate distinct ecosystem cultures, and may ultimately produce divergent business models.

As we've previously observed, two platforms that made very different openness decisions are Apple's Mac operating system/hardware combination and Microsoft's Windows operating system in the 1980s and 1990s. Although some critics describe Windows as a closed system, by comparison to Apple it has been much more open. Apple made the decision to charge extension developers a relatively high $10,000 for system development kits (SDKs), thereby ensuring a small, select pool of outside software developers. Microsoft, by contrast, basically gave the developer SDKs away and consequently attracted a much larger developer pool.

Meanwhile, IBM lost control of the hardware standard, partly as the result of regulatory action, making it possible for any manufacturer to enter the PC market, which drove costs rapidly down. The combination of a large developer pool with inexpensive hardware was compelling to consumers, and the so-called Wintel platform dominated the market for nearly twenty years—while the share of the industry enjoyed by the closed Apple system steadily dwindled. In this case, it seems clear that the open path was far more successful than the closed path.

More recently, as we've seen, Google and Apple made differing openness decisions regarding their mobile platforms. Google allowed the development of an open-source version of Android, which is freely available to any manufacturer, while Apple sponsored the proprietary iOS operating system and tightly controlled the hardware so that it is the sole device provider and therefore the sole manager of the system.

At first, this might look like a repeat of the Microsoft/Apple PC operating system battle. However, although Apple is much more closed than Google—for example, retaining control of the vital device manufacturing function rather than opening it to other companies— it is more open than it was in the previous technological generation. Having opened its system just enough to encourage developers, Apple now assists them with strong developer toolkits and gives them access to its user base through the iTunes store. A multitude of apps has appeared as a result.

Google, meanwhile, needed to be more open because it entered the market after Apple. As a result, AOSP quickly grew beyond Google's control, prompting Google to seek to restrict access to its platform through a variety of mechanisms. Because the underlying operating system is free to all, Google cannot easily close AOSP, but almost the same goal can be achieved by exerting control over critical functions. Journalist Ron Amadeo has described how Google closed the Android applications for functions such as search, music, calendar, keyboard, and camera, while also working hard to encourage handset manufacturers to join its so-called open handset alliance, dedicated to developing and maintaining open software and hardware standards for mobile devices. Amadeo explains the impact of Google's move toward closing AOSP on extension developers:

If you use any Google APIs and try to run your app on a Kindle, or any other non-Google version of AOSP: surprise! Your app is broken. Google's Android is a very high percentage of the Android market, and developers only really care about making their app easily, making it work well, and reaching a wide audience. Google APIs accomplish all that, with the side effect that your app is now dependent on the device having a Google Apps license.[20]

By requiring a license to access Google Play, the official app store for AOSP, the firm is able to control access to the platform even though the underlying technology is open source. In this way, Google can manage potential competition as well as ensure a more orderly technology environment for users and developers.

Stories like these illustrate the complicated competitive factors that impact openness decisions—as well as the never-ending balancing act that platform sponsors and managers need to practice to ensure that their platforms remain relevant, vibrant, and valuable to a growing base of users.

OPENING OVER TIME:
THE BENEFITS AND THE RISKS

As we've seen, platforms can expand and develop stronger network effects by opening out over time. More rarely, as in the case of Android, they can choose to become more closed over time.

The choice to become more open or more closed depends on whether a platform was originally structured as a proprietary or shared platform. Naturally, a proprietary platform, which is sponsored, managed, and completely controlled by a single company, can only become more open. By contrast, a fully open, shared platform (Linux, for example) can only become more closed.

As we noted in chapter 5, which deals with launching a platform, a new platform will often choose to execute virtually all of its processes internally simply because there are no partners willing to make the necessary investment. In these cases, employees must provide both content and curation. Over time, as the platform grows and outside developers are attracted, the openness pattern may change, which means that curation processes need to evolve as well.

A forward-looking platform management team must design ways to continually evaluate the platform's openness level. Preferably, the platform will use a consistent strategic framework to make decisions for opening over time. Eventually, as the maturing platform moves processes outside the firm from employees to partners, it may need to develop algorithms to automate curation or to decentralize curation to the entire base of users. YouTube now depends upon its large user base to evaluate content, provide feedback, and flag content that should not be on the platform.

As the platform's openness policies evolve, the challenge is always to find balance. If a platform is too closed—for example, if it extracts excessive rents in the form of unreasonable and arbitrary fees—its partners may refuse to make platform-specific investments. On the other hand, platforms face trouble when extension developers begin to insert themselves too aggressively between the platform and its users. If a particular developer successfully displaces other competitors, a platform manager should be careful to ensure that the developer does not seek to displace the platform itself.

There are a number of examples of such struggles for control of a particular platform's user base. Consider SAP, the German-based multinational giant that produces software for large enterprises to use in managing their internal operations, customer relationships, and other processes. SAP, which operates a large business processes platform, has partnered with the U.S.-based firm ADP to provide payroll processing services to its users, partly in order to take advantage of ADP's superior access to cloud computing capabilities. However, ADP has substantial customer relationships of its own and can serve as the platform host linking customers to a number of data/computing/storage partners. Thus, the partnership creates an opportunity for ADP to displace SAP as the primary manager of the customer relationship. This is an instance in which the platform manager (SAP) is in danger of losing control of the customer connection to an extension developer (ADP).

The unique power and value of the platform lies in its ability to facilitate connections among participants from outside the platform itself. But defining exactly who should have access to the platform and precisely how they can participate is an enormously complex issue with ever-changing strategic implications. That's why the question of openness needs to be at the top of every platform manager's agenda—not just during the initial design process, but throughout the life of the platform.

TAKEAWAYS FROM CHAPTER SEVEN

❑ There are three kinds of openness decisions that managers face: those regarding manager/sponsor participation, developer participation, and user participation.

❑ Management and sponsorship of a platform may be controlled by a single firm, by different firms, or by groups of firms. The four possible combinations lead to differing patterns of openness and control, with various advantages and disadvantages.

❑ The open/closed dichotomy isn't black or white. There are shades of gray, and benefits and drawbacks to every point on the spectrum. Sometimes, similar platforms choose to compete on the basis of differing openness policies.

❑ Maturing platforms often evolve in the direction of greater openness. This demands continually reevaluating and adjusting curation processes to ensure consistently high quality of platform content and service value.

8

GOVERNANCE

Policies to Increase Value
and Enhance Growth

In the first quarter of 2015, Brian. P. Kelley, the CEO of Keurig Green Mountain coffee company, had some explaining to do. The company had just launched the Keurig 2.0, a next-generation coffee brewer touted as the future king of brewing. The reigning king, the Keurig 1.0, had become ubiquitous in homes, offices, and hotels, and Green Mountain's expensive coffee cartridges had helped fuel the growth of what had been a regional brewer into a firm worth more than $18 billion.

Yet with the launch of Keurig 2.0, sales did not rise further. Instead, they fell by 12 percent.

The problem had its origins back in 2012, when key patents on Keurig's coffee pod design expired. Taking advantage of this change, competing coffee makers began selling pods that were compatible with Keurig's machines and significantly cheaper. These rivals were like extension developers offering new sources of value to Keurig users. Of course, their existence, and the competition they presented to the official Keurig pods, caused an erosion of Keurig's market share.

To fight back, Keurig included in its brewer version 2.0 a scanning device that prevented the use of any pods not marked with a special proprietary emblem. Consumers were furious. Many denounced Keurig on shopping websites; thousands watched You-Tube videos purporting to demonstrate how to hack the system, tricking it into accepting coffee pods unauthorized by Keurig. Buyers lamented the firm's "ridiculous corporate greed" and bemoaned the fact that the Amazon rating system made it impossible for them to give the new Keurig a zero star rating.[1]

By attempting to grab an even bigger share of the profits from its coffee-making platform, Green Mountain had angered its community and forfeited profits. The king of coffee had violated three fundamental rules of good governance:

- Always create value for the consumers you serve;
- Don't use your power to change the rules in your favor; and
- Don't take more than a fair share of the wealth.

Governance is the set of rules concerning who gets to participate in an ecosystem, how to divide the value, and how to resolve conflicts.[2] To understand good community governance is to understand the set of rules for orchestrating an ecosystem.[3]

Green Mountain failed at the task of ecosystem governance. The Keurig in all its incarnations is simply a product platform, a single one-sided market serving a community of coffee drinkers. It could be much more successful as a beverage ecosystem with other value-adding options, a range of vetted suppliers, and an array of other high-quality services that customers would appreciate. Instead, Green Mountain chose to exclude suppliers that its customers found valuable, eliminating variety and freedom of choice in order to retain control. It overreached for a share of the value produced by its system. And it unilaterally placed its interest ahead of all others. Keurig users were the losers—and soon enough, so was Green Mountain.

WHY GOVERNANCE MATTERS:
PLATFORMS AS STATES

The goal of good governance is to create wealth, fairly distributed among all those who add value. As we saw in chapter 2, the new technology-driven communities known as platform businesses are creating a vast amount of new wealth outside the firm, and these external benefits must be designed and managed fairly. Because these value-creating networks grow faster outside the firm than inside, ruling the ecosystem wisely puts a premium on not ruling it selfishly.

If navigating the rules for governance is hard for one-sided platforms like the Keurig brewing system, it's exponentially harder when platforms are multisided. After all, multisided platforms involve numerous interests that don't always align. This makes it difficult for platform managers to ensure that various participants create value for one another, and it makes it likely that conflicts will emerge that governance rules must resolve as fairly and efficiently as possible.

This is a juggling act that even giants and geniuses often get wrong. Facebook, for example, has alienated users with its privacy policies.[4] LinkedIn has angered its developers by turning off their access to APIs.[5] And Twitter has expropriated technologies developed by other members of its ecosystem while permitting Twitter users to harass one another. As Twitter's CEO Dick Costolo said, "We suck at dealing with abuse."[6]

In the complexity of the governance issues they face, today's biggest platform businesses resemble nation-states. With more than 1.5 billion users, Facebook oversees a "population" larger than China's. Google handles 64 percent of the online searches in the U.S. and 90 percent of those in Europe, while Alibaba handles more than 1 trillion yuan ($162 billion) worth of transactions a year and accounts for 70 percent of all commercial shipments in China.[7] Platform businesses at this scale control economic systems that are bigger than all but the biggest national economies. No wonder Brad Burnham, one of the lead investors at Union Square Ventures, responded to the introduction of Facebook Credits— a short-lived system of virtual currency for use in playing online games—by wondering what the move said about Facebook's monetary policy.[8] In a similar vein, we might ask: In choosing to apply unilateral software standards as opposed to multilateral standards (as we saw in chapter 7), what kind of foreign policy is Apple pursuing? Is Twitter following an industrial policy based on investment in "state-owned" services or one relying on decentralized development by others? What does Google's approach to censorship in China tell us about the company's human rights policy?

Like it or not, firms like these already serve as the unofficial and unelected regulators of millions of lives. For this reason, platforms have much to learn from cities and states, which have had thousands of years to evolve principles of good governance. Like the platform businesses of today, cities and states have long had to wrestle with the question of how best to create wealth and distribute it fairly. Increasing evidence suggests that just governance is a crucially important factor in the ability of a state to create wealth—even more important than such obviously valuable assets as natural resources, navigable waterways, and favorable agricultural conditions.

Consider the modern city-state of Singapore. In 1959, when Lee Kuan Yew became prime minister, it had almost no natural resources. For defense and clean water, it relied on the Federation of Malaya, the predecessor of the nation of Malaysia (established in 1963). Corruption was rampant. Per capita GDP hovered below $430.[9] Ethnic strife between Malays and Chinese, religious strife between Muslims and Buddhists, and political strife between capitalists and communists hamstrung progress.

Lee Kuan Yew brought economic vitality to Singapore by changing its system of governance. Having studied at the London School of Economics and with a law degree from Fitzwilliam College, Cambridge, Yew introduced the British system of justice and rule by law. Then he attacked corruption. To make graft less attractive, he raised the salaries of civil servants to match those of similar workers in the private sector. New public servants had to wear white as a sign of purity when they assumed office. The anti-corruption rules were enforced strictly: the minister of state for the environment, a staunch supporter of Yew, committed suicide rather than face prosecution on bribery charges.[10] Fairer, more open government was encouraged by the creation of multicultural councils empowered to give voice to religious and ethnic groups willing to work within the system. Singapore now boasts a government that ranks with those of New Zealand and the Scandinavian countries as one of the least corrupt in the world. This is significant, in part, because each 1 percent drop in corruption and misuse of public power for private gain is associated with a 1.7 percent rise in GDP.[11]

Although Yew has been criticized in the West for throttling political dissent, the economic results produced by his good-governance campaign are impressive. By 2015, Singapore's per capita GDP was $55,182, higher than that of the United States. During the fifty-five years from 1960 to 2015, Singapore's annual growth rate was 6.69 percent, almost 2 percent higher than that of Malaysia, from which it separated in 1965.[12]

Similar evidence of the importance of good governance to wealth creation can be seen by comparing the GDP growth and innovation rates in communist East Germany and North Korea with those in their near-twin siblings, West Germany and South Korea.[13] Good governance matters.

MARKET FAILURE AND ITS CAUSES

Good governance is important in both nation-states and platform businesses because absolutely free markets, in which people and organizations interact with no rules, restrictions, or safeguards, can't always be relied upon to produce results that are fair and satisfactory to those involved.

An example can be seen on eBay, where some participants inevitably have greater knowledge, market savvy, and bargaining skill than others. In most cases, the interactions that result are basically fair, even when a particular interaction produces a "winner" and a "loser." But sometimes, outcomes that appear manipulative or even deceptive occur. For example, a group of eBay members, noticing that some inexperienced sellers were prone to misidentifying goods— for example, by misspelling Louis Vuitton with one "T" or Abercrombie and Fitch as "Abercrombee" or "Fich"—began taking advantage of these errors as middlemen. They would actively seek out mislabeled items, which were usually languishing unnoticed on the auction site, snatch them up at bargain prices, and then resell them for a huge markup under their proper names.

In one celebrated example, the owner of an antique beer bottle that had been kept in his family for fifty years decided to list it on eBay. Unfortunately, the seller had no idea of the true value of his heirloom. The beer had been produced in the 1850s as the result of a brewing contest intended to provide "life-sustaining ale" to a crew navigating the Arctic in hopes of discovering the fabled Northwest Passage from the Atlantic to the Pacific. (At the time, it was believed—erroneously—that ale could prevent scurvy.)[14] The expedition failed, but a little of the original brew survived, and by the time of the eBay sale, two bottles were known to exist, both eagerly sought after by beer collectors and history buffs.

Unaware of all this—and careless to boot—the seller listed the precious bottle on eBay under the heading "Allsop's Arctic Ale—full and corked with wax seal," and proposed an opening bid of $299. The brand name should have been spelled "Allsopp's," with an extra P—a tiny error, but one big enough to confuse the serious collectors who would have been interested in the item. A shrewd scavenger for mislabeled bargains spotted the listing and jumped in as the sole bidder. He bought the bottle for $304 and relisted it on eBay three days after receiving it. When collectors heard about it, the brew fetched bids exceeding $78,100.[15]

The Case of the Ambiguous Ale is an example of *market failure*—a situation in which "good" interactions (fair and mutually satisfactory) fail to occur, or "bad" interactions do. If you can't find an item you want on eBay, then a good interaction has failed to occur. If you did find an item you wanted but got cheated, abused, or deceived, then a bad interaction has occurred. In general, there are four main causes of market failures: *information asymmetry, externalities, monopoly power,* and *risk*.

Information asymmetry arises whenever one party to an interaction knows facts that other parties don't and uses that knowledge for personal advantage. Consider the problem of counterfeit goods, when the seller knows that the goods are fake but does not inform the buyer. Fakes account for Skullcandy headphones with lousy sound quality, Gucci handbags with broken stitching, Duracell batteries that don't hold a charge, OtterBox mobile phone cases that are not drop-proof, and Viagra that provides no lift. Estimated at more than $350 billion worldwide, the size of the counterfeit goods market exceeds the trade in illegal drugs (estimated at $321 billion).[16]

Externalities occur when spillover costs or benefits accrue to anyone not involved in a given interaction. Imagine that one of your friends provides your private contact information to a gaming company in exchange for a few digital points. This would be a bad interaction because it violates your privacy rights, and so it is an example of a *negative externality*.

The concept of a *positive externality* is a bit more ambiguous. Consider what happens when Netflix analyzes the movie-watching behavior of someone whose tastes match yours and uses this data to give you a more accurate movie recommendation. This would be a positive externality, because it provides you with a benefit based on an interaction in which you're not directly involved. Individuals who benefit from positive externalities aren't likely to complain about them— but they are considered problems from a business design standpoint, since they reflect value that is not being fully captured by the platform. In an ideal world—at least, according to economic theory—every value created would somehow be accounted for and credited accurately to the entity responsible for it.

A concept closely related to the positive externality is the *public good*, whose value is not fully captured by the party that created it. Individuals generally create too few public goods unless some governing mechanism is designed to recognize and reward them.

Monopoly power arises when one supplier in an ecosystem becomes too powerful because of its control of the supply of a widely sought good, and uses this power to demand higher prices or special favors. At the height of its popularity (2009–10), game-maker Zynga became excessively powerful on Facebook, leading to conflicts over issues such as the sharing of user information, the split of gaming revenues, and the cost to Zynga of ads on the social network. eBay has experienced similar problems dealing with so-called power sellers.

Risk is the possibility that something unexpected and essentially unpredictable may go wrong, turning a good interaction into a bad one. Risk is a perennial problem in all markets, not just on platforms. A well-designed market generally develops tools and systems that serve to mitigate the effects of risk, thereby encouraging participants to engage in more interactions.

TOOLS FOR GOVERNANCE: LAWS, NORMS, ARCHITECTURE, AND MARKETS

The literature on corporate governance is vast, especially in the field of finance. However, platform governance involves design principles that traditional finance theory overlooks. The single most heavily cited article on corporate governance is a literature survey that considers only "the ways in which suppliers of finance to corporations assure themselves of getting a return on their investment."[17] The focus here is on the information asymmetry arising from the separation of ownership and control—a critical element of governance design, but far from sufficient.[18] Information asymmetry between the community of users and the firm also matters, and their interests too must be aligned.

Additionally, platform governance rules must pay special heed to externalities. These are endemic in network markets, since, as we've seen when examining network effects, the spillover benefits users generate are a source of platform value. Understanding this forces a shift in corporate governance from a narrow focus on shareholder value to a broader view of stakeholder value.

Market designer and Nobel Prize-winning economist Alvin Roth described a model of governance that uses four broad levers to address market failures.[19] According to Roth, a well-designed market increases the *safety* of the market via transparency, quality, or insurance, thereby enabling good interactions to occur. It provides *thickness*, which enables participants from different sides of a multisided market to find one another more easily. It minimizes *congestion*, which hampers successful searches when too many people participate or low quality drives out high. And it minimizes *repugnant activity*—which explains why platform designers forbid porn on iTunes, human organ sales on Alibaba, and child labor on Upwork. According to Roth, good governance occurs when market managers use these levers to address market failures.

A broader view of platform governance uses insights borrowed from the practices of nation-states as modeled by constitutional law scholar Lawrence Lessig. In Lessig's formulation, systems of control involve four main sets of tools: *laws, norms, architecture,* and *markets.*[20]

A familiar example can be used to clarify these four kinds of tools. Suppose leaders of a particular ecosystem want to reduce the harmful effects of smoking. Laws could be passed to ban cigarette sales to minors or forbid smoking in public spaces. Norms—informal codes of behavior shaped by culture—could be applied by using social pressure or advertising to stigmatize smoking and make it appear "uncool." Architecture could be used to develop physical designs that reduce the impact of smoking—for example, air filters that clean the air, or smokeless devices that substitute for cigarettes. And market mechanisms could be used by taxing tobacco products or subsidizing "quit smoking" programs. Historically, those who want to control social behavior—including platform managers—have employed all four of these tools.

Let's consider some of the ways in which these four kinds of tools can be used by platform managers as part of a governance system.

Laws. Of course, many laws created and enforced by nation-states—laws, in the traditional sense of the term—apply to platform businesses and their participants. Sometimes, the application of such laws can be tricky. For example, legal sanctions that punish bad actors offer one traditional way of addressing the problem of risk. However, applying these sanctions requires determining who is responsible for problems that arise and who should bear the blame when they do— something that is not always simple or straightforward.

When it comes to platform businesses, this is far from a purely theoretical issue. We've mentioned some of the serious legal problems faced by platforms earlier: individuals who listed properties on Airbnb had their homes used for brothels and raves; people offering personal services on Craigslist have been murdered.[21] Case law does not generally hold platforms accountable for misdeeds of platform users, even though the owners of the platform may be reasonably well positioned to regulate and control the behavior of the users. Thus, individual platform participants usually have to bear the downside risk, at least as far as national and local laws are concerned. (We'll return to this topic in chapter 11, on regulation.)

Applying Lessig's concept of "law" to governance *within* the platform business takes us into a different arena. The "laws" of a platform are its explicit rules—for example, the terms of service drafted by lawyers or the rules of stakeholder behavior drafted by the platform's designers. These laws moderate behavior at both the user and the ecosystem level. For example, at the user level, the Apple rule that allows a user to share digital content among up to six devices or family members prevents unlimited sharing while nonetheless providing economic incentives for the purchase of Apple services and making a reasonable amount of sharing convenient.[22] At the ecosystem level, the Apple rule compelling app developers to submit all code for review, combined with the rule that releases Apple from any duty of confidentiality, allows Apple to proliferate best practices.[23]

Platform laws should be, and usually are, transparent. Stack Overflow, the most successful online community for answering programming questions, offers an explicit list of rules for earning points as well as the rights and privileges those points confer. One point confers the right to ask and answer questions. Fifteen points confers the right to vote up someone else's content. At 125 points, you gain the right to vote down content—which also costs one point. And at 200 points, you've added so much value that you earn the privilege to see fewer ads. This system of explicit, transparent laws solves a public goods problem by encouraging members to share their best insights with everyone else on the platform.[24]

An exception to the principle of transparency applies to laws that might facilitate bad behavior. Dating sites discovered this the hard way. When the sites applied laws that gave stalkers a quick "hand slap" when they misbehaved, the stalkers soon learned to avoid the specific trigger that flagged them. If, instead, the platform delayed the negative feedback, the stalker had a harder time learning how he'd been caught, which led to a more powerful and lasting disincentive.

Similarly, when a troll on a user-generated content site has his account deleted, he often returns under a new identity. Smart platform managers started making nuisance posts invisible to everyone but the troll. Unable to inflame community sentiment, the troll retreated.

The underlying principle: Give fast, open feedback when applying laws that define good behavior, but give slow, opaque feedback when applying laws that punish bad behavior.

Norms. One of the greatest assets any platform—indeed, any business—can have is a dedicated community. This doesn't happen by accident. Vibrant communities are nurtured by skilled platform managers in order to develop norms, cultures, and expectations that generate lasting sources of value.

iStockphoto, today one of the world's largest markets for crowdsourced photographs, was originally founded by Bruce Livingstone to sell CD-ROM collections of images by direct mail. As that business tanked, Bruce and his partners hated the thought that their work might go to waste. So they began giving away their images online.[25] Within months, they were discovered by thousands of people who not only downloaded images but asked to share their own images as well. To maintain the quality Bruce prided himself on and to eliminate spam, pornography, and copyright infringement, he made sure that every image was scrutinized by an iStockphoto inspector. This was a painstaking and costly process. Bruce found himself working sixteen-hour days.[26]

Realizing that individual human inspection could not scale, Bruce turned to crowd curation. He devised a system under which people who uploaded quality content could earn their way to becoming inspectors and community organizers. Groups emerged to handle specific categories of images—for example, images linked to locations like "New York" or categories like "Food." Bruce himself worked relentlessly to praise, give feedback, and build his community. Under the online name Bitter, he regularly posted comments on the platform's homepage promoting members and their work, such as when he noted "great new stuff from Delirium, also tasty food series from Izusek."[27]

These efforts established a powerful set of norms that came to govern the iStockphoto community. These norms included feedback, high-quality content, open engagement, and a natural role progression to greater levels of authority. Applying these norms, the community produced a remarkable body of stock photos, a classic and valuable public good.

As the story of iStockphoto suggests, norms do not arise in a vacuum. They reflect behaviors, which means that they can be constructed through the intelligent application of the discipline of *behavior design*.

Nir Eyal, who has worked in both advertising and game development, describes behavior design as a recurring sequence of *trigger, action, reward,* and *investment.*[28]

The trigger is a platform-based signal, message, or alert such as an email, a web link, a news item, or an app notification. This prompts the platform member to take some action in response. The action, in turn, produces a reward for the member, usually one with some variable or unanticipated value, since variable reward mechanisms like slot machines and lotteries are habit-forming. Finally, the platform asks the member to make an investment of time, data, social capital, or money. The investment deepens the participant's commitment and reinforces the behavior pattern platform managers want to see.

Here's an example of how the process works. Barbara is a member of Facebook. One day, an interesting photo shows up in Barbara's news feed—perhaps a picture of a gorgeous sunlit beach in Maui, Barbara's favorite vacation spot. This is the trigger. The action in response is designed to be as easy as possible (frictionless), which encourages Barbara to take the next step. In this case, the next step is clicking on the photo, which takes Barbara to Pinterest, the photo-sharing platform, which happens to be entirely new to Barbara. There she receives her reward: a variety of additional tantalizing, carefully curated photos selected specifically to engage her curiosity. (Imagine a photo collection titled "Ten Best Unknown Beaches of the South Pacific.") Finally, Pinterest asks Barbara, whom they just rewarded, to make a small investment. She may be asked to invite friends, state preferences, build virtual assets, or learn new Pinterest features.[29] Any of these actions will set up a new set of triggers for Barbara and others, and the cycle starts over.

In the case of Pinterest, the norms fostered by this system of behavior design have produced a body of content that is a valuable public good. Of course, behavior design is not always used to benefit participants. It can also be used as a tool of selling and manipulation— which is one reason why users themselves should be aware of how such governance mechanisms work.

As a rule, it's desirable to have users participate in shaping the systems that govern them. Elinor Ostrom, the first woman ever to receive the Nobel Prize in Economics, observed that successful creation and policing of public goods by communities follows several regular patterns. Clearly defined boundaries delineate who is and who is not entitled to community benefits. People affected by decisions regarding how community resources will be appropriated have recognized channels they can use to influence the decision-making processes. People who monitor community member behavior are accountable to the community. Graduated sanctions apply to those who violate community rules. Members have access to low-cost dispute resolution systems. And, as community resources grow, governance should be structured in nested tiers, with certain simple issues controlled by small, local groups of users, and increasingly complex, global problems managed by larger, more formally organized groups.[30] Norms that emerge in successful platform communities generally follow the patterns outlined by Ostrom.

Jeff Jordan, former senior vice president at eBay, recounts the problems the company encountered when it sought to add a fixed-price sale format to the traditional auction format.[31] The two main categories of market participants reacted quite differently to the plan. Buyers liked the idea of fixed prices, but the sellers who paid eBay's marketplace fees feared that fixed-price listings would effectively kill the golden goose of auction-driven price escalation.

The process Jordan used to resolve the dispute paralleled several of Ostrom's ideas. eBay used focus groups and a "Voices" program to reflect user perspectives and gauge the strength of their feelings. Jordan's team deployed thoughtful communications to alert buyers and sellers about proposed rule changes. They tested programs on smaller groups and pulled back if changes turned out badly. Ultimately, eBay's leadership sided with the buyers, reasoning that the sellers would ultimately remain loyal to the platform because "merchants go where the consumers are."[32] The decision succeeded. Today, "Buy it Now" fixed-price listings account for about 70 percent of eBay's $83 billion in gross merchandise volume.

Architecture. In the world of platform businesses, "architecture" refers basically to programming code. Well-designed software systems are self-improving: they encourage and reward good behavior, thereby producing more of the same.

Online banking platforms such as peer-to-peer lending businesses are using software algorithms to displace traditional, labor-intensive, and expensive loan officers. They calculate a borrower's likelihood of repaying using both conventional data such as credit scores and nontraditional data such as a Yelp rating (for a restaurant), the stability of the borrower's email address, her connections on LinkedIn, and even how thoroughly she interacts with the loan assessment tools before applying.[33] As the platform architecture becomes better at predicting borrower behavior, participation risk declines, attracting more lenders. Meanwhile, the low overhead costs allow the platform to offer lower rates, which attracts more borrowers. Greater participation further improves the data flow, and the cycle repeats.

No wonder peer-to-peer lending platforms like the British firm Zopa have been enjoying such notable success. When Zopa proudly announced that it had provided more than $1 billion in loans, one of this book's authors, Sangeet Choudary, congratulated the company leaders and politely asked, "Wouldn't your loan default rate be a more significant measure of success?" Zopa responded by publicizing the fact that its loan default rate had fallen to 0.2 percent from 0.6 percent three years earlier.[34] Such is the power of well-designed platform architecture.

Architecture can also be used to prevent and correct market failures. Recall the middlemen on eBay who took advantage of seller misspellings. Although one might lament the lost opportunity for the hapless sellers to complete the deal, these middlemen provided market liquidity ("thickness" in Alvin Roth's formulation) through the process known as *arbitrage*. If no one bids on misspelled items, the interaction never happens—so arbitrageurs can be viewed as providing a valuable service. Yet the existence of arbitrage opportunities also highlights market inefficiencies. eBay now uses automated systems to provide spelling assistance, so sellers can have more confidence that they'll receive what their items are worth. In a case like this, wise governance may disenfranchise a specific group of stakeholders, such as arbitrageurs, in order to increase the overall health of the ecosystem.

High-speed trading on the New York Stock Exchange offers another example. Firms like Goldman Sachs use supercomputers to determine when an order placed in one market will spill over to another market. Then they swoop in to intercept the deal, buying low, selling high, and skimming the margin. This methodology gives a few market participants who can afford massive computing power an unfair advantage over others.[35] Such asymmetric market power risks driving away players who feel cheated. To solve this problem, competing exchanges, such as the alternative trading system IEX, are using their own supercomputers to precisely time the order of bids, thereby eliminating the advantages of a Goldman Sachs.[36] Architecture can level the playing field, making markets more competitive and fair for all.

One of the most innovative forms of architectural control ever invented made its appearance in 2008, when an anonymous coding genius known as Satoshi Nakamoto published a paper on the Cryptography mailing list defining the Bitcoin digital currency and the so-called blockchain protocol governing it. Although Bitcoin is notable as the world's first unforgeable digital currency that cannot be controlled by a government, bank, or individual, the blockchain is truly revolutionary. It makes possible fully decentralized, completely trustworthy interactions without any need for escrow payments or other guarantees.

The blockchain is a distributed public ledger that enables storage of data in a container (the block) affixed to other containers (the chain).[37] The data can be anything: dated proof of an invention, a title to a car, or digital coins. Anyone can verify that you placed data in the container because it has your public signature, but only your private key can open it to see or transfer the contents. Like your home address, a blockchain container is publicly, verifiably yours, but only people you authorize have a key that permits entry.[38]

The blockchain protocol makes decentralized governance possible. Normally, when you sign a contract, you must either trust the other party to honor the terms or rely on a central authority such as the state, or on an escrow service like eBay, to enforce the deal. Public blockchain ownership empowers us to write self-enforcing smart contracts that automatically reassign ownership once contract terms are triggered. Neither party can back out because the code, running in a decentralized public fashion, is not under anyone's control. It simply executes. These smart, autonomous contracts can even pay people for the output of their work—in effect, machines hiring people, not the other way around.

For example, imagine a smart contract between a wedding photographer and a couple planning their nuptials. The blockchain-stored contract could specify that payment of the final installment of the photographer's fee will be made promptly when the edited photo files are delivered electronically to the newlyweds. The automatic digital trigger ensures that the photographer is incentivized to deliver the photos promptly, while it also relieves her of any concern that her clients might fail to pay.

Nakamoto's invention has given birth to a new kind of platform—one with open architecture and a governance model but no central authority. Having no need for gatekeepers, it will put serious pressure on existing platforms that rely on costly gatekeepers. Financial services that claim 2–4 percent of transactions simply for passing them may in the future be hard pressed to justify their rake.

Furthermore, while most platforms address the problem of the market power of particular participants, Nakamoto's platform addresses the problem of monopoly power of the platform itself. Not even Nakamoto, whose real identity remains a mystery, can remake the rules of the open source code to favor one participant over another.

Markets. Markets can govern behavior through the use of mechanism design and various incentives—not money alone, but the trifecta of human motivations that may be summarized as fun, fame, and fortune. In fact, on many platforms, money is far less important than the more intangible, subjective form of value known as *social currency*.

The idea behind social currency is to give something in order to get something. If you give fun in a photo, you can get people to share it. Social currency, measured as the economic value of a relationship, includes favorites and shares.[39] It also includes the reputation a person builds up for good interactions on eBay, good news posts on Reddit, or good answers on Stack Overflow. It includes the number of followers a user attracts on Twitter and the number of skill endorsements she garners on LinkedIn.

iStockphoto evolved a useful market mechanism based on social currency to manage exchange of photos. Every photo download cost the downloader one credit and earned one credit for the person who'd originally uploaded the photo.[40] Credits could also be purchased for 25 cents each, and photographers received cash payment for accumulated credits valued at $100 or more. This system created a fair social exchange that allowed professional photographers and non-photographers to participate in the same market. The mechanism simultaneously encouraged supply and market "thickness," giving birth to the micro stock photo industry.

Social currencies have a number of remarkable and underappreciated properties. We can even use them to answer Brad Burnham's interesting question about the "monetary policy" of a platform.

The enterprise management platform company SAP uses a social currency like that of iStockphoto or Stack Overflow to motivate developers to answer one another's questions. Points earned when the employee of a development company answers a question are credited to a company account; when the account reaches a specified level, SAP makes a generous contribution to a charity of the company's choice. The system has saved SAP $6–8 million in tech support costs, generated numerous new product and service ideas, and reduced average response time to thirty minutes from the one business day that SAP promises.[41] SAP estimates that knowledge spillovers from these activities account for a half-million-dollar gain in annual productivity for a typical enterprise software partner.[42]

Even more interesting, SAP has used the social currency supply to stimulate its developer economy in the same way as the Federal Reserve uses the money supply to stimulate the U.S. economy. When SAP introduced a new customer relationship management (CRM) product, it offered double points on any answer, code, or white paper relating to CRM. During the two-month duration of this "monetary expansion" policy, developers found gaps in the software and devised new features at a vastly higher rate.[43] Used as a money supply, the increased flow of social currency caused overall economic output to rise. In effect, SAP employed an expansionary monetary policy to stimulate growth—and it worked.

In addition to promoting economic growth, well-designed market mechanisms can incentivize the creation and sharing of intellectual property and reduce the riskiness of interactions on the platform.

Beautiful, useful ideas are public goods. Which raises the question: what is the optimal intellectual property policy for a platform business? If a developer working on a platform invents a valuable idea, who should own it, the developer or the platform? It's possible to imagine arguments on both sides of the issue. Giving ownership to the developer provides incentives for idea creation. Giving ownership to the platform facilitates standardization and sharing, and enriches the platform ecosystem as a whole. State-mandated laws regarding patents and other forms of intellectual property protection are clumsy and expensive to enforce. A more elegant platform-based solution is required.

SAP has tackled this problem through two practices. First, it publishes an 18–24-month advance road map indicating what new products and services it intends to build to enhance its offerings to its corporate clients. This not only tells SAP's outside developers what digital real estate will be available for their own innovations but also gives them up to two years before they face competition. The two-year window thus serves as a metaphorical patent period.[44] Second, SAP has made a policy of partnering with developers financially or buying them out at a fair price. This assures developers that they will be fairly compensated for their work, reduces partner risk, and encourages outside investment in the SAP platform.

The issue of risk reduction on a platform is a perennial one. History shows that platform owners generally seek to avoid responsibility for the risks faced by platform participants, especially in the early days of the platform. For example, in the 1960s, credit card companies, which host the two-sided merchant and cardholder platform, resisted insuring cardholders against fraud on their cards. They argued that insurance would promote fraud as consumers would become careless with their cards, and that banks forced to absorb more risk would become more reluctant to extend credit, hurting low-income consumers.

Over the vigorous objections of major banks, the Fair Credit Reporting Act (1970) and a subsequent amendment required fraud insurance, imposing a limit of $50 on consumer liability for fraudulent use of a credit card. The disaster predicted by the credit card companies did not occur. Freed from the fear of fraud, consumers used their cards so much more often that the increase in interaction volume more than offset the increase in fraud. The business benefit from fraud insurance is so powerful that, in order to encourage adoption and use, many banks now waive the $50 charge if consumers report a lost or stolen card within twenty-four hours.[45]

In recent years, new platform businesses have made the same mistake as credit card companies did in the 1960s. Initially, Airbnb refused to indemnify hosts against bad guest behavior, and Uber refused to insure riders against bad driver behavior.[46] Eventually, both companies realized that this refusal was hurting the growth of their platforms. Today, as we've noted, Airbnb offers its host members $1 million in homeowners' protection, and Uber is partnering with insurance firms to create new types of policies to protect its drivers.[47]

Rather than seeking to minimize their own risk, platforms should use market mechanisms such as risk pooling and insurance to reduce risk for their participants and thereby maximize overall value creation. Good governance means looking after the health of one's ecosystem partners.

PRINCIPLES OF SMART SELF-GOVERNANCE FOR PLATFORMS

Kings and conquerors like to make the rules; they don't always like to abide by them. Yet results improve when smart rules of governance are applied to platform companies themselves as well as to platform partners and participants.

The first big principle of smart self-governance for platforms is *internal transparency.* In platform companies, as in virtually all organizations, there's a tendency for divisions or departments to become "siloed"—to develop unique perspectives, languages, systems, processes, and tools that are difficult for outsiders to understand, even those in another department of the same company. This makes it extremely hard to solve complex, large-scale problems that span two or more divisions, since it means that members of different work teams lack a shared vocabulary and tool set. It also makes it much harder for outsiders—including platform users and developers—to work effectively with the platform management team.

To avoid this kind of dysfunction, platform managers should strive to give all their business divisions a clear view across the entire platform. Such transparency promotes consistency, helps others develop and use key resources, and facilitates growth to scale.

The so-called Yegge Rant, executive Steve Yegge's attempt to summarize a mandate issued by Amazon's Jeff Bezos, captures the spirit of this principle very effectively. Bezos insisted that all members of the Amazon team must learn to communicate with one another using "service interfaces"—data communication tools specifically designed to be clear, understandable, and useful to everyone in the organization as well as to outside users and partners. The idea is to treat everyone you do business with—including your colleagues in other departments and divisions of the organization—as customers with legitimate and important information needs that you are responsible to meet. Hence the seven rules presented in the Yegge Rant:

1. All teams will henceforth expose their data and functionality through service interfaces.
2. Teams must communicate with each other through these interfaces.
3. There will be no other form of interprocess communication allowed: no direct linking, no direct reads of another team's data store, no shared-memory model, no back-doors whatsoever. The only communication allowed is via service interface calls over the network.
4. It doesn't matter what technology they use. HTTP, Corba, Pubsub, custom protocols—doesn't matter. Bezos doesn't care.
5. All service interfaces, without exception, must be designed from the ground up to be externalizable. That is to say, the team must plan and design to be able to expose the interface to developers in the outside world. No exceptions.
6. Anyone who doesn't do this will be fired.
7. Thank you; have a nice day!

Astute application of this principle of transparency underlies the success of Amazon Web Services (AWS), the platform's giant cloud services company. Andrew Jassy, Amazon's vice president of technology, had observed how different divisions of Amazon kept having to develop web service operations to store, search, and communicate data.[48] Jassy urged that these varied projects should be combined into a single operation with one clear, flexible, and universally comprehensible set of protocols. Doing this would make all of Amazon's vast body of data accessible and useful to everyone in the organization.

Even more important, Jassy recognized that solving this problem for Amazon could have broader external applications. He reasoned that if multiple business units within Amazon had to solve this problem, then a reliable data management service that had solved the problem effectively might well be useful to outside firms with similar needs. AWS was born—one of the first businesses to offer cloud-based information storage and management services and expertise to companies with massive data challenges. Thanks to Jassy's vision, AWS today has more market capacity than the next dozen cloud services combined.[49]

By contrast, companies that limit their own ability to see across business units are likely to fail to establish viable platforms or to build their platform businesses to scale.

Sony Corporation provides a sobering example. The Sony Walkman had dominated portable music since the 1970s. In 2007, when the Apple iPhone was introduced, Sony's dominance of the world of electronic devices seemed unshakeable. Sony had a world-class MP3 player, it had a pioneering e-reader, and it made some of the best cameras. In the fall of that year, Sony introduced the next-generation PlayStation Portable (PSP), the best gaming device in the world. Sony even owned Time Warner movie and television studios, giving it the opportunity to offer unique content. Yet despite these piecemeal advantages, Sony never developed the vision to offer a platform. Instead, the firm embraced separate product lines and focused on individual systems.

Sony's siloed business vision prevented it from creating a unified platform ecosystem. Within a few years, Apple's iPhone and the apps built on its growing platform had swept the field. Two years after the crash of 2008, Sony's stock price was still almost one-third below its prior value, while Apple's price had soared to historic highs.

The second big principle of platform self-governance is *participation*. It's crucial for platform managers to give external partners and stakeholders a voice in internal decision processes equal to that of internal stakeholders. Otherwise, the decisions made will inevitably tend to favor the platform itself, which will eventually alienate outside partners and cause them to abandon the platform.

In their book *Platform Leadership*, Annabelle Gawer and Michael A. Cusumano offer a vivid example of how giving partners a voice can be great platform governance. The ecosystem built around the universal serial bus (USB), promoted by Intel, was one of the first standards to facilitate data and power transfer between peripherals—keyboards, memory devices, monitors, cameras, network connectors, and so on—and computers. Yet peripherals were outside Intel's core microchip business.[50] This meant that Intel faced a particularly acute version of the chicken-or-egg launch problem that we discussed in chapter 5. No one wants to produce peripherals for a computer standard no one else has adopted, but no one wants to buy a computer for which no one else has made peripherals. And potential hardware partners were reluctant to link with Intel since, as the owner of the standard, Intel would have the option of making future changes to the standard that could render competing products incompatible, thereby capturing all the long-term value of partner investments.

Intel cracked the chicken-or-egg conundrum by entrusting USB to its Intel Architecture Labs (IAL) division. As a new business unit, IAL did not fall under the authority of any internal product line. Its job was to serve as a neutral negotiator between ecosystem partners and internal business units, which it could only achieve through independence. IAL earned the trust of partners by advocating and enacting policies that advanced the health of the ecosystem even at the occasional expense of Intel business units. Over the course of a year, the IAL team visited over fifty companies, inviting them to help define the standard and design licenses that made them comfortable. Through IAL, Intel also committed not to trample partner markets. Intel used both reputation and contracts to limit its own future behavior. (See the sidebar on page 180 for a summary of IAL's self-governance principles.)

These efforts paid off. A consortium of seven companies—Compaq, DEC, IBM, Intel, Microsoft, NEC, and Nortel—united behind USB, producing an ecosystem standard that has evolved successfully for more than a decade.

This returns us to the deep design principle we introduced early in this chapter: *Just and fair governance can create wealth*. We saw this principal operate in the story of Singapore's rise; we see it here in the story of IAL and the launch of the USB standard.

SELF-GOVERNANCE RULES FOLLOWED BY INTEL ARCHITECTURE LABS
IN LAUNCHING THE USB STANDARD

1. Give customers a voice in key decisions. Use a separate business unit, with a "Chinese wall," to handle conflicting agendas.
2. For trusting relationships, open standards must remain open.
3. Treat IP [intellectual property] fairly, yours and theirs.
4. Communicate a clear road map and stick to it. Commitments to act or not act must be credible.
5. Reserve the right to enter strategically important markets with notice. Don't surprise people and don't play favorites with news.
6. In case of big investments, share risk and bet your own money.
7. Do not promise to not change the platform. Do promise early notice. Have skin in the game, so change bites the platform, not just the partner.
8. It's okay to offer differential benefits to partners with differentiated assets. Just make sure everyone understands how to qualify.
9. Promote the long-term financial health of partners, especially smaller ones.
10. As the business matures, decisions increasingly favor outward progression from core platform, to complements, to new businesses that cannibalize the platform.[51]

Fairness helps create wealth in two ways.[52] First, if you treat people fairly, they are more likely to share their ideas. Having more ideas creates more opportunity to mix, match, and remake them into new innovations.

Second, one of this book's authors (Marshall Van Alstyne) has shown formally that fair governance leads participants in a market to allocate their resources more wisely and productively.[53] Consider the USB standard. If each of the seven firms involved in creating the standard is sure to get a fair share of the value created, then each will willingly participate. By contrast, if five of the firms could gang up to steal the value of the other two—and those two know this could happen—the two may never join the coalition. This fracturing caused by the possibility of unfairness could have split the USB standard into competing standards, or, worse, prevented the development of any standard at all.

This is not to say that fairness always creates wealth or that wealth can never be created without it. Keurig, Apple, Facebook, and others have all, at times, treated their communities badly yet thrived financially. But in the long run, designing fair participation into ecosystem governance prompts users to create more wealth than if the rules grant a platform owner the ability to make arbitrary decisions without accountability. Many platform managers choose governance principles that favor themselves over their users. Yet platforms that respect their users more can expect more from their users—with benefits ultimately accruing to all.

Governance will always be imperfect. Whatever the rules, partners will find new forms of private advantage. There will always be information asymmetries and externalities. Interactions lead to complications, which lead to interventions, which lead to new complications. Indeed, if good governance allows third parties to innovate, then, as they create new sources of value, they will simultaneously create new struggles to control that value.

When such conflicts arise, governance decisions should favor the greatest sources of new value or the direction where the market is headed, not where it used to be. Firms that choose only to guard their aging assets, as Microsoft has done, stagnate. The governance mechanism must therefore be self-healing and promote evolution. Sophisticated governance achieves efficiency at the level of "design for self-design"—that is, it encourages platform members to collaborate freely and experiment fearlessly in order to update the rules as necessary. Governance should not be static. When signs of change appear on the horizon—such as new behaviors by platform users, unanticipated conflicts among them, or encroachments by new competitors—information about the change should spread rapidly through the organization, encouraging creative conversations about how the governance system may need to evolve in response.

No matter what kind of business or social ecosystem your platform inhabits, it will always include both fast-moving parts and slow-moving parts. Smart governance systems are flexible enough to respond to both.[54]

TAKEAWAYS FROM CHAPTER EIGHT

❑ Governance is necessary because absolutely free markets are prone to failures.

❑ Market failures are generally caused by information asymmetry, externalities, monopoly power, and risk. Good governance helps prevent and mitigate market failures.

❑ The basic tools for platform governance include laws, norms, architecture, and markets. Each must be designed and implemented with care in order to encourage platform participants to engage in positive behaviors, incentivize good interactions, and discourage bad interactions.

❑ Self-governance is also crucial to effective platform management. Well-run platforms govern their own activities following the principles of transparency and participation.

9

METRICS

How Platform Managers Can Measure What Really Matters

L eaders have always needed to focus on a handful of key metrics to guide them. This has been true for thousands of years in every domain of human activity, from business to government to warfare. Consider Jonathan Roth's description of the key factors for Julius Caesar's army in the Gallic campaigns (58–50 BCE):

> The Roman army took a vast array of materiel into the field: clothing, armor, edged weapons, missiles, tents, portable fortifications, cooking gear, medical supplies, writing materials, and much more . . . Yet, approximately ninety percent of the weight of the supplies needed by an ancient army was made up of only three elements: food, fodder and firewood. All military decisions from the basic strategic concept to the smallest tactical movements were affected by, and often determined by, the need to provide these supplies to the army.[1]

Given a certain number of soldiers and animals, Caesar's quartermaster could quickly determine how far the army could march and how long it could campaign before reprovisioning, simply by tabulating the quantity of food for the men, fodder for the animals, and firewood for warmth and cooking. These three key metrics shaped many of Caesar's most fundamental strategic choices.

Leaders of traditional for-profit companies that have linear value chains (pipelines) have, similarly, achieved success by working with a relatively limited set of standard metrics. For example, firms that manufacture goods such as automobiles or washing machines must source raw materials or subassemblies and then assemble these into complete products that are offered for sale to end customers through a variety of sales and marketing channels. The details of the work may be very complex, but as long as the revenue exceeds the total cost of compensating pipeline participants, along with a margin to justify the risk and cover future development costs, all is well. While line workers and middle managers all along the pipeline need to be immersed in the fine points of design, manufacturing, production, marketing, and delivery, leaders at the C-suite level, as well as board members and outside investors, can focus on a few key numbers to get a quick sense of the relative health of the business.

Traditional measures from pipeline businesses, which are familiar to most managers, include cash flow, inventory turns, and operating income. These work in combination to create a useful, broad-brush picture of a business, and their simplicity and clarity helps company leaders stay focused on the factors that are crucial to long-term success rather than getting distracted by secondary details.

FROM PIPELINE TO PLATFORM: THE NEW MEASUREMENT CHALLENGE

Unfortunately, the traditional metrics used in organizing and running pipeline businesses quickly break down in the context of a platform—and developing alternative metrics that effectively measure the true health and growth prospects of a platform business is far from easy.

Consider the story of BranchOut. Launched in July 2010, BranchOut was a professional networking platform based mainly on an app that enabled users to make job-hunting connections via Facebook. Think of BranchOut as a variant of LinkedIn piggybacked on the vast Facebook network. In a world where the majority of jobs are filled *not* through help-wanted ads or Internet postings but through friend-to-friend word of mouth, BranchOut struck many people as a brilliant innovation. Its founder and CEO Rick Marini managed to attract $49 million in three rounds of investment.

The company's rocket-propelled ride to the top of the professional networking world was astonishing. BranchOut's user base expanded from fewer than a million to a whopping 33 million between the spring and summer of 2012. But its implosion occurred as quickly. Before another four months had passed, the number of members had plummeted to fewer than two million. And by the following summer, the company was groping for an entirely new business strategy, hoping to become a "workplace chat" platform that teams of coworkers could use to stay in touch. Rich Marini admitted to reporters that "active users aren't very big right now," while saying that BranchOut was "not a failure, it's still alive."[2]

Postmortems pointed to a variety of reasons for BranchOut's collapse. Some blamed changes in Facebook's app developer platform, which put a crimp in BranchOut's communications system. Others pointed out that the whole notion of blending job search capabilities with Facebook's social networking ambience was misguided. "Looking for a job is stressful," as one observer put it. "It's a lot of work. When I hang out with my friends, the last thing I want to do is talk about my job search. I want to escape it."[3]

These may have been factors in BranchOut's failure. But the most significant mistake BranchOut made appears to have been *focusing on—and measuring—the wrong things.* Flush with investment capital and riding an incredible upsurge in "active user" enrollments, during those fateful months in the middle of 2012, BranchOut kept directing its efforts to boosting membership numbers. It incentivized users to invite as many friends as possible, and made it easy for Facebook members to invite everyone in their network to join BranchOut. As hundreds of millions of invitations flooded cyberspace, BranchOut's enrollment figures skyrocketed.[4]

Having a person's name and email address on a membership list doesn't promise success for a platform. What matters is *activity*—the number of satisfying interactions that platform users experience. If BranchOut had tracked the activity numbers as diligently as it tracked membership, it might have realized that its millions of members weren't finding much value in the service—which led, of course, to plummeting membership rolls.

The BranchOut story illustrates a vital truth about the world of platforms. Just as platforms transform traditional value chains, competitive strategy, and management techniques, they also demand new forms of internal measurement.

Let's return for a moment to the metrics that are most commonly used by pipeline managers: key numbers like cash flow, inventory turns, and operating income, as well as ancillary metrics like gross margin, overhead, and return on investment. These tools, in their varied ways, help to measure the same thing: *the efficiency with which value flows through the pipeline*. A successful pipeline business is one that produces goods and services with minimal waste of resources and then delivers a large quantity of these goods and services to customers through well-managed marketing, sales, and distribution systems, thereby generating revenues that are more than sufficient to recoup costs and produce profits to reward investors and finance future growth.

Pipeline metrics are designed to gauge the efficiency of this value flow from one end of the pipeline to the other. They help managers recognize bottlenecks, logjams, and breakdowns in the flow that require improved process efficiencies or system enhancements that will facilitate a larger, faster, and more rewarding stream of value through the pipeline. Thus, when a statistic like inventory turns unexpectedly plummets, it's generally a sign of overstocking, product obsolescence, or marketing failure, while an excessively high rate of turnover may indicate understocking and consequent loss of sales. Carefully monitoring this metric can help managers make necessary adjustments to keep the business humming.

This kind of (admittedly simplified) analysis doesn't work when we shift our focus to a platform business. As we've seen, platforms create value primarily through the impact of network effects. Platform managers in search of metrics that reveal the true health of their business need to focus on positive network effects and on the platform activities that drive them.

In specific, platform metrics need to measure *the rate of interaction success and the factors that contribute to it*. Platforms exist to facilitate positive interactions among users—particularly between producers and consumers of value. The greater the number of positive interactions the platform creates, the more users will be drawn to the platform, and the more eager they will be to engage in activities and interactions of various kinds on the platform. Thus, the most important metrics are those that quantify the success of the platform in fostering sustainable repetition of desirable interactions. The end result: positive network effects and the creation of enormous value for everyone involved, including the users of the platform as well as the sponsors and managers of the platform.

Note the difference between this core metric and the core metric of the pipeline. Whereas a pipeline manager is concerned with the flow of value from one end of the pipeline to the other, the platform manager is concerned with the creation, sharing, and delivery of value throughout the ecosystem—some occurring on the platform, some elsewhere. For a platform manager, process efficiencies and system enhancements may be quite important—but only insofar as they facilitate successful interactions among users. The big goal on which platform managers must remain focused is the creation of value for all users of the platform, which strengthens the community, improves its long-term health and vibrancy, and encourages the continual growth of positive network effects.

DESIGNING METRICS THAT TRACK
THE LIFE CYCLE OF THE PLATFORM

In this chapter, we'll consider some of the key issues related to developing and using appropriate metrics for platform businesses, following the life cycle of a platform from startup to maturity. In the startup phase, it is critical to have simple measures to guide decision-making around key questions of platform design and launch, including the design of the core interaction; the development of effective tools to pull users, facilitate interactions, and match producers with consumers; the creation of effective systems of curation; and decisions about how open the platform should be to various kinds of participants.

In particular, firms in the startup phase must track the growth of their most important asset: active producers and consumers who are participating in a large volume of successful interactions. These users and the interactions they engage in are the key to generating the positive network effects that will ultimately make the platform successful. Notice that some of the traditional metrics generally regarded as crucial in the early years of a pipeline business—revenues, cash flow, profit margins, and the like—are largely irrelevant when evaluating a platform during the startup phase.

Once the platform has reached critical mass and users are gaining significant value from the platform, the focus of metrics can shift to customer retention and the conversion of active users to paying customers. This is the phase in which monetization becomes a crucial issue. As we explained in chapter 6, decisions about how to monetize the platform are fraught. Platform managers will need to devise metrics that focus on some of the key issues related to monetization, for example: Which user groups are enjoying the greatest value from platform activities? Which user groups may need to be subsidized to ensure their continued participation? What fraction of the value creation unleashed by the platform is occurring on the platform rather than outside it? How much additional value can be created through services such as enhanced curation? Which groups outside the platform might find value in access to specific user groups on the platform? And most important, how can the platform capture and retain a fair share of the value being created on the platform without impeding the continued growth of network effects? During the growth phase, thoughtfully designed metrics can help platform managers develop accurate answers to questions like these.

Finally, as the platform matures and a self-sustaining business model has been developed, the challenge of user retention and growth requires the platform to innovate. This is the best way to maintain and enhance the business's value proposition relative to competing platforms. Metrics then must sensitively gauge the ongoing engagement of users and the degree to which they continue to discover new ways to create value on the platform. It's crucial to measure and track the degree to which both producers and consumers are repeatedly participating in the platform and increasing their participation over time.

Other competitive concerns include attempts by adjacent platforms to drain users and reduce the platform's comparative advantage, as well as the possibility that participants in the platform (such as extension developers) may create platforms of their own that could eventually pull users away. These, too, call for the development of metrics that will enable platform leaders to recognize such threats and respond to them in time.

STAGE 1:
METRICS DURING THE STARTUP PHASE

At startup companies—whether they operate as pipelines or as platforms—resources are usually stretched. With money, time, and talent at a premium, people find themselves doing multiple jobs, often in domains far from their expertise. In this kind of environment, deciding the categories of information to which to dedicate resources in collection and processing can be both critically important and challenging.

Furthermore, the *kinds* of metrics that work in a startup context may be quite different from those that apply to a conventional, mature business. Entrepreneur Derek Sivers describes the problem:

> Most tools from general management are not designed to flourish in the harsh soil of extreme uncertainty in which startups thrive. The future is unpredictable, customers face a growing array of alternatives, and the pace of change is ever increasing. Yet most startups—in garages and enterprises alike—still are managed by using standard forecasts, product milestones, and detailed business plans.[5]

So what kinds of metrics are most valuable during the startup phase of a platform business? Platform managers should focus on the core interaction and the benefits it creates for both producers and consumers on the platform. To define success or failure for a platform, and to identify how to improve it, there are three main metrics: *liquidity, matching quality,* and *trust.*

Liquidity in a platform marketplace is a state in which there are a minimum number of producers and consumers and the percentage of successful interactions is high. When liquidity is achieved, interaction failure is minimized, and the intent of users to interact is consistently satisfied within a reasonable period of time. Achieving liquidity is the first and most important milestone in the life cycle of a platform. Therefore, the most valuable metric in the early months of a platform is one that can help you determine when liquidity is reached. Depending on the precise workings of the platform and the nature of its user base, the formula for this metric may vary.

One reasonable way to measure liquidity is by tracking *the percentage of listings that lead to interactions within a given time period.* Of course, both the definition of "interactions" and the appropriate time period will vary depending on the market category. On an information and entertainment platform, an interaction might be the click-through that takes a consumer from a headline to a complete story; on a marketplace platform, it might be the purchase of a product; on a professional networking platform, it might be the offer of a recommendation, the swapping of contact information, or a posted response to a question on a discussion page. Any of these interactions would signify a greater degree of engagement by the user and represent the moment when the user has recognized, used, and enjoyed a value unit available on the platform.

On the negative side, it's important to look for and track the occurrence of illiquid situations. These are circumstances in which a desired transaction is impossible—for example, when an Uber user opens the app and discovers that no car is available. Illiquid situations discourage users from participating in the platform and so must be kept to a minimum.

Note that user commitment and active usage of the platform are the vital metrics of platform adoption, not sign-ups. That's why our definition of liquidity includes both user totals and the level of interactions occurring. New reports and investor pitches that emphasize impressive raw numbers of platform members can be very misleading and may be a sign that the platform, far from flourishing, is struggling to convert curiosity-seekers into active participants and value creators.

Also note that the most meaningful metrics are comparative ones, which draw helpful distinctions between groups of users or over periods of time (a useful recommendation from Alistair Croll and Benjamin Yoskovitz, authors of *Lean Analytics*). A good example of an inherently comparative measure is a ratio or rate, which is calculated by dividing one number by another—for example, *the ratio of active users*, which is calculated by dividing the number of active users by the number of total users, or *the rate of growth in active users*, which is calculated by dividing the number of new active users by the number of total active users.[6]

A second crucial category of metric for the startup platform is *matching quality*. This refers to the accuracy of the search algorithm and the intuitiveness of the navigation tools offered to users as they seek other users with whom they can engage in value-creating interactions. Matching quality is critical to delivering value and stimulating the long-term growth and success of the platform. It is achieved through excellence in *product or service curation*.

As the definition implies, matching quality is closely related to the effectiveness with which products or service offerings on the platform are curated. Users generally participate in a platform with highly interactional intent; they want to find what they're looking for as quickly as possible. Precision in matching leads to lower search costs for users—that is, they need to invest less time, energy, effort, and other resources in finding the matches they want. Thus, if the platform does a great job of linking users to one another quickly and accurately, those users are likely to become active participants and long-term members of the platform; if matching quality is poor, slow, and disappointing, users will soon dwindle in number, interactions will slow to a trickle, and the platform may be doomed to an early demise.

Of course, it's necessary to translate the abstract term "matching quality" into a concrete quantity with a clear operational definition in order to make it the basis of a meaningful metric. One way to measure the efficiency of the platform in successfully matching producers to consumers is by tracking the *sales conversion rate,* which can be expressed as the percentage of searches that lead to interactions.

Obviously, the higher the percentage, the better—but where does the threshold between "poor" and "good" matching quality lie? There's no single answer that applies to every kind of platform. However, the manager of a particular platform may be able to develop a useful rule of thumb by correlating the interaction percentage for particular users with the long-term rate of activity of those users— say, over a period of one to three months. Calculations like these may enable you to determine, for example, that an interaction percentage of 40 percent appears to represent a significant cutoff point for users of your platform: the majority of users who experience interaction percentage higher than 40 percent during their first week on the platform remain active members for at least three months, while a majority of those with an interaction percentage lower than 40 percent stop participating in activities on the site.

Once you've calculated a number of this kind—whether it is 40 percent, higher, or lower—you can use it as a working target that serves as one measure of the health of your site. The daily interaction percentage can be measured, its trend over time can be observed, and improvements to the platform's matching system can be developed, tested, and evaluated based on changes in this metric.

The third crucial category of startup metric is *trust.* Trust refers to the degree to which users of a platform feel comfortable with the level of risk associated with engaging in interactions on the platform. It is achieved through excellent curation of participants in the platform.

Building trust, of course, is central to marketplaces, especially those in which interactions carry some level of risk—and in the world of online platforms, where initial connections among users as well as many interactions are conducted entirely in cyberspace, the perception of risk may be even more significant. A well-run platform is one in which participants on both sides have been successfully curated so that users are comfortable with the level of risk involved in engaging in interactions on the platform. As we've noted, Airbnb is an example of a player in a high-risk category that has succeeded so far because of its ability to curate its participants successfully. It allows hosts and guests to review each other and has one of the highest review rates among platforms. It also takes additional measures to build trust, including having photographers certify the accuracy of the information contained in a host's listing. By contrast, Airbnb's competitor Craigslist has earned relatively low scores on the trust metric and has experienced a number of embarrassing scandals involving apparently sleazy platform users engaged in disreputable, even illegal activities.

These three crucial categories of metrics—liquidity, matching quality, and trust—combine to provide the managers of startup platforms with an accurate picture of the platform's rate of interaction success and the key factors that contribute to it. As we've noted, this measurement is at the heart of the platform's purpose and plays a central role in determining its ability to create positive network effects.

The specific formulas you use to define the metrics for a particular platform business need to be carefully devised to be appropriate for the kind of platform business involved—the nature of the platform, the types of users, the forms of value being created and exchanged, the variety of interactions performed, and so on.

There are a number of specialized metrics that are potentially valuable for particular platform businesses. You might choose to measure *engagement per interaction*, *time between interactions*, and *percentage of active users*, all of which focus on the degree of user commitment to the ecosystem.

Alternatively, you might choose to measure *number of interactions*, as, for example, the graphics and design platform Fiverr does. Since Fiverr has a fixed value per interaction—every "gig" traded on the site is priced at five dollars—the sheer number of interactions is a perfectly adequate and complete measurement of the current activity flow on the site.

Other platforms need to develop more sophisticated interaction metrics. Airbnb, for example, tracks the number of nights booked, which is a better indicator of value creation for this platform than simply recording the number of interactions. The freelance work marketplace Upwork measures interaction volume by counting the hours of work delivered by a particular freelancer, which is a key measure of value creation in that ecosystem. In a similar fashion, Clarity can track the duration of a consulting call between an expert and the information seeker.

Platforms whose revenue is based on claiming a share of the value of any interaction—a commission fee based on a percentage of the interaction, for example—may choose to measure *interaction capture*, which will reflect the value of interactions that occur on the platform. Amazon Marketplace, for instance, uses this metric, tracking the gross value of interactions processed by the platform as a key indicator of its activity level.

Platforms that focus on content creation require different metrics. For example, some measure *co-creation* (the percentage of listings that are consumed by users) or *consumer relevance* (the percentage of listings that receive some minimum level of positive response from potential consumers). These metrics focus on interaction quality and reflect the skill with which production is being curated.

Finally, other platforms focus on *market access*—the effectiveness with which users have been able to join the platform and find or connect with one another, regardless of whether a complete interaction has occurred. Some measure *producer participation*—that is, the rate at which producers join the platform and the growth of this rate over time. Dating and matrimonial sites often talk about number of women registered, since this metric serves as a useful proxy for the value that other users of the site can expect to receive. In a somewhat different fashion, OpenTable tracks restaurant reservations. These are not the actual interactions, in which restaurants are paid for meals served (information not readily available to the platform), but they serve as a fairly accurate proxy for the value created.

The three key factors of liquidity, matching quality, and trust remain crucial to measuring the health of virtually any kind of newly launched platform. But as you can see, specific characteristics of a particular platform may dictate the need for additional, more specialized measurement tools. The variety and range of metrics that may be suitable during a platform's startup phase is limited only by your ingenuity and the nature of the activities occurring in your burgeoning ecosystem.

STAGE 2:
METRICS DURING THE GROWTH PHASE

The metrics that best measure the number and quality of interactions in your ecosystem will change over the life cycle of the platform, and it's critical to identify points at which these transitions occur. Companies often make the mistake of clinging to metrics that their business has outgrown. Identifying and vetting the core metrics that are most relevant to the decisions you face *today* is important at every point in the platform's development.

For example, once the platform reaches a critical mass of users, new issues arise. Managers must still ensure that the core interaction is creating value and that the inflow of engaged users exceeds the outflow so that the platform is still growing. However, as growth continues, the platform must monitor the change in size of the user base over time. In particular, platform managers will want to work to ensure balance on the two sides of its market. This balance can be monitored by calculating the *producer-to-consumer ratio*, with an adjustment to include only active platform users—those who've engaged in interactions on the platform at a specific minimum rate of frequency that you consider appropriate. Experience shows that this ratio is a crucial factor in the rate of interaction success achieved by the platform.

Consider the core interaction that the dating website OkCupid is facilitating: introductions between men and women. As we noted in chapter 2, one of the critical things for this platform to manage is the access of straight men (who may be considered "consumers" in this context) to straight women (who play the role of "producers").*

---

*We recognize the unpleasant implications of this language. It reflects the currently prevailing dynamic of many male–female dating interactions in U.S. society at this time, including the fact that most online dating sites find it easier to attract male participants than

As a result, OkCupid tracks the ratio of straight women to straight men, and platform managers work hard to adjust that ratio when it diverges from the level they deem optimal. They manage these adjustments by asking users to rate the attractiveness of those on the opposite side of the platform.[7] The website then introduces a filter to reduce the number of men who can participate in the platform by seeing women's profiles—especially women who are rated as particularly attractive.[8] In this way, the OkCupid platform is helping to maintain positive network effects and fostering market liquidity by avoiding an imbalance that might otherwise alienate a segment of its female users. Continually measuring and monitoring the male–female ratio makes this maintenance possible. In similar fashion, the freelance platform Upwork focuses on keeping the number of freelancers proportional to the number of job postings, since a surfeit on either side causes participants to leave.

For a traditional two-sided platform with producers on one side and consumers on the other, it is best to find ways to calculate the value of each user type. In *Lean Analytics*, the entrepreneur/author team of Alistair Croll and Benjamin Yoskovitz provide a useful illustration of metrics for a two-sided platform, which we adapt below.[9]

On the producer side, the platform should monitor figures that include the *frequency of producer participation, listings created*, and *outcomes achieved*. The platform should also monitor *interaction failure*—the percentage of cases in which interactions, such as sales, are initiated but fall through for some reason. This is a crucial metric that many platform managers overlook. If users are being retained but the rate of successful interaction is falling, there is a serious problem.

It's especially important to monitor instances of *producer fraud*—for example, the failure of a producer to describe a product offering accurately or to deliver it in a timely fashion. Producer fraud is, of course, a particularly egregious, painful, and costly form of

---

females. Thus, females are "in demand" in a way that is analogous to the demand for highly-sought-after products on an auction site like eBay. As social norms evolve in the direction of greater gender equality, we hope and expect that this dynamic will also evolve, with implications for the effective management of dating platforms.

interaction failure. Examination of the characteristics of users and interactions repeatedly linked to fraud may be used to create predictive models that can help the platform prevent future fraud.

Combining all these forms of data, the value of a producer can be calculated using traditional *lifetime value* (LTV) models used in many kinds of businesses. These models capture the mechanism by which repeat producers provide recurring platform revenues without incurring additional acquisition costs—that is, expenses incurred by the platform in attracting and engaging these producers. Because repeat producers are especially profitable to a platform, well-managed platform firms will work hard to create active repeat producers, just as subscriber-based services like magazines and cell service providers work to keep the rates of subscriber turnover (or *churn*) as low as possible.

On the consumer side, the growing platform should monitor the *frequency of consumption, searches,* and *rate of conversion to sale* (the percentage of click-throughs that result in completed interactions). This information, along with the likelihood of repeat interactions, provides the data necessary to calculate each consumer's LTV. Once both producer and consumer LTV measures have been created, the platform can run experiments in an effort to impact the critical determinants of LTV—churn rate, for example.[10]

Most of today's successful platform businesses have programs designed to encourage loyalty on the part of the most valuable active users and to discourage those who are less valuable. If you've ever had a platform like Facebook or LinkedIn ping you with an invitation to return to the platform after a falloff in your usage, you've been targeted by such a program. Similarly, Twitter has introduced the "popular in your network" feature to alert you to content that might be particularly relevant even if you have not subscribed to those authors' feeds—another activity-building program that is driven by metrics and designed to stimulate more interactions around users with a proven track record of value-creating activity.[11]

A critical variable from the startup phase that remains highly relevant during the growth phase is the *interaction conversion rate*—that is, the percentage of searches or queries that result in interactions. Well designed and consistently monitored metrics focusing on the sales conversion rate can help platform managers develop smart strategies that will enhance the platform's continued growth—as when Airbnb introduced its professional photography service after discovering that high-quality photos increase property rental rates.[12]

Interestingly, Airbnb has also discovered that its best source of hosts is people who have been guests. Consequently, it is now working hard to convert consumers on its platform into producers. In this case, the *side switching rate*—the rate at which people convert from one type of user to another—offers an important metric that the platform can use to track the health of its user base and to maintain balance across its network.

New metrics are continually being devised by platform managers based on their specific objectives and interests as well as the unique characteristics of their users. Haier Group is a rapidly growing manufacturing company based in Qingdao, China. It is currently building a platform to connect its customers with the design and production teams, both inside and outside the organization, that create the products, which include home appliances and electronics. Haier's CEO, Ruimin Zhang, spoke with the authors about a unique metric that the company is eager to capture and use—namely, the *distance between consumers and producers*.[13] In this case, the word "distance" is metaphorical, not literal; it refers to the frequency of direct interaction and the size, reach, and influence of the social networks that connect producers of Haier products to their users.

To measure this distance, Haier has devised metrics based on interactions on WeChat, a social instant messaging and photo sharing tool developed by the Chinese company Tencent. The goal: to minimize the distance between Haier and its customers, thereby improving the fit between products and consumer needs, enhancing the company's innovative capacities, and making its marketing and promotional efforts less costly and more effective.

As CEO Zhang pointed out to us, the size of a company's advertising budget might be viewed as a reflection of the distance between the company and its customers. For example, the annual brand value report issued in 2013 by the consulting firm Interbrand noted that Google's advertising budget is just a tiny fraction of Coca-Cola's. The likely reason: Google is deeply integrated into people's lives through its many productivity and social applications, giving it constant user feedback that Coca-Cola doesn't receive.

Based on analogies like this, Haier's leadership team hypothesizes that a reduction in its user distance measure may improve its product design, customer service, and marketing efficiency. Thus, a seemingly abstract metric like user distance may have a highly practical, dollars-and-cents impact on your bottom line.

STAGE 3:
METRICS DURING THE MATURITY PHASE

Once a platform business has moved past the phases of startup and early growth, new challenges and issues emerge. Eric Ries, the writer and entrepreneur known for pioneering the "lean startup" movement, emphasizes that, for the mature company, incremental innovation and metrics must be closely related to each other. "When making improvements to your product," Ries observes, "the only arbiter of whether or not it was successful is the metrics. And, when you are implementing an improvement to your product, you should be testing that improvement against a baseline."

Somewhat in line with Ries's thinking, Amrit Tiwana, a professor at the University of Georgia, suggests that metrics suitable for information technology platforms that have reached the maturity phase should meet three major requirements: they should *drive innovation*, have a *high signal-to-noise ratio*, and *facilitate resource allocation*.[14]

First, let's focus on the role of metrics in driving innovation. In order to remain vibrant, a platform must be able to adapt to the needs of its users and to changes in the competitive and regulatory environment. One way for a platform to identify necessary adaptations is by studying the extensions provided by developers. These innovations may represent functionalities missing from the core platform, which the platform may choose to absorb. For example, during the era of the desktop computer, Microsoft Windows absorbed a number of applications that were once provided by stand-alone companies, such as disk defragmentation, file encryption, media playing, and more.[15]

Cisco has followed the same absorption strategy in the router business, where it operates a platform known as the Cisco Application Extension Platform. The Cisco AXP (as it is called) is a Linux-based platform that allows third-party developers to create applications that work on Cisco routers, providing new capabilities that Cisco customers find useful—for example, enhanced security measures and customized monitoring systems. When we asked Cisco's chief technology officer, Guido Jouret, how the company decided which functions to bundle into the Cisco AXP, his answer was illuminating:

> The issue is to embed into the platform multiple independent solutions to the same problem. Then this becomes common for everyone else. It's a question of timing. If you do it right away, your ecosystem is scared that you'll cannibalize their cash cows. If one provider builds a particular functionality, you don't want to co-opt it. But if a whole slew of them have [developed the same capability], then competition reduces benefits anyway, and you can fold it in.[16]

To enable this strategy, Cisco employs metrics that seek out instances in which the same capability is provided across multiple industry verticals—health care or the automotive business, for example. That is a sign that the platform is missing important features that should be part of the next round of continuous platform innovation.

A platform may also choose to innovate when features provided by third parties become a large part of the overall value enjoyed by users. As we saw in chapter 7, this helps to explain Apple's 2012 introduction of Apple Maps in response to the enormous popularity of Google Maps.

Some kinds of platforms need still other customized metrics during their maturity phase. These include labor platforms such as Upwork, data platforms such as Thomson Reuters, connection platforms such as Skype, and platforms that connect machines such as GE's Industrial Internet. Although these are distinct platform types with disparate needs, they all face the challenges of facilitating a core interaction, measuring the drivers of value, and innovating to maintain the platform's ability to produce significant value for users.

ELEMENTS OF SMART METRICS DESIGN

The metrics dashboard you develop for your platform can be quite complex, allowing you to get a real-time glimpse of activities at a very fine level. However, simplicity is a virtue when developing metrics for your platform business. Overcomplex metrics make management *less* effective by introducing noise, discouraging frequent analysis, and distracting from the handful of data points that are most significant.

At one time, oDesk (now known as Upwork) had so many metrics (measuring job postings, registered workers, service variety, and many other factors) that one board member complained, "You're over-measured and under-prioritized." Having learned from this mistake, Gary Swart, former CEO of oDesk, writes eloquently about the need for highly focused metrics, especially in the critical early period of a startup:

> As a business leader you need to figure out the metric that matters most for your company and understand that the more you measure, the less prioritized you'll be. Don't fall into the trap of trying to measure everything. What I've learned is that in the early days, what matters most is having customers who love and use your product. Figure out the one or two best measures to determine this.[17]

Lean startup guru Eric Ries echoes the need to be selective in the design and use of metrics. In particular, he cautions against what he calls "vanity metrics," such as total sign-ups—a relatively meaningless statistic that often increases even as the volume of interactions is flat or actually declining. Vanity metrics fail to indicate accurately whether the business is really achieving critical mass or the liquidity it needs.

Instead, Ries suggests, "you should make sure your metrics meet the '3 A's test' where your metrics are actionable, accessible, and auditable." They must be actionable in that they provide clear guidance for strategic and managerial decisions, and in being clearly related to the success of the business. They must be accessible in that they are comprehensible to the people who gather and use the information. And they must be auditable in the sense that they are real and meaningful—based on clean, accurate data, precisely defined, and reflecting the reality of the business as perceived by users.[18]

In the end, the most important metric is a simple one: the number of happy customers on every side of the network who are repeatedly and increasingly engaged in positive, value-creating interactions. The real question, which you should never lose sight of, is: are people happy enough with the ecosystem to continue participating in it actively? No matter how you end up designing the metric dashboard for your specific platform business, it should ultimately serve to accurately measure the answer to this key question.

TAKEAWAYS FROM CHAPTER NINE

❑ Since the value of a platform is derived primarily from network effects, platform metrics should ultimately seek to measure the rate of interaction success and the factors that contribute to it. Interaction success attracts active users and thereby enhances the development of positive network effects.

❑ During the startup phase, platform companies should concentrate on metrics that track the strength of characteristics that enable core interactions on the platform, including *liquidity, matching,* and *trust.* These characteristics can be measured in a variety of specific ways, depending on the nature of the platform.

❑ During the growth phase, platform companies should focus on metrics that are likely to impact growth and enhanced value creation, such as the relative size of various portions of the user base, the lifetime value of producers and consumers, and the sales conversion rate.

❑ During the maturity phase, platform companies should focus on metrics that drive innovation by identifying new functionalities that can create value for users, as well as metrics that can identify strategic threats from competitors to which the platform needs to respond.

10

STRATEGY
How Platforms Change Competition

I n the world of platforms, the nature of competition is being transformed. Companies find themselves struggling to make sense of new competitive threats posed by unexpected, often counterintuitive rivals.[1] The educational book publisher Houghton Mifflin Harcourt doesn't fear McGraw-Hill as much as it fears Amazon. Broadcaster NBC worries less about ABC than about Netflix. Legal information purveyor Lexis feels less threatened by Westlaw than by Google and by the online legal services purveyor LegalZoom. Appliance maker Whirlpool fears GE and Siemens less than it fears Nest, the maker of smart home monitoring and control devices that is rapidly becoming a key element in the emerging "Internet of things." And the social network Facebook was less worried about a rebooted Myspace than about Instagram and WhatsApp—which is why it bought them.

What has changed is not simply the types of competitors but the very nature of the competitive battle. The result is a series of seismic upheavals that are making one business landscape after another almost unrecognizable. We're not speaking only of the dramatic disruptions produced by the advent of platform businesses in traditional marketplaces (as described in chapter 4 and elsewhere in this book). We're also referring to the dramatic competitive battles being waged *within* the world of platforms, between platform companies—with results that are often startling, even shocking.[2]

It's probably safe to say that the $25 billion initial public offering of shares in Alibaba Group in September 2014—the largest IPO in history—was one of the most unexpected business stories of the year.

Many Westerners who had not obsessively followed the world of e-commerce had never heard of the company. Those who had were mainly familiar with it through its connection with the floundering Yahoo, which owned a significant stake in Alibaba. Much U.S. coverage of the Alibaba story was vaguely dismissive, treating the company's amazing growth and impressive size as fluky results of the sheer vastness and parochialism of the Chinese market and the impact of government protectionism.

A 2010 story in the *New York Times* was typical. Reporter David Barboza acknowledged Alibaba as one of several "fast-growing local firms that are making huge profits" through online sales. But in the future, Barboza wrote, "China's Internet market could increasingly resemble a lucrative, walled-off bazaar, experts say. Those home-grown successes . . . could have trouble becoming global brands." Barboza quotes one analyst as predicting, "When the Chinese companies go outside of China, they will find that they fail to understand their competitors as well as they did when they were competing in China."[3]

By the summer of 2014, with Alibaba's U.S. stock debut just weeks away, U.S. business analysts were singing a different tune. In *Businessweek*, Brad Stone warned of "the Alibaba invasion" and explained how the Chinese giant was suddenly posing the first ever significant threat to U.S. domination of the Internet. Stone recounted how Alibaba had outcompeted eBay in China, had become a huge source of Chinese goods for businesses around the world, had successfully opened the Chinese consumer market for global companies such as Nike and Apple, and was quickly building the infrastructure to challenge Amazon and eBay in their own home market—the U.S. Stone concluded, "China's Web entrepreneurs are positioning themselves to compete in—and win—the race to build the first truly global online marketplace."[4]

In most traditional industries, such a rapid emergence from relative obscurity to global leadership would be virtually impossible. Glancing back at business history, we see that it took American businesses in industries like steel and heavy machinery decades to overtake once-dominant rivals in Britain and Germany. After World War

Two, Japanese upstarts required three decades to seize leadership roles in auto making and electronics from industry leaders in the U.S. But Alibaba today has the potential to outstrip companies like eBay and Amazon a decade or so after entering the battle for platform marketplace dominance.

How did it happen?

As with most big business stories, there are many contributing elements in the Alibaba saga, including the strategic insights of CEO Jack Ma, the explosive growth of China's middle class, and, yes, government-imposed restrictions on foreign companies operating in China, which gave Alibaba a bit of space to grow without being crushed by American competitors. But the swiftness of Alibaba's ascent is largely a function of the new realities of platform competition.[5]

Explosive network effects and strong economies of scale enabled this relatively new company to expand so rapidly on the stage of international commerce. Alibaba.com, one of five major businesses operating under the corporate umbrella, allows companies around the world to source goods, products, and parts from Chinese manufacturers. One California cosmetics maker marvels that, through Alibaba.com, "I have access to hundreds of suppliers at my fingertips." Conversely, Tmall, another Alibaba subsidiary, sells foreign goods to millions of Chinese consumers, bypassing the country's traditional broker system, which slowed imports and added layers of paperwork and cost. One U.S. shoe retailer says Alibaba "has compressed the whole middle layer of retail." The result is near-frictionless cross-border trading that connects thousands of merchants with millions of customers—a phenomenon scarcely imaginable before the advent of the platform.

Furthermore, Alibaba is shrewdly leveraging another enormous competitive strength of platforms—the ability to seamlessly incorporate the resources and connections of outside partners into the activities and capabilities of the platform. For example, to expand its ability to offer U.S. goods to Chinese consumers, Alibaba has now forged a partnership with ShopRunner, a U.S.-based logistics company in which Alibaba owns a stake. ShopRunner already has arrangements with U.S. brands including Neiman Marcus and Toys"R"Us that enable Alibaba to ship American products to customers in China in two days.[6]

Back in the nineteenth and early twentieth centuries, it took decades and vast investments in retailing, warehousing, product testing, management, printing, shipping, service, and fulfillment systems for Sears, Roebuck to make itself into America's merchant. Today, a platform business like Alibaba can assemble the capabilities of dozens of preexisting entities and swiftly become a contender for the title of merchant to the world. And, of course, Alibaba's chief rivals for the crown are other platform companies such as Amazon and eBay. Such is the world of competition that the rise of platforms has brought.

But to fully understand how the rise of the platform is transforming the nature of competition, we need to reexamine the traditional concepts of competition that have dominated business thinking for decades—and that many businesspeople still take for granted.

STRATEGY IN THE TWENTIETH CENTURY: A CAPSULE HISTORY

For three decades, the five forces model of competition outlined by Michael Porter of Harvard Business School has dominated the world of strategic thinking.[7] As one measure of Porter's influence, his writings have received more than a quarter million citations, exceeding those of any Nobel Prize-winning economist.

Porter's model identifies five forces that affect the strategic position of a particular business: the threat of new entrants to the market, the threat of substitute products or services, the bargaining power of customers, the bargaining power of suppliers, and the intensity of competitive rivalry in the industry. The goal of strategy is to control these five forces in such a way as to build a moat around the business and thereby render it unassailable.

Thus, when a firm can erect barriers to entry, it can keep competitors out, and entrants with substitute products cannot storm the castle. When a firm can subjugate suppliers, competition among them weakens their bargaining power so the firm can keep its costs low. When a firm can subjugate buyers by keeping them relatively small, disunited, and powerless, the firm can keep its prices high.

In this model, the firm maximizes profits by avoiding ruinous competition for itself but encouraging it for everyone else in the value chain. Advantage is found in industry structures that create a protective moat—one that enables the firm to segment markets, differentiate products, control resources, avoid price wars, and defend its profit margins.

For decades, companies have studied the five forces model and used it to guide their decisions about which markets to enter and exit, what mergers or acquisitions to consider, what sorts of product innovation to pursue, and what supply chain strategies to employ. Approaches like horizontal integration (in which a firm controls most or all of a specific product or service marketplace) and vertical integration (in which a firm controls an entire value chain, from raw materials to manufacturing to marketing) have been analyzed and implemented based on the strategic implications of the five forces model. Under this model, Houghton Mifflin Harcourt competes with McGraw-Hill by striving to control the best authors and content and by using copyright to construct a moat around its fortress of value. Whirlpool competes with GE by engineering differentiated products, squeezing the supply chain, and continually improving its manufacturing efficiencies, thereby constructing a moat that makes it hard for GE to poach Whirlpool's customers.

Later thinkers have added nuance and fresh insights to Porter's approach. In 1984, MIT's Birger Wernerfelt first described in detail what he called the resource-based view of the firm, a variation on strategic thinking with roots in the work of several earlier scholars.[8] The resource-based view highlights the fact that a particularly effective barrier to entry is control of an indispensable and inimitable resource. A firm with such a resource is safe from new entrants who lack and cannot acquire means to produce it. A simple example is De

Beers, whose control of a worldwide diamond marketing cartel enabled it to maintain a near-monopoly over the diamond industry for the entire twentieth century. The De Beers cartel broke down after 2000 when some diamond producers decided to market their product outside the De Beers-controlled system, reducing the cartel's share of the market from 90 percent in the 1980s to about 33 percent in 2013.[9] Until then, however, De Beers's control of an irreplaceable resource gave it a sustainable advantage that yielded a hundred years' worth of profits.

In the twenty-first century, a number of strategy scholars have challenged the resource-based view, pointing out that nimble firms are using new technologies to ford the moats established by control of scarce resources. In separate works, Richard D'Aveni and Rita Gunther McGrath have argued that, in an age of "hypercompetition" (D'Aveni's term), sustainable advantage is illusory. Technological advances drive shorter and shorter cycle times on everything from "microchips to corn chips, software to soft drinks, and packaged goods to package delivery services."[10] Connecting across the Internet also allows firms to redraw industrial and geographic boundaries so that stable, slow-moving oligopolies fall to nimbler competitors attacking with new tools and technologies.

McGrath describes how the Internet era has created radically new tools and techniques with which to attack incumbent firms. Imagine a company that wanted to compete with the Union Pacific Railroad in 1915—a firm with a five-decade head start thanks to its authorization by Congress in 1862. The would be competitor would have needed to make investments in locomotives, rolling stock, depots, terminals, warehouses, and the legal right-of-way required to build a nationwide rail network. The massive investment in these and other fixed costs already spent by Union Pacific provided a mile-wide moat that made the railroad incumbent virtually impregnable.[11]

By contrast, imagine a firm that wants to compete with any of the Global 500 companies in 2015. Depending on the specific industry, such an upstart could buy production resources from manufacturing firms around the world, cloud and computing services from a range of suppliers, marketing and distribution services from various intermediary companies, and professional services from many online networks of freelancers—all at near marginal cost. In today's hyper-competitive environment enabled by technology, ownership of infra-structure no longer provides a defensible advantage. Instead, flexibility provides the crucial competitive edge, competition is per-petual motion, and advantage is evanescent.

Other analysts have offered additional insights into the evolving nature of competition. Author Steve Denning has highlighted the weakness of Porter's assumption that the purpose of strategy is to avoid competition. Denning pointed instead to management guru Peter Drucker's dictum that the purpose of business is "to create a customer." According to Denning, in a world where sustainable advantage is an illusion, a company's relationships with customers are its only lasting source of value.[12]

It would be an exaggeration to say that events of the last decade have demolished the five forces model—but they suggest that the nature of competition has become more complicated and dynamic than Porter's model might imply.

THREE-DIMENSIONAL CHESS: THE NEW COMPLEXITIES OF COMPETITION IN THE WORLD OF PLATFORMS

Enter platforms. Many of the insights embodied in the five forces, resource-based, and hypercompetition models remain valid, but two new realities are now shaking up the world of strategy.

First, firms that understand how platforms work can now inten-tionally manipulate network effects to *remake* markets, not just *respond* to them. The implicit assumption in traditional business strategy that competition is a zero-sum game is far less applicable in the world of platforms. Rather than re-dividing a pie of more-or-less static size, platform businesses often grow the pie (as, for example, Amazon has done by innovating new models, such as self-publishing and publishing on demand, within the traditional book industry) or create an alternative pie that taps new markets and sources of supply (as Airbnb and Uber have done alongside the traditional hotel and taxi industries). Actively managing network effects changes the shape of markets rather than taking them as fixed.

Second, platforms turn businesses inside out, moving managerial influence from inside to outside the firm's boundaries. Thus, a firm no longer needs to seize every new opportunity on its own; instead, it can pursue only the best opportunities while helping ecosystem partners seize the others, with all partners sharing the value they jointly create.[13]

These two new realities add a dramatic layer of complexity to business competition. Platform strategy resembles traditional strategy much the way three-dimensional chess resembles the traditional game.[14] Within the ecosystem, the lead firm negotiates dynamic tradeoffs involving competition at three levels: platform against platform, platform against partner, and partner against partner.

At the first level, one platform competes with another, as in the video game console battles among Sony (PlayStation), Microsoft (Xbox), and Nintendo (Wii). Strategic advantage is based not on the attractiveness of particular products or services but rather on the power of entire ecosystems. The Sony PlayStation Portable was a stronger gaming device than the iPhone, which lacked specialized left and right controls. When Sony released the PSP-2000 in fall of 2007, after Apple's summer release of the iPhone, Sony's stock rose about 10 percent. But before long, the iPhone ecosystem vastly outstripped that of the PSP. As we've already noted, Apple has subsequently enjoyed far great financial success than Sony, thanks in large part to the size and value of its ecosystem.

At the second level, a platform competes with its partners—for example, when Microsoft appropriates such partner innovations as browsers, multithreading, streaming media, and instant messaging and incorporates them into its operating system, or when Amazon operates as a platform for independent merchants while also selling some of the same goods on the same platform in competition with those merchants. This is a delicate and dangerous move. It can strengthen the platform, but at the expense of weakening partners—a short-term gain that can lead to painful long-term consequences.

At the third level, two unrelated platform partners compete for positions within the platform ecosystem, as when two game app developers strive to attract the same consumers on the same console.[15]

Let's consider some of the specific impacts that these platform-driven changes have on traditional views of strategy.

As we've seen, platforms expand the boundaries of the firm. The shifting horizons of managerial influence now make competition less significant for strategists than collaboration and co-creation—or, as scholars Barry J. Nalebuff, Adam M. Brandenburger, and Agus Maulana call it, "co-opetition."[16] The shift from protecting value inside the firm to creating value outside the firm means that the crucial factor is no longer ownership but opportunity, while the chief tool is no longer dictation but persuasion.

The five forces model depends on the distinct boundaries that characterize traditional product markets. Each of the five forces—customer power, supplier power, and so on—is a separate entity that must be managed independently. By contrast, in platform markets, a winning strategy blurs the boundaries among market participants, thereby increasing valuable interactions on the platform. A Skillshare student today can become a teacher tomorrow; an Etsy customer one day can begin selling her own crafts on the site the next. Platform competition requires treating buyers and suppliers not as separate threats to be subjugated but as value-creating partners to be wooed, celebrated, and encouraged to play multiple roles.

The resource-based view assumes that a firm must own, or at least control, the inimitable resource. In the world of platforms, the nature of the inimitable resource shifts from physical assets to access to customer–producer networks and the interactions that result. In fact, it can be better for the firm *not* to own physical resources, since eschewing ownership enables it to grow more quickly. As the examples of Airbnb and Uber remind us, the resource pool that a platform company can access is capable of growing much faster than the platform company itself.

HOW PLATFORMS COMPETE (1):
PREVENTING MULTIHOMING BY LIMITING
PLATFORM ACCESS

In traditional business, Porter's five forces and the ability to control inimitable resources—as modified by the dynamic of technology-driven hypercompetition—have largely shaped business strategy. In the world of platforms, new competitive factors have moved to the fore. These new factors help determine who participates in a platform ecosystem, the value they help to create, who controls that value, and ultimately the size of the market. These new factors have become the focus of a series of new competitive strategies.

Let's consider them one by one, beginning with the strategy of limiting platform access so as to control and capture a greater share of the value created on the platform.

As we've seen, the resource-based view of business value must be modified when applied to platform businesses. However, the resource-based emphasis on inimitable resources has its parallel in the world of platforms: *Platforms seek exclusive access to essential assets.* They do this, in part, by developing rules, practices, and protocols that discourage *multihoming*.

Multihoming occurs when users engage in similar types of interactions on more than one platform. A freelance professional who presents his credentials on two or more service marketing platforms, a music fan who downloads, stores, and shares tunes on more than one music site, and a driver who solicits rides through both Uber and Lyft all illustrate the phenomenon of multihoming. Platform businesses seek to discourage multihoming, since it facilitates *switching*—when a user abandons one platform in favor of another. Limiting multihoming is a cardinal competitive tactic for platforms.

Here's an example of how the effort to limit multihoming plays out in the new world of strategy. Adobe Flash Player is a browser app that delivers Internet content to users, including audio/video playback and real-time game play. Flash could have been used by app developers on Apple's iPhone operating system—but Apple prevented this by making its iOS incompatible with Flash and insisting that developers use similar tools created by Apple itself.

Developers and users responded with dismay, and some observers called the policy an anti-competitive gambit that might be subject to governmental sanction under antitrust regulations. The furor grew so heated that, in 2010, Apple's Steve Jobs felt compelled to defend the policy in an open letter—a highly unusual step for a CEO to take. In his "Thoughts on Flash," Jobs argued that Flash was a closed system and technically inferior to other options, consuming excessive energy and otherwise delivering poor performance on mobile devices. Keeping Flash off the iPhone, Jobs claimed, would preserve the quality of the Apple user experience.[17]

The real reasons were much deeper and more strategic. Adobe had designed Flash developer tools to allow content and program porting from Apple iOS to Google Android and to web pages more generally. Apps developed in Flash could multihome, reducing the iPhone's distinctiveness. Adobe also released extensions that allowed in-app purchases. By allowing developers to take interactions off the iTunes platform, Flash would cause Apple to lose its 30 percent cut of every interaction as well as control over the associated usage data—information that provides valuable clues concerning trends in the marketplace.

If Apple had supported Flash, it would have granted users access to enormous amounts of Flash content already on the web while giving developers more ways to monetize their investments by multihoming across platforms.[18] But it would have been a big loss for Apple. So they used licensing rules and technology to keep interactions from going off platform.

Another example of how the strategic battle for control of access to the customer can play out is the story of Alibaba.

Ming Zeng is chief strategy officer of Alibaba. At the MIT Platform Strategy Summit hosted by the authors in 2014, Zeng explained how denying a powerful competitor access to Alibaba helped change the shape of the market and enabled at least a portion of Alibaba's remarkable growth.[19]

Early in the evolution of Alibaba, the company was scrambling for ways to attract users and generate significant network effects. The company's "great explosion" in network effects didn't occur until it devised a policy requiring every employee to find and list 20,000 items for sale by some person or merchant. The resulting increase in product listings generated two-sided demand. Alibaba and its companion consumer site Taobao quickly became the fastest-growing site for online purchases, attracting any Chinese consumer looking to purchase almost any imaginable product.

Prior to that great explosion, when Alibaba was struggling to attract traffic, CEO Jack Ma and his team had made a counterintuitive decision: they created technological barriers that prevented Baidu from searching their website. Baidu is China's biggest Internet search engine—the Google of China. Blocking Baidu's bots from searching Alibaba for products being sought by Baidu users cut off a vast supply of potential customers. Doing this at a time when Alibaba was desperate for shoppers must have seemed a bit crazy.

But Alibaba's leaders were playing a long-term strategic game. They had their eye not just on the shopping interactions that would take place on their platform but on the potential to monetize the platform by selling advertising. They were determined to retain control of the community of would-be shoppers that they were gradually building on Alibaba—so that Alibaba alone would be able to sell ads aimed at those shoppers. Barring Baidu's bots from Alibaba's listings was a way of preventing Baidu from hosting the consumer-oriented ads that companies would ultimately want to direct to the growing numbers of Chinese online shoppers—and making sure that those ads would appear on Alibaba's platform instead.

The strategy worked. As Alibaba's user base expanded, it gradually displaced Baidu as the most valuable online advertising platform in China. It's as if eBay or Amazon had found a way to capture the targeted advertising revenues now enjoyed by Google. The income generated helps to explain why Alibaba earned more profits in 2014 than Amazon has earned *in its entire history*.

HOW PLATFORMS COMPETE (2):
FOSTERING INNOVATION,
THEN CAPTURING ITS VALUE

The open-ended nature of platforms creates enormous opportunities for users to create new value. Platform managers can build their businesses by, first, giving partners frictionless opportunities to innovate, then capturing some or all of the value created by acquisition or duplication. As we saw in chapter 8, SAP encourages innovation by partners on its business services platform by periodically publishing a road map of the platform real estate it plans to open to developers over the next 18–24 months. This tells developers where they can build, giving them up to two years of lead time before they face competition from SAP itself, and prevents developers from wasting time and resources developing a site for SAP users only to find its work undermined by the arrival of SAP's own bulldozers.

Over the long haul, it is in the interest of platform managers to take control of the major sources of value created by and for users in their ecosystem. This leads to what we might call the platform-world variant of the resource-based theory of value: *A platform business need not own all the inimitable resources in its ecosystem, but it should seek to own the resources whose value is greatest.* This is why Alibaba (rather than Baidu) owns search on its platform, why Facebook (rather than Google) owns search on its platform, and why Microsoft (rather than some outside software developer) owns Word, PowerPoint, and Excel on its platform. These are all crucial resources that create value for the majority of the platforms' users—that's why it is critical for the platform owners to control them. Less valuable, or more niche, resources can be ceded to ecosystem partners without significantly weakening the competitive position of the platform itself.

This principle explains why platform managers need to keep a careful watch on new features or apps that appear on the platform. These will usually make their first appearance far down the "long tail" of adoption, with relatively few platform participants using them to co-create value. Most will stay there, but a few will show the ability to jump rank, climbing rapidly toward the head of the distribution curve. A few will even show signs of attracting their own interactive communities, which means they have the potential to become platforms themselves. Recall that social gaming company Zynga and the photo-sharing services Instagram and Snapchat all started off as mere blips on the Facebook platform. But their social sharing and network effects enabled them to grow fast.

Growth of this kind often launches a strategic tug-of-war. The platform may seek to absorb the function of the innovative partner and the value it creates by acquisition. As we've noted, Facebook succeeded in acquiring Instagram, purchasing the company for $1 billion in 2012; it has (so far) failed to acquire Snapchat, having made a $3 billion offer that company cofounder Evan Spiegel rejected in December 2013.

The platform may also seek to weaken the startup by promoting competitors, as Facebook has done with Zynga. As of 2011, there were more than three thousand games on Facebook, collectively weakening Zynga's individual bargaining power.[20] The startup's response may be to sell, to fight back through multihoming, or to expand into other business arenas. Zynga, for example, now multihomes on Tencent's QQ social network and on the Apple and Google mobile platforms, as well as offering its own cloud service.

HOW PLATFORMS COMPETE (3): LEVERAGING THE VALUE OF DATA

One of the clichés of the Internet economy is the saying "Data is the new oil"—and like most clichés, it contains a lot of truth. Data can be a source of enormous value to platform businesses, and well-run firms are using data to shore up their competitive positions in a wide variety of ways.

Platform businesses can use data to improve their competitive performance in two general ways—tactically and strategically. An example of tactical data use is in the performance of A/B testing, to optimize particular tools or features of the platform. If Amazon wants to determine whether placing the buy-it-now button at the top right or the bottom left on a web page will generate more sales, it can run an experiment by randomly alternating the button placement and tallying the results, possibly cross-tabulated against various customer characteristics. Tactical data analysis is quite effective—and it's the reason why Amazon now places the buy-it-now button at the top right of a web page.

Strategic data analysis is broader in its scope. It seeks to aid ecosystem optimization by tracking who else is creating, controlling, and siphoning value both on and off the platform and studying the nature of their activities. When Facebook uses data about member activity to observe Zynga doing something unexpected or to spot Instagram diverting traffic in novel ways, that is strategic data analysis.

Some notable platform strategy battles have been won by companies that took advantage of data supremacy to outcompete their rivals.

By most measures, Monster should have won the battle for supremacy among job placement platforms. As one of the earliest entrants into the market, it had a first mover advantage, and it quickly generated strong network effects in the two-sided market of employers and employees seeking one another. However, there were built-in limitations to the data Monster gathered. Because Monster targeted only active job seekers, it captured no information concerning users' broader social networks. And once a particular job search interaction was completed, both employer and employee would leave the platform, halting the flow of data altogether.

By contrast, LinkedIn targeted the social networks of all professionals, not just active job seekers. This led to a higher degree of ongoing engagement and captured data from those who were happily employed but willing to consider new job opportunities—a vastly expanded user base. LinkedIn also captured data from interactions among professionals interacting with one another as well as with recruiters, providing two separate feedback loops on the same platform. Later, LinkedIn began emphasizing content creation and sharing by its users to foster additional reasons for them to spend time on the platform. LinkedIn's big edge in the scope, depth, and volume of marketplace data has given it a huge advantage in competing against Monster.

Platform design can be optimized in various ways to generate better user data. Guided by a two-sided network analysis, the authors developed a set of recommendations for the design of data analysis tools to provide improved ecosystem leverage for SAP.

We emphasized the value of search tools that help clients find solution providers among SAP ecosystem partners. Better matches facilitated by enhanced data make both sides happier. We also noted that solution providers can find clients by identifying *unsuccessful* user searches, reflecting the existence of potential clients in need of business solutions. In addition, we noted the need for tools that help clients benchmark their capabilities against other, similar companies on the platform, as well as tools to help developers benchmark their capabilities against other developers on the platform. Such tools can help SAP users compete more effectively with rivals who are not on the platform.

A final set recommendation that we developed with SAP is to look for new business service capabilities that cut across industry verticals and new features that are rapidly climbing the long tail, meaning that they are growing in popularity among business users. These represent new sources of value that platforms like SAP can absorb into its platform for the benefit of ecosystem partners who have yet to discover them.

Data analytics can thus significantly augment the capabilities of both the platform company and its ecosystem partners, making the platform more successful and greatly increasing its ability to generate value for users. Analytics can guide investments in product design and in customer and partner success, reinforcing the platform's network effects. Collectively, these new data tools create a formidable barrier to entry—a platform version of Porter's competitive moat. If competitors don't have the data, they can't create the value—which means they can't create the interactions, which further limits their access to the data.

HOW PLATFORMS COMPETE (4):
REDEFINING MERGERS AND ACQUISITIONS

Classic merger and acquisition (M & A) strategy suggests that business leaders should pursue targets that either add complementary products or market access or subtract supply chain costs. In a world dominated by five forces competition, the key question driving M & A evaluation is whether or not the target company has a moat protecting a sizeable fortress of value.

Platform managers need to adjust this strategy. For them, the key question is whether the target company creates value for a user base that significantly overlaps with the one they are currently serving.

If the answer is yes, then a tentative conclusion that the target *may* be worth acquiring can be reached. However, there are additional hurdles to be surmounted before making the commitment to buy, such as the profitability of the target company and its ability to elicit a continuing stream of repeat interactions from platform participants. Fortunately, a platform business is in an unusually privileged position when it comes to measuring the value of a potential acquisition. Unlike a traditional pipeline company, a platform owner can delay an acquisition until it has observed how a partner transacts on the platform.

This solves the traditional challenge of information asymmetry in M & A evaluation. Instead of basing a buy decision on someone else's audited financial data, the purchaser can rely on firsthand observation of transaction data and even run real-world experiments to test various strategic scenarios. Managing a platform lets you take the partnership for a test drive before signing a purchase agreement.

Furthermore, based on the fact that platform businesses don't need to own all the critical assets as long as they have access to them in their ecosystems, platform companies can pursue fewer M & A deals than many traditional firms feel compelled to do. In the process, they enjoy at least two significant benefits.

First, claiming a portion of the value created by a platform partner is far less risky than buying that partner. Recall that, in 2011, Farmville and Mafia Wars were the biggest hits in gaming, driving the stock market value of game developer Zynga through the roof. It's easy to imagine that the leaders of Facebook must have been tempted to buy Zynga, which would have not only provided them with the full value of Zynga's game portfolio but also denied access to this key asset to rival platforms like Myspace.

But Facebook resisted the temptation—and wisely so. Game development is notoriously unpredictable; even the most successful games flame out after a few years, and there's no guarantee that another hit will follow. Rather than buying Zynga and shouldering the responsibility for creating the next big sensation, it was far better for Facebook to let hundreds of game companies compete to produce the next hit and then capture a fraction of the upside.

Second, keeping a partnership at arm's length reduces the platform's technological complexity. As the very term *vertical integration* implies, any new business a platform purchases must be *integrated* with the platform, which creates both technical and strategic challenges. A platform built from a dozen independently developed technologies will break sooner, cost more, and deliver a worse customer experience than one built on a lean architecture that conducts all its business activity through clean interfaces. Recall our discussion of the benefits of modular design in chapter 3: in a modular system, when a part or partner fails, a new one can be swapped in relatively easily. But when a part or partner fails in an integrated system, the whole system can grind to a halt.

For these reasons, managers of platform businesses can afford to approach the challenge of M & A strategy in a more thoughtful, deliberate fashion than leaders of traditional companies, who often feel compelled to snap up the next hot startup before someone else does.

HOW PLATFORMS COMPETE (5):
PLATFORM ENVELOPMENT

Platform managers need to continually scan the horizon, observing the activities of other platforms—particularly platforms that serve similar or overlapping user bases. We call these *adjacent platforms*. When a new feature appears on an adjacent platform, it may represent a competitive threat, since there's a possibility that users of your platform may find the new feature attractive enough to begin multihoming or even to abandon your platform altogether.

To respond, the platform manager can choose either to provide a similar feature directly or to offer it indirectly via an ecosystem partner. When used most successfully, this strategy leads to the phenomenon we call *platform envelopment*. This occurs when one platform effectively absorbs the functions—and the user base—of an adjacent platform.

For example, back in the 1990s, RealNetworks invented streaming audio in the form of its 1995 product, Real Audio. It soon owned 100 percent of the market. But once Microsoft decided to capture this market, the enormous scope of its existing platform gave it an almost unstoppable advantage. Since MS Windows had a market share of over 90 percent in operating systems, almost everyone who was interested in media streaming already had an operating system from Microsoft. All Microsoft had to do was develop a software product similar to Real Audio and offer it as part of a bundle with its Windows operating system. The Windows streaming audio platform soon enveloped the much smaller platform created by Real Audio— despite the older software's superior performance.

The envelopment strategy is a common one that we can see in operation in many platform arenas. Apple is now endeavoring to use its iPhone platform to envelop the markets for mobile payment systems and wearable technology. Similarly, China's Haier Group is expanding its appliance platform in an effort to envelop the market for connected home applications.

Of course, the opportunities and threats run both ways. If Platform A is trying to envelop adjacent Platform B by developing a feature that competes with Platform B's most attractive offering, Platform B may try to envelop Platform A by mounting the same kind of attack in reverse. In this kind of envelopment battle, the larger platform, with its more numerous initial user base and more powerful network effects, is generally triumphant. But as the story of Monster versus LinkedIn demonstrated, a platform that offers superior value to users can win a competitive battle despite an initial size disadvantage.

By comparison with traditional pipeline businesses, platform companies are able to move very rapidly to respond to competitive moves—and to mount competitive assaults of their own. The winners will usually be those platforms that are able to consistently create the greatest value for users. But in today's business, no victory is permanent, which means that platform companies must be at least as vigilant in guarding against complacency as traditional firms.

HOW PLATFORMS COMPETE (6): ENHANCED PLATFORM DESIGN

In the world of traditional business, companies compete by attempting to create higher-quality products and services. In an analogous fashion, platforms compete by trying to improve the quality of the tools they provide to pull in users, facilitate interactions, and match producers with consumers (the basic elements of platform design we described in chapter 3).

We saw a simple example of how this works in chapter 5, when we explained how video hosting platform Vimeo managed to coexist with YouTube despite serving an overlapping market, differentiating itself through better hosting services, greater bandwidth availability, more valuable viewer feedback, no obtrusive pre-roll advertisements, and other features that attract more selective video producers despite YouTube's much larger viewer base. Vimeo's competitive stance in relation to YouTube resembles that of many traditional businesses that coexist with a market-dominating rival by identifying a specialized niche and creating a higher-end product designed to cater to that audience.

In some cases, superior platform design enables a platform to dramatically outcompete a preexisting rival. Airbnb initially had far fewer users than the much older Craigslist, which also provides listings of rooms and apartments for short-term rent. However, Airbnb did a much better job at the key platform functions of facilitation and matching. On Craigslist, a person seeking a room for rent had to drill down through an unmanaged list of options clustered by city and organized by time of posting. By contrast, Airbnb allowed a person to search through options organized not only according to these characteristics but also by quality, number of rooms, price, and mapped geolocation. Furthermore, users could also strike deals directly through Airbnb, whereas Craigslist users had to go off platform to make a rental agreement. This made Airbnb far easier to use and enabled the platform to rapidly outgrow the erstwhile category leader.

WHEN ADVANTAGE *IS* SUSTAINABLE: WINNER-TAKE-ALL MARKETS

In business, no victory is permanent—but on occasion, a particular firm is capable of enjoying a dominant position within its industry for a decade or longer. When this happens, we can say that the company has maintained a sustained advantage. This happens most often in a *winner-take-all market.* This is a market in which specific forces conspire to encourage users to gravitate toward one platform and to abandon others. The four forces that most often characterize winner-take-all markets are *supply economies of scale, strong network effects, high multihoming or switching costs*, and *lack of niche specialization.*

As we explained in chapter 2, supply economies of scale are an industrial-era source of market power driven by the massive fixed costs of production in such industries as railroads, oil and gas exploration, mining, pharmaceutical development, and auto and aircraft manufacture. In industries like these, volume matters, since amortizing costs over more buyers means that margins improve with scale. It might cost Intel $1 billion to develop a semiconductor fabrication plant, but once the plant is built, the incremental costs of making a million chips—or a billion—are negligible. The greater the supply economies of scale, the greater the tendency toward market concentration. In the U.S., despite competitive markets and the regulatory pressure created by antitrust legislation, a handful of firms dominate industries in which supply economies of scale play a large role—for example, the auto industry.

As we also saw in chapter 2, network effects are the Internet-era source of market power. Thanks to positive network effects, the value created and the profit margins enjoyed by the company both increase as more users join the ecosystem.[21] This is why firms with network effects can enjoy a 10x multiple in value relative to other firms that have comparable revenues but lack network effects.[22] With their current product focus and business models, Houghton Mifflin Harcourt, NBC, Lexis, and Whirlpool do not have strong network effects. Amazon, Netflix, LegalZoom, and Nest do. Because positive network effects attract more users to whichever platform is larger, they are a second force that is likely to strengthen a market's winner-take-all tendency.

A third factor driving the winner-take-all effect is high multihoming and switching costs. As we discussed earlier in this chapter, multihoming takes place when users participate on more than one platform. Of course, multihoming enables users to take advantage of the benefits provided by multiple platforms—but it always comes with a cost, monetary (such as multiple subscription fees) or otherwise (such as the inconvenience of having to upload data to more than one platform website).

Somewhat comparable to multihoming costs are switching costs—the costs associated with leaving one platform and moving to another. Again, these costs may be monetary (such as the penalty assessed when a cell phone user switches service providers in mid-contract) or non-monetary (such as the inconvenience of moving all your family photos from one web hosting service to another).

Both higher multihoming costs and higher switching costs tend to push a market toward higher concentration, dominated by fewer, larger companies. For example, because most people cannot afford to carry both an Android phone and an Apple phone, they tend to choose one of these two alternatives and stay with it for at least a few years. By contrast, lower costs encourage people to participate in two or more platforms at once. Because most credit cards carry a low annual fee or none at all, many people carry Visa, MasterCard, and American Express cards in their wallets, perhaps accompanied by a couple of department store cards, choosing among them in various circumstances based on convenience and other factors.

In markets where multihoming and switching costs are low, late entrants can gain market share more easily, leading to markets that are more open and fluid. For example, because most social networks offer free basic service, multihoming on two platforms is virtually costless—which is one reason Facebook and LinkedIn were able to compete successfully with their forerunners, Myspace and Monster. By contrast, high multihoming costs are one reason Microsoft has had such difficulty entering the mobile market behind Apple and Google, despite its advantage in desktop operating systems and the market share it gained when it acquired mobile phone maker Nokia.

The fourth and final factor affecting demand-side scale is users' taste for niche specialization. When a particular set of users has distinctive needs or tastes, they can support a separate network, thereby weakening the winner-take-all effect. In the 1990s, when Windows enjoyed strong advantages in the world of desktop operating systems due to its strong network effects and the high multihoming costs in the market, Apple survived thanks to niche specialization—it was inordinately popular among graphic artists and musicians. Similarly, LinkedIn was able to establish a foothold among social networks against the overwhelming network effects of Facebook because it served the distinctive needs of business professionals.

A market with little or no niche specialization is particularly susceptible to the winner-take-all effect. And the greater the winner-take-all forces, the more vicious the platform competition. In the market for ride-sharing transportation services, the absence of distinct user needs and the presence of strong network effects explains the fierce rivalry between Uber and Lyft. Each side has ruthlessly poached the other's drivers by offering referral bounties and cash incentives. Some of the alleged tactics border on the unethical. For example, Lyft has accused Uber of ordering, then cancelling, more than 5,000 rides in order to clog the Lyft service. Uber denied the specific charge. But there's no doubt that both companies are convinced that only one is likely to survive their rivalry, and that each is determined to do whatever it takes to be the one left standing.[23]

■ ■ ■

As we've seen, the nature of competition in the world of platforms is very different from that in the world of traditional pipeline businesses. It's a natural next step to wonder whether and how these differences are impacting the nature of business regulation. Do definitions of fundamental concepts like monopoly, fair trade, price fixing, anticompetitive practices, and restraint of trade need to be reconsidered in their application to platform companies? Are existing rules designed to protect the interests of consumers, workers, suppliers, competitors, and entire communities effective and reasonable in the world of platforms? These are some of the questions we'll examine in the next chapter.

TAKEAWAYS FROM CHAPTER TEN

❑ Platform competition is like 3D chess, involving competition at three levels: platform against platform, platform against partner, and partner against partner.

❑ In the world of platforms, competition becomes less important that cooperation and co-creation. Control of relationships becomes more important than control of resources.

❑ Among the methods that platforms use to compete with one another are preventing multihoming by limiting platform access; fostering innovation, then capturing its value; leveraging the value of information; nurturing partnerships rather than pursuing mergers and acquisitions; platform envelopment; and enhanced platform design.

❑ Winner-take-all markets exist in certain platform markets. They are driven by four main factors: supply economies of scale, network effects, multihoming and switching costs, and the lack of niche specialization. In winner-take-all markets, competition is apt to be particularly fierce.

11

POLICY

How Platforms Should
(and Should Not) Be Regulated

In the fall of 2014, the New York City subways were suddenly filled with ads for a business many city residents were just beginning to learn about—Airbnb. These were not ordinary ads aimed at convincing potential customers to try out the room rental services provided by Airbnb. They were what advertising people call corporate image ads, designed to burnish the reputation of the company itself. "Airbnb is great for New York City," read the slogan on every ad.

But not all subway riders agreed. Within days, many of the ads had been "edited" by marker-wielding graffiti writers with their own thoughts about Airbnb. Journalist Jessica Pressler recorded some of the choicest comments in *New York* magazine. One poster had been supplemented with the observation, "Airbnb accepts NO Liability." Another had been marked with the scrawl, "The dumbest person in your building is passing out a set of keys to your front door!" And on several posters, the phrase "for New York City" had been replaced with a different handwritten conclusion: "Airbnb is great *for Airbnb*."

The war of the posters reflected a bigger conflict already being waged in New York City and in other cities around the world where Airbnb was expanding its foothold. Airbnb's corporate image advertising campaign was part of an expensive lobbying and public relations program designed to counter what the company viewed as an unfair assault by regulators, business rivals, and misinformed members of the media and the general public. The issues under debate: Is Airbnb a blessing and a boon to New York and its citizens, or a cancer that is undermining the quality of life and the economic soundness of the city? And who should have the right and the power to decide?

THE REGULATORY CHALLENGE: REWORKING OLD RULES FOR A NEW WORLD

The emergence of the world of platforms is giving rise to an increasingly important social challenge: the need to design balanced internal governance systems and external regulatory regimes to ensure they operate fairly.[1] As platforms such as Airbnb, Uber, Upwork, RelayRides, and many more play a growing role in the economy and in the social and political spheres, issues about the rights of participants as well as the impact of platform businesses on other sectors and on society as a whole are becoming increasingly salient. Thus, the unprecedented growth of platforms is bringing regulatory issues to the front of the popular consciousness in ways that have not been seen since the financial meltdown of 2008–09.

As debates about these issues rage, many observers are beginning to recognize that much of what we all "know" about regulatory policy is wrong—at least when applied to today's rapidly evolving platform markets. There is significant tension between the social goals of promoting innovation and economic development, which argue for a relatively laissez-faire approach to regulating platforms, and the social goals of preventing harm, encouraging fair competition, and maintaining respect for the rule of law.

It's time for policymakers, legal scholars, and business advocates to reexamine old assumptions about regulation in light of the changes being brought about by the rise of the platform. In this chapter, we'll explore some of the key questions that leaders must grapple with in the years to come as platforms continue to transform the economy. Some of the issues we will explore include possible effects on tax policy, affordable housing, public safety, economic fairness, data privacy, labor rights, and more.

THE DARK SIDE OF THE
PLATFORM REVOLUTION

We have already noted the many benefits that the explosive growth of network platforms is providing. However, we must also acknowledge that the spread of platforms will not usher in some kind of new-economy nirvana. Like every business, social, or technological innovation, the rise of platforms has the potential for harm.[2]

Some of the complaints about the rise of platforms reflect the disruptive impact of platform businesses on traditional industries. It's natural that companies and workers whose profits and livelihood may be threatened by new business models will fight back by any means available, including seizing on evidence, meaningful or not, that the new models are causing economic, environmental, social, or cultural harm. Some of the attacks on platform businesses certainly fall into this category. It's not hard to understand why large publishers and bookstore chains might hate Amazon, why record companies might hate iTunes, why taxi companies might hate Uber, and why hotel chains might hate Airbnb. Naturally, when criticism of platforms— including calls for strict regulation to limit their impact—comes from interested sources like these, it should be taken with a grain of salt.

But this doesn't mean that there are no legitimate complaints to be raised about the impact of platform businesses. Visitors to New York who take advantage of Airbnb to enjoy affordable accommodations are fans of the service, as are the hosts who make extra money by renting out their spare rooms. But some of their neighbors are unhappy. Horror stories about orgies in Airbnb rentals, assignations with prostitutes (one of whom reportedly ended up getting stabbed), and parties with uncontrolled groups of rowdy young drunks have found their way into the tabloid press. One worried Manhattan landlord, Ken Podziba, felt driven to install surveillance cameras to prove that a tenant was renting out her place in violation of a state law forbidding short-term sublets. He succeeded in having her evicted. "Airbnb is making money while letting people do whatever they want," Podziba exclaims. "It's crazy."[3]

As we saw in chapter 8, the impacts of Airbnb on third parties uninvolved in the rental arrangement are what economists call *externalities*. A recurring economic problem is when the cost of negative externalities is borne not by the people or companies that created them but by "innocent bystanders" who are stuck with the problem. Externality issues are a great way for a business to antagonize its neighbors and invite intervention by regulators—and Airbnb is currently grappling with a number of them.

Lack of consistent insurance coverage has been one of the most serious externality questions around Airbnb. In December 2014, after years of complaints, Airbnb announced a new policy that would provide $1 million of liability coverage to protect its U.S. hosts from damages caused by wayward guests. The problem: this is so-called secondary coverage, which only kicks in after the host's personal homeowner's policy is used up. And nearly all personal homeowner's policies in the U.S. specifically *exclude* coverage for "commercial activity" in the home—including rentals. Airbnb appears to be hoping that the cost of damages will somehow get pushed onto personal insurance policies administered by companies that aren't diligent about investigating claims—or that are deceived by homeowners who lie about their role as Airbnb hosts.

Naturally, this partial insurance coverage is worrisome to many Airbnb hosts. But as financial journalist Ron Lieber points out, it also creates an externality that could impact thousands of otherwise uninvolved citizens. "If Airbnb succeeds in sharing risk with personal insurance companies," he writes, "then everyone's premiums have to rise to cover it."[4]

Of course, as we've noted, some externalities are positive—economic and other benefits that businesses provide to uninvolved third parties. Some data suggest that hotel prices fell slightly after the entry of Airbnb, likely increasing the tourism business and ultimately benefiting local restaurants and other attractions.[5] Other data suggest that the number of drunk driving deaths has fallen slightly after the entry of Uber.[6] But such positive externalities are often difficult to document and quantify, while negative externalities tend to be vivid, unmistakable, and painful. Is it fair for Airbnb to slough off those external costs onto individuals who are not part of the platform, or onto the society at large?

These issues are far from theoretical. Some platform businesses have actually been shut down because of concerns about negative externalities. Consider the MonkeyParking app. Launched in San Francisco in January 2014, this system encouraged drivers to vacate parking spaces by auctioning off the empty places to other users of the system, splitting the proceeds with the driver who vacated. Many observers considered it unfair that the system encouraged the privatization and monetization of a public good—parking spaces—and thereby affected the openness and accessibility of a public transportation system on which countless individuals and businesses depend. It also had a negative impact on privately owned parking lots, whose owners had invested in their businesses to serve the same need. In response to the complaints, in June 2014, regulators stepped in to close the platform.[7]

The MonkeyParking story isn't a black-and-white judgment call. It raises the question of whether, when, and how the social harm of privatizing a public resource outweighs the benefit of providing planned access to a scarce resource. A case can be made that a system like MonkeyParking produces environmental benefits by reducing the need for drivers to roam downtown streets in search of parking spaces, burning fossil fuels and adding to traffic congestion in the process. But if we permit MonkeyParking to auction off public parking spaces for private profit, are we opening up to other questionable market activities? Should platform users be permitted to claim choice locations in public parks or beaches on summer weekends and auction them off to the highest bidders? What about seats in the most desirable public schools? Or private rooms in the best-run public hospitals? Do we want to live in a society where those with the most money can claim an ever larger share of the most attractive public goods? These are some of the questions about external impacts that a seemingly simple case like the MonkeyParking story raises.

Labor platforms, bulwarks of what some call the freelance or 1099 economy, raise still other issues of social impact and equity. Platforms like Upwork, TaskRabbit, and Washio are fine for people who value a flexible work schedule above all, but are much more problematic for people who find themselves with no choice except to operate as full-time employees on a freelance basis without the benefits and worker protections normally mandated by law. It's understandable that businesses want to take advantage of the agility and low overhead costs that labor platforms make possible. But in a society like the United States, where basic services such as health care are provided largely through employer programs, is it desirable to create an economic advantage to companies that offload the costs of such services onto their freelance employees—or onto government support programs that are already financially stressed?[8]

Platforms certainly create benefits for their users—if they didn't, they wouldn't be exploding in popularity. But they also create unintended side effects, including negative externalities, that society as a whole must consider and address.

THE CASE AGAINST REGULATION

Despite the problems illustrated by platform business like Monkey-Parking, there are many who would argue that the potential abuses and social dislocations caused by platforms are a small price for the tremendous innovation, new value, and economic growth they produce. Platform businesses are here to stay, and they are bringing undoubted benefits to millions of people. Why run the risk of discouraging innovation through the heavy hand of regulation?

Opponents of regulation are quick to point out the many cases in which it fails or backfires. Nobel Prize-winners Ronald Coase and George Stigler, members of the famous laissez-faire-oriented Chicago School of economics, argue that the vast majority of market failures are best addressed by market mechanisms themselves—for example, by encouraging the free growth of competitors who provide goods and services that produce greater social benefits than their rivals. In their view, the evidence of history suggests that government regulators tend to be incompetent or corrupt, which means that regulation generally fails to solve the problems it is intended to address. In specific instances where the free market fails to resolve a significant problem of market fairness or consumer protection, it can be addressed by private litigation in the courts.

One of the most common mechanisms of regulatory failure was labeled by Stigler "regulatory capture."[9] The basic premise is that market participants will act to influence regulation in their own interests, often making the underlying market problems worse rather than better. In his 1971 article, Stigler illustrated the point with examples drawn from oil import quotas, the prevention of new firms entering the airline, trucking, and banking industries, and the control of access to labor markets through licensing requirements for workers such as barbers, embalmers, physicians, and pharmacists. Thanks to regulatory capture, government rules are often used to block competition and thwart innovation rather than to protect consumers and benefit society. Stigler and his followers argue that the economy and society as a whole will benefit when regulatory capture is eliminated—and that this requires the elimination of most government regulation of business. Jean-Jacques Laffont and Jean Tirole (the latter the 2014 winner of the Nobel Prize in Economics) extended Stigler's analysis using an agency perspective, making the point that "principals," like voters, have imperfect control over their "agents," including elected and appointed officials. Laffont and Tirole show that it would be impossible for firms to benefit from regulatory capture if the principals involved had more complete information about and control over the behavior of their agents.[10]

There's no doubt that regulatory capture does exist. Managers of government agencies charged with devising and enforcing business regulations must often turn to business leaders for advice and guidance on how to craft those regulations, which often means that the rules end up benefiting companies—or certain highly influential companies—rather than the public at large. In some powerful industries, such as financial services, executives have been known to divide their careers between Washington and the private sector, so that the same people who design regulatory regimes later advise corporations on the best ways to evade those regimes or manipulate them for profit (a practice that Laffont and Tirole specifically highlighted).

Today, some of the regulatory battles about platform businesses reflect, in part, efforts by traditional industries to use government regulation as shields against the competitive models that platforms introduce. Thus, as commentator Conor Friedersdorf puts it, "The car service Uber is fighting in cities all over America to end the regulatory capture enjoyed by the taxicab industry."[11] Airbnb is facing similar battles with regulators who are influenced by long-standing relationships with the hospitality industry.

In the eyes of some observers, the phenomenon of regulatory capture sharply undercuts the claims to legitimacy of most economic regulation by government. For example, in a post on his blog *Cafe Hayek*, libertarian economist Don Boudreaux summarizes the way Uber enables drivers to transform their personal cars from private goods into part of the economy's capital stock, then goes on to criticize "government interventions against Uber and other sharing-economy innovations" as both "obstacles to market forces that improve consumers' access to goods and services" and "assaults against market forces that increase the amount of wealth-producing capital that ordinary people are able to own, control, and profit from."[12]

You may or may not agree with Boudreaux that attempts to restrict the spread of Uber constitute today's "single most obnoxious example of government intervention." But the existence of the phenomenon of regulatory capture is not necessarily a fatal blow to the argument in favor of regulation—or even the argument in favor of regulating platforms in particular. It's possible to argue that, rather than eliminating regulation altogether, we need to design political, social, and economic systems that reduce the likelihood of regulatory capture—for example, through laws that restrict the "revolving door" between business and government.

Economist Andrei Shleifer, a scholar in the areas of corporate governance and government regulation, points out that there are strong differences in the prevalence of regulatory capture across countries. When governments are relatively unchecked by their citizens, strong regulation often leads to high levels of corruption and expropriation by government officials. And, indeed, this is widely seen in authoritarian countries. However, in countries with more accountable governments, such as those seen in northern Europe, higher levels of regulation appear to be relatively free of such corruption, which reduces the level of regulatory capture. In these circumstances, Shleifer argues, regulation can be compatible with promotion of social welfare and economic growth.

Shleifer notes, moreover, that the reliance of the Chicago School on litigation as an alternative to regulation assumes and depends upon the existence of an independent and honest judiciary. This ignores the fact that judges and lawyers are just as subject to manipulation and capture as other government employees.[13] More broadly, Shleifer's argument is consistent with the argument made by Laffont and Tirole in favor of regulation that is specific to countries and technologies.[14]

In general, the historical record doesn't support the arguments of people who favor no regulation of business. In fact, it's difficult to identify any developed marketplace that has been completely free of intervention by government authorities. Regulation to prevent anti-competitive practices goes back at least as far as ancient Greece and Rome, where state authorities took swift action to mitigate grain market price fluctuations that occurred due to natural (weather) events as well as deliberate market manipulation by merchants and shipping agents.[15] In the same way, modern societies depend upon regulators to enforce rules of fair play in markets. When regulation fails, we get the scandals of insider trading, the meltdown of the mortgage securities market, or the high prices enjoyed by incumbent monopolists.

Relatively few people want to live in a world free of all regulation, and in a complex society like the one we live in today, regulation serves a number of important social functions. The airline system in the developed world is astonishingly safe, given the complexity of the technologies involved and terrorist attempts to sabotage it.[16] This record is a result both of improved technology and training and of relentless post-crash investigations by government agencies like the National Transportation Safety Board, which have led to a systematic elimination of risk factors. In similar fashion, we depend upon regulation to maintain the purity of our drinking water, the safety of our transportation systems, and our ability to respond to and control infectious diseases.

For all these reasons, only a relatively small fraction of the population would endorse the extreme libertarian position of calling for a complete elimination of business regulations—which means that the question is not whether, but precisely how, platform businesses should be covered by regulatory regimes.

Of course, there is a tradeoff between the benefits and costs of regulation. A complete absence of regulation is likely to produce high social and economic costs through the persistence of problems like business fraud, unfair competition, monopolistic and oligopolistic practices, and market manipulation. On the other hand, the most extreme level of government intervention into markets, as seen in some totalitarian countries, leads to other problems, including corruption, inefficiency, waste, and lack of innovation. Usually the existence of such tradeoffs implies that an intermediate solution is best, and indeed the world's most vibrant economies have typically employed some intermediate level of government regulation via oversight agencies, judicial review, or some combination of the two.

Economist Simeon Djankov and colleagues have classified the range of possible regulatory regimes on a spectrum from private orderings (what we call private governance), through systems that rely on court rulings administered by independent judges or regulation by state employees, to direct government ownership of assets (socialism).[17] Their visual depiction of this spectrum (Figure 11.1) reflects the tradeoff between social losses because of private misdeeds and social losses because of government misbehavior.

Over the last two generations, as Andrei Shleifer has noted, most economists and political theorists have shifted from viewing government intervention in a positive light to preferring privatization.[18] Today, there's a trend toward regulation that was once provided by governments now being provided by private entities acting in their own self-interest—for example, the gradual shift from nationally mandated accounting standards like the Generally Accepted Accounting Principles used in the United States toward the International Financial

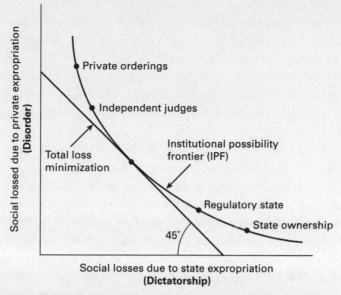

FIGURE 11.1. Djankov's depiction of the curve of "social losses" produced by either the complete absence of regulation (on the left) or total control of business by government (on the right). Reprinted by permission.

Reporting Standards promulgated by the International Accounting Standards Board, a private organization based in London. We believe this trend will continue and that governments must rethink what they choose to regulate and what kinds of regulation private entities can provide more efficiently. One purpose of this chapter will be to suggest the circumstances in which regulators should consider intervention in platform markets and those in which platforms might best govern themselves.

REGULATORY ISSUES RAISED BY THE GROWTH OF PLATFORM BUSINESSES

Let's consider some of the most significant regulatory issues that have come to the fore as a result of the rise of platform businesses over the last two decades.

Platform access. As platforms become increasingly important markets for goods and services, access to platforms can be a legitimate subject for inquiry by regulatory authorities. When certain potential participants are excluded from a platform, it raises questions about who benefits from the exclusion, whether that exclusion is fair, and what its long-term impact on the overall marketplace is likely to be.

For example, the Alibaba Group handles 80 percent of e-commerce transactions in China.[19] The threat of exclusion presents a serious challenge to any firm conducting business online. Access is also a concern of every startup hoping to break into the top listings, among millions, when they have no transactions history to raise their page ranks. In the computer game console market, the platform sponsors (Sony, Microsoft, and Nintendo) have been known to offer category exclusivity to certain firms such as Electronic Arts in exchange for their support of the platform. Firms can achieve the same ends when they buy producers that provide critical components or software for their platforms. For example, Microsoft acquired the game studio Bungie in order to ensure exclusive access to the popular Halo video game franchise when the Xbox was launched in 2001.

Access and exclusivity also play a role in platform compatibility. In 1997, Sun Microsystems filed suit against Microsoft for intentionally "forking" the Java programming language—that is, creating an incompatible branch in the code base—in order to limit its appeal on operating systems other than Microsoft Windows. Sun filed another suit in 2002 when Microsoft excluded Java from desktop distribution in favor of .NET, a proprietary Microsoft language.[20] In 2015, the mobile operating system Android has split into open and proprietary versions. Commercial and regulatory inducements to maintain compatibility can be necessary to preserve the interests of consumers.

The issue of exclusion is especially significant when network effects are strong, as business professor Carl Shapiro argues. "[S]uch exclusionary contracts and exclusive membership rules," Shapiro notes, "can be especially pernicious in network industries, posing a danger that new and improved technologies will be unable to gain the critical mass necessary to truly threaten the current market leader."[21]

He goes on to say: "Ultimately, this is not a story about consumer harm based on monopoly pricing, although that can be part of the problem. The graver problem is that the pace of innovation may be slowed, denying consumers the full benefits of technological progress that a dynamically competitive market would offer." This phenomenon has been dubbed *excess inertia,* referring to the power of network effects to slow or prevent the adoption of new, perhaps better, technologies. When one or a few platforms can dominate a particular market because of the power of network effects, they may choose to resist beneficial innovations in order to protect themselves from the costs of change and other disruptive effects.

It's certainly arguable that regulators should consider whether government intervention would be appropriate in cases where arbitrary denial of access to a particular platform seems likely to lead to excess inertia.[22] However, it's not always easy for observers to judge what the true impact of a particular competitive move may be. In some instances, the apparent outcome may change dramatically when viewed over time.

For example, in a 2014 article, two of the authors of this book (Geoffrey Parker and Marshall Van Alstyne) argued that platform policies that limit competition among developers can actually benefit consumers in the long run by fostering higher rates of innovation.[23] The process works like a short-term micro-patent: a platform grants temporary category exclusivity to a particular extension developer in exchange for substantial investment in new products or services. (SAP has used this "preferred partner" strategy with developers like ADP, and Microsoft has used it with selected game developers.) Over time, the innovations created under this time-limited arrangement tend to be folded into the core platform. They then become available to all consumers for their direct consumption and also become available to the next generation of developers to foment new innovation.

For these reasons, we'd urge regulators to move with caution when considering intervention in cases that concern platform access.

Fair pricing. A practice that has traditionally drawn regulatory interest is *predatory pricing*—the situation in which a firm prices goods or services so low that it cannot possibly be making money. The low prices temporarily benefit consumers, but in the long run harm them by driving competitors out of business, which permits the remaining supplier to raise prices to monopoly levels. This, of course, is the objective of the predatory pricer in the first place, and it explains why government regulators have sometimes stepped in to prohibit pricing practices they view as predatory in nature.

However, two of the authors of this book (Parker and Van Alstyne) have done research that calls into question the traditional interpretation of lower-than-cost prices and therefore the regulator's definition of predatory pricing. Our analysis shows that in fact firms with strong two-sided network externalities can maximize profit even when they distribute services to one side of the market at a price of zero. They achieve this result by earning attractive profits through sales of the goods or services they provide to the *other* side of the market.[24]

Along with other authors, including Jean Tirole, this line of research in two-sided networks has overturned the conventional wisdom and required regulators to retool their predation tests to incorporate network effects.[25] In particular, regulators have viewed the practice of selling goods or services at or below cost as evidence of intent to drive competitors out of business with the intent of then raising prices once those competitors are gone. However, as discussed above, when firms take cross-market externalities into account, they can rationally price their goods or services at zero when selling to certain groups of customers, even in the absence of competition.

Despite these changes in competition analysis, there are still open issues of platform law to be decided. The case brought against Google's search service by the European Union in 2015, which accuses Google of favoring its own comparison shopping service over that of rivals, illustrates this point.[26] Interestingly, a similar complaint to the Federal Trade Commission (FTC) in the U.S. was dropped in 2013.[27] Another platform giant, Amazon, is facing scrutiny over its role in the book market. The concern is that Amazon is lowering prices in order to gain market share and that, once competitors exit, prices will rise.[28] We are skeptical about the specific charge against

Amazon—namely, that book prices will rise significantly once the company's dominance is complete—but we are somewhat more sympathetic to the idea that Amazon might act as too powerful a gatekeeper for an important cultural industry, perhaps establishing its own proprietary format for digital content, as it has tried to do with Amazon Word (AZW), the format used on the Kindle reader. Free pricing of book chapters given away in the AZW format, for example, could be used as a Trojan horse, attracting readers as part of a long-term strategy leading to increased platform control and a shift from an open to a closed proprietary standard.

Data privacy and security. Citizens have long had reason to wonder about what firms might be doing with the personal data they collect about their customers. The ability of businesses to gather finely detailed data about individual households expanded dramatically with the introduction of the consumer credit card. This financial innovation helped increase consumer spending by making it much easier to access credit. But this, of course, meant banks had a significant incentive to use data to measure the creditworthiness of customers. To provide this analysis, three major consumer credit information agencies arose: Equinox, Experian, and Transunion. In exchange for interaction-level detail from the banks, the agencies computed credit scores for consumers that banks could use to decide whether to extend credit and if so, at what rates. If you've ever taken out a car loan or a mortgage, you're familiar with the importance and impact of your credit score.

Early data security regulation focused on the need to provide transparency around the criteria used to compute credit scores. Stories of racial and geographic discrimination abounded.[29]

In 1974, Congress passed the Equal Credit Opportunity Act, which prohibited credit discrimination on the basis of sex and marital status. It was amended in 1976 to include race, color, religion, national origin, source of income, and age. In 1977, the FTC began to devote a significant fraction of its resources toward enforcing the act and addressing the discriminatory practices that had led to its passage.[30]

Today, however, issues regarding the use of consumer data have grown in scale and complexity. The credit agencies have been plagued by problems such as stolen and mistaken identities that can take years for consumers to resolve, causing untold harm.[31] The use and abuse of consumer information by the credit agencies and the lenders who rely upon them are also the subject of fierce debate. Practices like predatory lending—the deliberate targeting of consumers who can't afford credit by lenders eager to profit from exorbitant interest rates and fees for missed payments—have been blamed for contributing to economic inequality and even market instability.

It's against this backdrop that the FTC came to be the leading U.S. player in regulating the practices of data service providers.

Most consumers appear to be willing to trade access to detailed data about their spending behavior for easy access to credit. But many may not fully appreciate the fact that the same dynamics that power the credit agencies underlie the services provided by "free" information service businesses—the data aggregators we described in chapter 7. If you've gone online to search for or simply research information about a camera, a book, or any other consumer product, you probably noticed that advertisements for the same product subsequently popped up on every website you visited. This is data-driven marketing in action, and the sale of the underlying personal information about consumers is a significant source of income for many platform businesses.

You may find those customized ads on the Internet a bit unsettling. Even more unsettling are some of the less obvious ways in which personal data are used. Many firms—both platform businesses and others—track consumers' web usage, financial interactions, magazine subscriptions, political and charitable contributions, and much more to create highly detailed individual profiles. In the aggregate, such data can be used for cross-marketing to people who share profiles, as when a recommendation engine on a shopping site tells you, "People like you who bought product A often enjoy product B, too!" The anonymity of this process renders it unobjectionable to most people. But the same underlying data can be, and is, sold to prospective employers, government agencies, health care providers, and marketers of all kinds. Individually identifiable data about sensitive topics such as sexual orientation, prescription drug use, alcoholism, and personal travel (tracked through cell phone location data) can be purchased through data broker firms such as Acxiom.[32]

Consumer concern over the practices of the data broker industry has led to a number of investigations, including a major FTC inquiry that resulted in a report titled "Data Brokers: A Call for Transparency and Accountability."[33] But very little has actually changed to prevent practices that many find objectionable.[34]

Skeptics say that, in reality, citizen concerns about data privacy are superficial. They point out that consumers routinely share intimate personal information about themselves on social media platforms such as LinkedIn and Facebook, and that they are increasingly "instrumenting themselves" using fitness, health, and diet tools like Fitbit, Jawbone, and MyFitnessPal. Although these platforms have privacy policies that are available to consumers, they are written in dense legalese that very few users bother to read. The readiness with which consumers publicly expose information about themselves through platforms suggests that few citizens care passionately about the issue of data privacy—which makes it unlikely that either regulators or platform managers will rein in the use of personal data any time soon.

One final point with respect to privacy is the issue of data ownership. Data aggregators and other firms with access to information are, in effect, asserting an ownership interest in data that might otherwise be viewed as belonging to individuals. In a provocative act designed to shed light on the issue, a young woman named Jennifer Lyn Morone has incorporated herself in order to assert an ownership interest in the data stream that she generates.[35] Companies that profit from the use and sale of personal data, of course, are unlikely to find Morone's gesture either amusing or persuasive. But the issue is not going to disappear. J. P. Rangaswami, chief data officer for Deutsche Bank, predicts:

> As we learn more about the value of personal and collective information, our approach to such information will mirror our natural motivations. We will learn to develop and extend these rights. The most important

change will be to do with collective (sometimes, but not always, public) information. We will learn to value it more; we will appreciate the trade-offs between personal and collective information; we will allow those learnings to inform us when it comes to mores, conventions, and legislation.[36]

In a world where data is widely described as "the new oil," it's clear that the issue of data ownership will need to be resolved through some combination of regulatory action, court rulings, and industry self-regulation.[37] Each new scandal involving the release of sensitive information, such as the 2014 disclosure that Sony Pictures had leaked access to the viewing history of millions of users, is likely to increase the push to establish ownership rights over user data.[38] Such ownership rights would give victims a legal course of action after data breaches occur; the theory is that, given high enough liability, firms will take data security more seriously and act to prevent future leaks.[39] In some niche markets, agreements over data ownership are already being developed. For example, in November 2014, a collection of major agricultural companies and organizations, including Dow, DuPont, Monsanto, and the National Corn Growers Association, agreed on a set of principles defining the rights of farmers to own and control data about their crops.[40] Consider the implications: sensor data used to improve crop yield could just as easily be used to predict soybean futures. These secondary uses have the potential to create vast wealth in which the sources of that data would have a legitimate interest.

National control of information assets. The global reach of the Internet has added significant complication to business regulation. Developing sensible rules concerning the role of national borders in business transactions, and then finding ways to enforce those rules consistently and fairly, is far more difficult in a world that is electron-ically interconnected. One example of this difficulty is the applica-tion to platform businesses of rules regarding national control of data access.

When multinational firms expand into less developed countries, they are usually required to follow so-called local content regulations, which are designed to stimulate the local economy and to ensure that a portion of the economic growth created by the new venture remains in the host country rather than being transferred to the headquarters of the multinational. For example, when corporations like Siemens and GE expand into sub-Saharan Africa, they are often required to set up local operations, in activities such as training and service. This is why Siemens operates a Siemens Power Academy in Lagos, Nigeria, to train technicians for the electrical power industry.

Some industry observers believe it is possible that the local content requirement might extend to data services —requiring, for example, that business data be stored and processed locally rather than internationally. If this principle becomes widely established, the value of the data involved may be significantly diminished. For example, if GE or Siemens power turbines around the globe were connected into a single network for data collection and study, the resulting data flow could become the basis of comparative analysis that would yield a unique "usage signature" for each machine. This would enable data analysts to make more accurate predictions of turbine performance and create customized maintenance schedules that could save money for both the corporation and its customers. However, realizing this positive outcome requires access to tremendous amounts of information for real-time processing—access that local data content laws might thwart. It's a good example of the kind of regulatory restriction that governments should reconsider in the light of the new capabilities offered by platform ecosystems.[41]

Privacy laws in Europe represent another form of what might be called data nationalism. Rules concerning the flow of data have been established for the ostensible purpose of protecting citizens' privacy. The result is a hodgepodge of local data processing centers and a fragmentation of data that, if aggregated, could be used for commercial purposes. The number of billion-dollar startups in the U.S. is forty-two, but only thirteen in the EU.[42] An inability to scale network effects could be one reason. Recent evidence suggests that this EU data privacy regime is already having a notable economic impact. For example, ad placement firms, which rely on insights from big data to optimize their decisions, are significantly less effective in their European operations than in comparably wealthy regions such as the United States that lack restrictive data management rules.[43]

Tax policy. One of the hottest regulatory issues facing platforms is tax policy. As quickly growing platforms that do business around the country and even around the world reorganize the economy and put countless local "mom and pop" companies out of business, who benefits from the sales tax dollars generated? Should they be paid at the location of a central producer, or should they be collected at the point of consumption? The economic and political impact of questions like these can be substantial.

As the world's second biggest online retailer (based on revenues), Amazon has been the poster child for this issue. In most countries where Amazon operates, a national sales or value-added tax is levied, which Amazon must collect from all customers. However, the crazy quilt of state and local sales taxes in the U.S. creates opportunities for Amazon to minimize its tax collection obligations and thereby keep the perceived price of its goods as low as possible. The company has battled with numerous state regulators and legislatures over sales tax rules, often refusing to collect taxes until specifically compelled to do so by the passage of new laws. In some states, Amazon claims not to maintain a "legal presence" sufficient to require payment of sales tax, despite operating large warehouses and shipping centers in those states. And in some cases, Amazon has played one state off against another—for example, apparently rewarding Indiana for passing a law that exempted the company from collecting sales tax by locating no fewer than five of its regional warehouses in the state. Today, Amazon collects sales taxes in twenty-three U.S. states, including several of the largest, while holding out against tax collection requirements elsewhere.[44]

The same issue exists in regard to other online platforms, such as labor platform Upwork, which reduces local tax collections by putting local staffing agencies out of business. It would seem that the international reach of online platforms renders traditional local and state sales tax regimes obsolete, and that a national sales tax law would be a natural and logical solution. However, as of the mid-2010s, it seems highly unlikely that the U.S. Congress, with its strong anti-tax bias, will pass such a law.

A next-best solution would be a bill making it easier for states to impose sales tax on goods purchased online from out-of-state sources, and such a bill has in fact been introduced in Congress several times since 2010. An early version, called the Main Street Fairness Act, failed to advance beyond the committee stage, thanks in part to heavy lobbying against the bill by representatives of Amazon.

A newer version called the Marketplace Fairness Act was passed in the Senate in May 2013, though it has not yet been brought to a vote in the House. In a fascinating twist, the Marketplace Fairness Act has been publicly *supported* by Amazon (as well as by retail giant Walmart). The likely reason for the reversal: since Amazon now collects sales tax on most of the goods it sells, the company stands to gain from a simplified sales tax system that will apply equally to all Internet merchants—including the many smaller rivals of Amazon who currently skate by collecting little or no tax on most of their sales. It's a classic illustration of how regulatory debates that evoke majestic concepts such as equity, freedom, and the sanctity of the marketplace often turn, in the end, on nitty-gritty issues of dollars and cents and the political clout that various players bring to the legislative table.

Labor regulation. Those who operate labor platforms usually choose to describe their systems as intermediaries that serve solely to match labor with demand for services. In this view, the people who sign up for work through firms such as Uber, TaskRabbit, and Mechanical Turk are truly independent contractors, and the platform bears little legal (or moral) responsibility to the parties on either side of the interaction once the match has been made.

However, from the perspective of regulators who are charged with safeguarding the welfare of working men and women, this position is dubious. In the traditional world of offline business, a number of firms that classify full-time, permanent employees as contract labor for legal and regulatory purposes have been drawing unfavorable attention for the practice. For example, in August 2014, FedEx

lost a federal court case involving 2,300 full-time workers in California who were classified as contractors rather than employees. The
practice, which the court ruled was illegal, reduced FedEx's responsibility for benefits, overtime payments, Social Security and Medicare
contributions, and even reimbursement for work expenses such as
uniforms. (FedEx has said it plans to appeal the ruling.)[45]

Labor platforms will need to monitor the evolution of regulation
in this area very carefully. While government agencies and judges
vary in their attitudes and in their readiness to challenge widespread
business practices, many look askance at employment models that
seem to be designed solely to shield companies from responsibility for
the well-being of their workers.

Perhaps equally significant, the reputation of online labor platforms has already taken a serious hit in the unofficial "court of public
opinion"—as reflected, for example, in more than a million Google
results, many from respectable mainstream media outlets, in response
to the query "Internet sweatshop."[46] In the long run, public disap-
proval of business behavior can have a meaningful impact on the
value of a company's brand—which means that the court of public
opinion operates, at times, as an unofficial regulatory body that business leaders are wise to heed.

Similarly, there are limits to the extent to which labor platforms
will be able to evade responsibility for their practices in hiring,
screening, training, and supervising workers—even when those
workers are technically classified as independent contractors. Uber,
for example, has experienced significant criticism for alleged sexual
assaults committed by its drivers on passengers.[47] At a time when
Uber is engaged in a fierce battle over regulation with the traditional
taxi industry, it can ill afford the suspicion that its labor practices are
shoddy.

On a very different front, the emergence of online labor platforms is creating new challenges for regulators tasked with monitoring and measuring the national and local labor markets. Because of
multihoming, freelancers can switch between multiple platforms over
the course of a day—for example, drivers can accept jobs for both
Uber and Lyft. This makes it all the more complex for government

agencies to accurately capture labor and unemployment data, which in turn play an important role in economic and political policy debates. If employment platforms continue to grow, this will be an increasingly important issue.

Potential manipulation of consumers and markets. When platforms grow big enough, they have the potential to cease being mere participants in markets—serving to efficiently match existing supply with existing demand—and actually begin manipulating individual users and even entire markets through their great size and reach.

There are disturbing indications that this is already beginning to happen. Retail platform Amazon controls such a large share of the online book market that even giant publishers feel pressured to accept business terms they'd otherwise consider unacceptable. During a seven-month dispute with Amazon over price-setting policy, the French-based Hachette Book Group—one of the world's largest publishers—found online sales of its products being delayed and preorder buttons for some of its titles being removed. Since preorders play an important role in determining whether or not a book achieves bestseller status, these steps by Amazon impacted the long-term success of a number of Hachette publications. The two sides finally came to terms in November 2014, having apparently reached some kind of compromise and with neither side claiming outright victory.[48]

Facebook users and privacy experts were distressed in June 2014, when it was revealed that, two years previously, the newsfeeds of almost 700,000 members had been deliberately manipulated as part of a psychological experiment. The researchers, including Cornell professor Jeffrey Hancock as well as some Facebook employees, altered the news flows to include an abnormally low or an abnormally high number of either positive or negative posts. According to the study results, the status messages posted by the Facebook members in response showed that "emotional states can be transferred to others via emotional contagion, leading people to experience the same emotions without their awareness."[49]

The stakes get higher as influence moves to politics. In one study of 61 million Facebook users, news feeds with positive social pressure caused roughly 2 percent more people to vote or at least declare that they had voted relative to people who did not receive such messages. In fact, Facebook social messaging increased turnout directly by about 60,000 people and indirectly by about 280,000 more people via social contagion.[50] While there is no evidence that election outcomes changed, one can imagine close races where a 2 percent margin affects who wins.

It's an interesting finding—one that Facebook advertisers and others seeking to influence the attitudes and behaviors of large numbers of people might find valuable. But these studies were conducted without the knowledge or consent of their subjects. And not all the studies received prior approval by any institutional review board, which is normally required before experimentation on human subjects is conducted. Outside experts responded by challenging the ethics and possibly even the legality of Facebook's actions. Amidst the ensuing furor, Mike Schroepfer, Facebook's chief technology officer, announced that the company would henceforth conduct an "enhanced review process" before performing research dealing with sensitive emotional issues.[51]

In a third case, Uber was embroiled in controversy in July 2015, when a team funded by FUSE Labs, a research organization sponsored by Microsoft, reported on the existence of so-called "phantom cabs" on the Uber passenger app—cars that appear to be close to a passenger pickup location but which in fact do not exist. An Uber spokesperson explained the phantoms as a mere "visual effect" that riders should ignore, but some drivers and passengers suspect they may be a deliberate ploy to trick riders into thinking Uber cabs are closer than they really are. Other reported visual anomalies on the Uber app create misleading or confusing impressions of high-demand areas that forecast higher "surge" pricing.

The FUSE researchers say that both drivers and passengers are learning to game the system, trying to avoid being misled by Uber's inaccurate visual data. They conclude: "Uber's access to real-time information about where passengers and drivers are has helped make it one of the most efficient and useful apps produced by Silicon Valley in recent years. But if you open the app assuming you'll get the same insight, think again: drivers and passengers are only getting part of the picture."[52]

Cases like these illustrate the wide variety of ways that highly popular platforms can use their market power and their access to vast amounts of data to mislead people and manipulate their behavior without their knowledge or consent. The temptation for platform managers to engage in such practices for potential economic gain is likely to be huge. But defining this kind of ethically questionable behavior, developing clear and reasonable rules to discourage it, and then enforcing those rules without excessive intrusiveness and bureaucracy will be a huge challenge for regulators.

TIME FOR REGULATION 2.0?

Some observers say that the advent of the information age, in which vast amounts of previously inaccessible data are now available for evaluation, analysis, and use in smart decision-making, should drive a wholesale rethinking of traditional approaches to regulation. Nick Grossman, an entrepreneur, investor, and former MIT Media Lab Scholar, calls for a transition from today's Regulation 1.0, which emphasizes prescriptive rules, certification processes, and gatekeeping, to a new system he calls Regulation 2.0, based on open innovation tempered by data-driven transparency and accountability.[53] Both kinds of regulatory regime share the goal of creating trust and fostering fairness, security, and safety, but the means employed are very different.

In Grossman's view, regulation based on restricted access makes sense in a world of scarce information. Traditionally, it was difficult or impossible for a consumer to gather accurate information about the quality or safety of a particular taxi driver or hotel. That's why most governments have taken steps to screen and certify taxi drivers, require insurance coverage for drivers, and monitor the safety and cleanliness of hotel accommodations.

But in a world of abundant information, regulation based on data-driven accountability makes more sense. Firms like Uber and

Airbnb can be granted freedom to operate in exchange for access to their data. Because it is possible to know exactly who did what to whom and when, consumers and regulators can hold people and platforms accountable for their behaviors after the fact. Uber customers can use driver ratings to decide whether or not to accept a particular ride; Airbnb customers can use host ratings to pick a safe and comfortable place for a night's stay; and both organizations can be sanctioned or even shut down by regulators if their activities violate public expectations of safety and fair dealing.

Under Grossman's Regulation 2.0 scheme, government regulatory agencies would operate quite differently from the way they do today. Rather than establishing rules of market access, their primary job would be to establish and enforce requirements for after-the-fact transparency. Grossman imagines a city government responding to the arrival of Uber by passing an ordinance that states: "Anyone offering for-hire vehicle services may opt out of existing regulations as long as they implement mobile dispatch, e-hailing, and e-payments, 360-degree peer-review of drivers and passengers, and provide an open data API for public auditing of system performance with regards to equity, access, performance, and safety."[54]

It certainly makes sense for policy-makers to seek ways to take advantage of the vast new flows of data created by online business—and in particular by the rise of platforms—in developing new systems for monitoring and regulating economic activity. And in some arenas, enhanced transparency, perhaps under government mandate, can powerfully supplement or even replace traditional forms of regulation, reducing the costs and inertia associated with government intervention and encouraging innovation.[55] For example, mandated disclosures of food nutrition data, auto safety ratings, and the energy efficiency of appliances have helped millions of consumers to make wiser choices and encouraged companies to improve the quality of their products.[56]

Grossman's emphasis on the power of transparency to enforce high community standards of behavior is particularly relevant in an age driven by information. An interesting analogy can be drawn with the ideas promulgated by Richard Stallman, the programmer–activist who is a leader of the "free software" movement. Stallman points out that one of the key virtues of free (or open source) software is that anyone can inspect the code and see what it does. Of course, only experts are likely to do this. But those who take the opportunity will be in a position to offer an informed judgment about the virtues and vices of the program, and, when necessary, to alert the general public to the problems they detect. If software code allows a company to spy on customers, defraud them, or misappropriate their data, then making the code freely accessible to all will quickly expose the problem and likely force its correction.[57]

In this sense, free software resembles the free speech guaranteed to Americans by the Bill of Rights—in the hands of engaged citizens, both can serve as crucial weapons in the battle against private or public malfeasance. And the same can be said about the platform data that Grossman's new regulatory system would rely upon. As Supreme Court Justice Louis Brandeis famously said, "Sunshine is said to be the best disinfectant; electric light the most efficient policeman."

Of course, it's unlikely, especially in the short term, that a wholesale replacement of traditional regulation with a new, information-based system would produce results that most citizens would find acceptable. Would most families be satisfied to have government inspections of food processing plants eliminated, so long as statistics about deaths from salmonella and trichinosis associated with particular companies were widely available? In matters of life and death, traditional systems of standard-setting and certification make it easier for people to consume goods and services without anxiety, and it's hard to imagine that most consumers would want to completely eliminate those systems.

Furthermore, an effective Regulation 2.0 regime would require significant talent upgrades on the part of government agencies as well as complex revisions to existing statutory codes. As suggested by the cases of apparent customer and market manipulation we described earlier in this chapter, platform businesses can't necessarily be trusted to behave with consistent transparency and integrity unless independent outsiders are monitoring their actions. These outsiders could be teams of tech-savvy experts employed by government agencies; they could be employees of rival businesses who take advantage of open data access to study the behavior of their competitors and publicize instances of wrongdoing. In either case, Regulation 2.0 could still end up being fairly intrusive and costly.

Grossman cites the work of economist Carlota Perez, who has described how "great surges" in technology have led to "profound changes in people, organizations and skills in a sort of habit-breaking hurricane." Perez goes on to say that these surges also demand changes in regulatory regimes—and Grossman's contention is that the advent of the information age represents the latest such surge.[58]

There's much truth in the notion that the information age— including the rise of the platform—is a paradigm-altering shift that will profoundly impact every corner of society, including government regulation of business. But, as Grossman notes, Perez describes the great surges as cycles of change that take around fifty years to play out. That's about right—and this suggests that it will take time to determine in exactly what ways the traditional regulatory system can safely be discarded in favor of a system like Regulation 2.0. In many cases, we may conclude that maintaining at least a portion of the current permission-based regulatory apparatus while augmenting its effectiveness using systems of permissionless, data-driven account-ability will yield the best results.

OUR ADVICE FOR REGULATORS

We began this chapter by describing the basic economic tradeoff between private governance and government regulation. Corporate governance acts to mitigate negative externalities that affect the private interests of the firm. Platforms are adept at regulating market failures on-platform but less able to regulate them off-platform. Experience suggests that firms are usually quick to react to changing technology and market conditions, but they generally do not act to maximize social welfare unless forced to do so by the power of public opinion or by regulatory constraints.

Government regulation, on the other hand, is supposed to be focused on safeguarding the interests of the general public and those of private industry. It can wield tools of enforcement such as search warrants, the power of civil forfeiture, and the authority of law. Unfortunately, regulators are subject to capture, especially in countries with weak democracy and government oversight. Thus, neither private governance nor government regulation can be counted on to serve as a foolproof guardian of the public interest.

For policymakers who are taking on the challenging task of adapting traditional regulatory systems to the new conditions of the age of platforms, we recommend two sets of frameworks. The first, provided by economists Heli Koski and Tobias Kretschmer, suggests that industries with strong network effects can generate market inefficiencies and that the goal of public policy should be to minimize those. The market inefficiencies of particular concern are abuse of dominant position and the failure to ensure that new and better technologies are adopted as soon as they become available.[59]

The second framework, developed by David S. Evans, proposes a three-step process to test for the desirability of government regulatory action. The first step is to examine whether the platform has a functioning internal governance system in place. The second step is to see whether the governance system is mostly being used to reduce negative externalities that would harm the platform (such as criminal behavior by users) or to reduce competition or take advantage of a dominant market position. If, on balance, the firm is using its governance system to deter negative externalities, then no further action is necessary. However, if the governance system appears to encourage anticompetitive practices, then a third and final step is required. This step involves asking whether the anticompetitive behavior outweighs the positive benefits of the governance system. If so, then a violation has occurred, and a regulatory response is required. If not, then no further action is needed.[60]

Proponents of low regulation are likely to urge restraint in applying government pressure to platform businesses, especially during the startup phase. After all, they might reason, the harm done to the marketplace or to the general public by a startup company is likely to be relatively small, especially when compared with the potential positive effects to be derived from innovation, new business model development, and economic growth. The time to apply the rules more stringently will come later, once the start up has grown to the point where the costs and benefits of regulation are both reasonable.

Early in its history, YouTube had an informal though unacknowledged policy of allowing copyrighted material to be posted on its site. As YouTube grew, concern over this lax enforcement of intellectual property rights increased, putting pressure on the company to establish a stricter compliance standard. Over time, mechanisms have been worked out to compensate rights holders, and today there are many instances of musicians earning significant revenues from their YouTube channels.

However, this approach does not satisfy everyone. Harvard professor Benjamin Edelman observes:

> If we let tech companies launch first and ask questions later, we invite misbehavior . . . Perhaps some sectors suffer unnecessary or outdated regulation; if so, let's remove the regulations through proper democratic processes. If we let a few firms ignore the rules, we effectively penalize those that comply with the law, while granting windfalls to free-wheeling competitors. That's surely not a business model consumers are looking for.[61]

We close with some general principles of regulatory guidance:

Where possible, we would hope that regulators will move to make adjustments to law to more quickly adapt to technological change. Old regulatory practices, such as the predatory pricing tests developed for non-network industries, simply do not work for new technologies and business models. Regulation must incorporate the recent advances in economic theory that show that firms can still be maximizing their profits even when they choose to distribute certain products and services at zero price.

Regulators should also act to reduce the opportunities for arbitrage. Given that the number of New York City taxi medallions has not changed since 1937, it should surprise no one that an alternate market would develop to leap the regulatory hurdle. In this sense, Uber is a response to regulatory-driven market failure, much like the gypsy cabs that have long operated under the regulatory radar.

Another area where regulators can add value to new technologies is where consumers depend upon accurate information in order for markets to function. Gas stations have long had their pump accuracy checked, restaurants have had health inspectors, and buildings have had safety inspections. Such audits have provided the consumer confidence for those markets to function. Comparable systems for auditing ratings and service quality might help the new platform-based markets develop and thrive. Access to platform data represents a real opportunity to limit market failures both on and off platform.

Finally, we would encourage regulators to have a light touch in order to encourage innovation. Change often provokes anxiety, and there's an understandable impulse to slow the pace of technological and economic innovation in order to fend off unforeseeable consequences that may be harmful. But history suggests that, in most cases, allowing change to flourish leads mainly to positive results in the long run.

One of the most notable regulatory battles related to technological change took place in the early 1980s, when the major movie studios fought to prevent ordinary citizens from using the then-new video recording technology to create copies of movies and TV shows for their personal use. In the landmark 1984 case *Sony Corp. of America v. Universal City Studios, Inc.*, the Supreme Court ruled that such copying constituted fair use and therefore did not violate copyright law. From an economic standpoint, the Sony decision proved to be highly beneficial. To the surprise of the movie moguls, the studios that once opposed video recorders made more money after the new technology was allowed to emerge, through the creation of an entirely new secondary market for movie rentals that did not previously exist. In a similar fashion, new platform markets are likely to create unexpected new opportunities for growth and profit, even for many incumbent businesses that may be fearful of change. For this reason, regulator-induced industry sclerosis must be strenuously avoided, despite the pressures government officials may feel from anxious business leaders eager to protect their familiar turf.

TAKEAWAYS FROM CHAPTER ELEVEN

❑   Opponents of regulation point to phenomena like regulatory capture to argue that government intervention in business is usually ineffectual. But history suggests that some level of societal regulation of business is healthy and beneficial both to the economy and to society as a whole.

❑   There are a number of regulatory issues that are unique to platform businesses or that require fresh thinking in the light of the economic changes that platforms are causing. These include access to platforms, compatibility, fair pricing, data privacy and security, national control of information assets, tax policy, and labor regulation.

❑   The flood of new data made available by today's information age technologies suggests the possibility of new regulatory approaches based on after-the-fact transparency and accountability rather than restrictions on market access. But such new approaches will need to be designed thoughtfully and carefully to fully protect the public.

❑   Economic frameworks for industries with network effects suggest that dominance alone is not necessarily cause for government intervention. Rather, failure to manage externalities, abuse of dominance, manipulating populations, and delaying innovation can indicate when intervention in platform markets is necessary and appropriate.

12

TOMORROW

The Future of the Platform Revolution

As you've seen in the previous chapters of this book, platforms have been transforming entire sectors of the economy, marginalizing incumbents and enabling small startups to rise rapidly to global dominance. It's rare to see a single new business model sweep the field in so many industries so quickly.

Still, you might be feeling that we've been overstating the impact of the platform, at least a bit. After all, hasn't the platform revolution so far been restricted to a relative handful of sectors? Many of the most important aspects of our economy, our society, and our lives—education and government, health care and finance, energy and manufacturing—appear largely unaffected by the rise of the platform.

That's true—so far. But these and other arenas are already seeing the encroachment of platform business models. In the years to come, we believe it's likely that platform businesses, while not claiming control of every aspect of these economic sectors, will stake out significant areas of influence in all of them. In this final chapter, we want to sketch some of the future trends that are already taking shape and that you will want to be aware of as you make plans for your own future.

WHAT MAKES AN INDUSTRY READY FOR THE PLATFORM REVOLUTION?

In our research into the disruption of industries by platforms, we've noted characteristics that make a particular industry especially susceptible. Here are some of the types of businesses that are most likely to join the platform revolution in the years to come:

- **Information-intensive industries.** In most industries today, information is an important source of value—but the more crucial information is as a value source, the closer the industry is to being transformed by platforms. This explains why media and telecom are two of the industries that have already been disrupted so thoroughly by platforms. New entrants have created ecosystems that can create and disrupt content and software more quickly and easily than large firms with thousands of employees once did.

- **Industries with non-scalable gatekeepers.** Retailing and publishing are two examples of industries that traditionally have employed expensive, non-scalable human gatekeepers—buyers and inventory managers in the case of retail, editors in the case of publishing. Both are already undergoing disruption thanks to the rise of digital platforms, with millions of producers (artisans, craftspeople, writers) creating and marketing their own goods through platforms like Etsy, eBay, and Amazon.

- **Highly fragmented industries.** Market aggregation through a platform increases efficiencies and reduces search costs for businesses and individuals looking for goods and services created by far-flung local producers. Platforms ranging from Yelp and OpenTable to Etsy, Uber, and Airbnb have made it easy for customers to visit a single source to gain access to thousands of small suppliers.

- **Industries characterized by extreme information asymmetries.** Economic theory suggests that fair, efficient markets require that all participants have equal access to information about goods, services, prices, and other crucial variables. But in many traditional markets, one set of participants has far better access than others. Used car dealers, for example, knew much more about the condition and history of the cars they sold, as well as about supply and demand variables, than their customers—hence the distrust in which they were held. Data aggregating and sharing platforms such as Carfax are now leveling the field, making detailed information about used car values available to anyone willing to pay a small fee. Other markets where information asymmetries have made fair dealing difficult, from health insurance to home mortgages, are ripe for similar changes.

Based on the factors above, one may question why banking, health care, and education continue to be so resistant to transformation. All three industries are information-intensive. (Health care may seem like a service-intensive industry, but all of its efficiencies are powered by information.) However, industries that might seem to be susceptible to platform approaches, yet are likely to be resistant to such disruption, have certain other characteristics. These include the following:

- **Industries with high regulatory control.** Banking, health care, and education are all highly regulated. Regulations favor incumbents and work against the interests of startups trying to unlock new sources of value. Emerging platforms are starting to attack this problem in an effort to create new sources of value, but regulatory control is holding them back.
- **Industries with high failure costs.** The costs of a defaulted loan or matching a patient with the wrong doctor are much higher than the cost of showing inappropriate content on a media platform. Consumers are reluctant to participate on platforms when the perceived costs of failure are high.
- **Resource-intensive industries.** Resource-intensive industries have typically not been dramatically affected by the Internet. Winning participants in these markets still depend on their access to resources and their ability to manage efficient, large-scale processes such as mining, oil and gas exploration, and agriculture, in which information has a limited role to play.

The impact of these factors will change over time. As more and more processes and tools get connected to the Internet, every industry has the potential to become an information-intensive industry. For example, resource-intensive industries like mining and energy will increasingly need to leverage the power of platforms, creating efficiency gains and faster learning by connecting their resources—material, labor, and machines—over a central network to coordinate workflows. Over the next few years, we will see the start of transformation in large resource-intensive companies as they leverage platforms toward greater efficiency gains.

Even as we consider the relative likelihood that various industries will be susceptible to platform transformation in the near future, let's bear in mind that industry boundaries are becoming increasingly porous due to the impact of platforms. Think about the advertising industry, for example. In a world of pipelines, businesses' access to consumers was limited to media and retail channels: television networks, newspapers and magazines, department stores. Very few businesses could afford to own their own direct-to-consumer channels for promoting their goods and services. By contrast, in today's world of Internet-powered platforms, any business can engage with consumers directly, capturing data about their preferences, connecting them with external producers, and offering personalized services that provide individual customers with unique value.

In effect, every company can now be an advertising company. Uber, for example, has the potential to be the world's largest hyperlocal advertising business. Through its rider data, Uber can gain unique insight into where users live, where they work, when and how often they commute, and many other such aspects of behavior. The company could use such data to connect users with local merchants. Many other kinds of companies with vibrant platforms, from banks to retailers, could employ a similar strategy.

The power of the platform is modifying—even erasing—many other, similar barriers that once separated industries from one another. Thus, one of the most dramatic effects of the rise of the platform has been the emergence of unexpected new competitors from seemingly unrelated industry sectors. Bear this in mind as you consider the possible future impact of the platform model on your own industry, whatever it may be.

With these insights in mind, let's consider some of the most plausible and intriguing future scenarios for the expansion and evolution of platforms in specific sectors of the economy.

EDUCATION:
THE PLATFORM AS GLOBAL CLASSROOM

Education is perhaps the prime example of a major industry that is ripe for platform disruption. Information-intensive? Check. In fact, the fundamental product being sold by schools, colleges, and universities is information of various kinds. Non-scalable gatekeepers? Check. Ask any parent whose child has recently had to navigate the slow, complex, inherently arbitrary process by which a lucky handful of students are admitted to the most prestigious and selective colleges, and you'll hear plenty about the shortcomings of some of the world's most powerful gatekeepers. Highly fragmented? Check. Within the United States, there are over 13,000 public school districts, as well as thousands of private school systems, colleges, universities, and proprietary schools, each fiercely independent and proud of its unique programs and standards. Information asymmetry? Check. Only a small percentage of parents feel competent to judge the qualifications and reputations of schools and colleges—hence the proliferating, competing, and confusing array of rating systems and the ever-increasing pressure on students to earn entry to the handful of institutions that are universally admired—the Harvards and Yales of the world.

With millions of families forced to negotiate this non-system system every year, it's no wonder that most emerge frustrated and uncertain as to whether or not they've found the right school for their child. Then factor in the unsustainable cost inflation that education has experienced in the U.S.: having grown by twenty-five times over the past fifty years, higher education spending has skyrocketed even faster than health care spending. The overall picture is of an industry under tremendous pressure to change so as to deliver better value for the dollars being invested.

The drive to build education platforms is well under way, as businesses like Skillshare, Udemy, Coursera, edX, Khan Academy, and others suggest. Eager to avoid being rendered irrelevant or obsolete by upstart platform companies, a number of the world's greatest universities are moving to position themselves as leaders in this educational revolution. Institutions including Harvard, Princeton, Stanford, the University of Pennsylvania, and many others are offering online versions of some of their most popular classes in the form of "massive open online courses" (MOOCs)—many in partnership with companies like Coursera.

In the years to come, the spread and increasing popularity of teaching and learning ecosystems will have an enormous impact on public school systems, private schools, and traditional universities. Barriers to entry that have long made a first-class education an exclusive, expensive, and highly prestigious luxury good are already beginning to fall. Platform technologies are making it possible for hundreds of thousands of students to simultaneously attend lectures by the world's most skilled instructors, at minimal cost, and available anywhere in the world that the Internet is accessible. It seems to be only a matter of time before the equivalent of a degree from MIT in chemical engineering will be available at minimal cost in a village in sub-Saharan Africa.

The migration of teaching to the world of platforms is likely to change education in ways that go beyond expanded access—important and powerful as that is. One change that is already beginning to happen is the separation of various goods and services formerly sold as a unit by colleges and universities. Millions of potential students have no interest in or need for the traditional college campus complete with an impressive library, a gleaming science lab, raucous fraternity houses, and a football stadium.

The traditional university makes education available to a select few: professors with specific, laboriously obtained academic credentials and highly qualified students with the time and money to invest in campus life. For this relative handful of people, the old model of education may work well. But education platforms like Skillshare make high-level teaching and learning available to thousands who can't or won't fit the traditional mold. Suddenly, brilliant instructors and eager learners can find one another anywhere, anytime. It's a priceless opportunity that the online platform makes available at a tiny fraction of the traditional cost.

Education platforms are also beginning to unbundle the process of learning from the paper credentials traditionally associated with it. As of 2014, statistics show that only about 5 percent of students who enroll in MOOCs receive certificates of completion—a data point that has led many to conclude that online teaching is ineffective. But a study of more than 1.8 million MOOC enrollees at the University of Pennsylvania found that 60 percent of students become actively engaged with the course content, watching class videos, connecting with their peers, and completing one or more assignments. The researchers concluded that "students treat MOOCs like a buffet, sampling the material according to their interests and goals."[1] As students gravitate to MOOCs—especially those that teach specific work skills, like the many online courses in fields such as software engineering, design, marketing, and film editing—they appear to be more interested in the real-world abilities they are honing than in such traditional symbols of achievement as a class transcript or a diploma. A high ranking on TopCoder, a platform that hosts programming contests, will earn a developer a job at Facebook or Google just as fast as a computer science degree from Carnegie Mellon, Caltech, or MIT. Platform-based students for whom a conventional credential is important can often make special arrangements to receive one—for example, at Coursera, college credit is a "premium service" you pay extra for.

The platform-based unbundling of educational activities is separating the teaching of specific skills from reliance on vast, multipurpose institutions like traditional universities. Duolingo uses a crowdsourcing platform to teach foreign languages. Its founder, Luis von Ahn, is a computer scientist who never studied language instruction. After reading the most respected books on the topic, he performed comparative tests of the leading theories using the crowds that visited his website and an evolving set of testing tools to measure the results. Today, more people are using Duolingo to learn a language than all the students in high school in the U.S. combined.[2]

Duolingo separates language teaching from traditional educational institutions. The same thing is happening with the teaching of programming on TopCoder, marketing on Salesforce, or guitar on Microsoft Xbox.

Learning platforms are facilitating many other experiments with the form, structure, and substance of traditional education. For example, the Minerva Project, launched in September 2014, with an initial class of thirty-three students, aims to replace the traditional liberal arts college with an online platform that allows students to attend interactive seminars with professors located anywhere in the world. The students themselves will live for a year at a time in dorms in various cities—San Francisco, Berlin, Buenos Aires—where local cultural, professional, and recreation facilities will be incorporated into the curriculum. Minerva hopes to grow to admit some 2,500 students per year, each paying a total fee of around $28,000 (including room and board)—about half the cost of attending a selective college or university.

"The Minerva boast," journalist Graeme Wood observes, "is that it will strip the university experience down to the aspects that are shown to contribute directly to student learning."[3] Will Minerva succeed? Only time will tell. But whether it does or not, many other educational experiments are sure to follow. The flexibility and power of the platform to facilitate connections between teachers and students makes this virtually inevitable.

The long-term implications of the coming explosion in educational experimentation are difficult to predict with certainty. But it wouldn't be surprising if many of the 3,000 colleges and universities that currently dominate the U.S. higher education market were to fail, their economic rationale fatally undercut by the vastly better economics of platforms.

HEALTH CARE: CONNECTING
THE PARTS OF AN UNWIELDY SYSTEM

Like education, health care is an information-intensive industry that features non-scalable gatekeepers (in the form of insurance company networks and much-in-demand physicians whose referrals are needed before any consultation can occur), a high degree of fragmentation (among hospitals, clinics, labs, pharmacies, and millions of individual practitioners), and enormous information asymmetries (thanks in part to professionals who sometimes encourage an attitude of "doctor knows best" among patients who are often overwhelmed by the complexities of modern medicine). And like education, health care is an industry widely felt to be in crisis, particularly in the United States. The fragmented U.S. health care delivery system imposes huge costs in missed diagnoses, garbled data, wasted time, and squandered resources.

In its simplest form, the platform model can make accessing health care faster and more convenient by providing an Uber-like interface that permits people to summon medical help wherever they are. Such a system has already been launched in several cities, including Miami, Los Angeles, and San Diego, by a company called Medicast. Click the Medicast app, describe your symptoms, and a physician is guaranteed to arrive within two hours. The service is popular among doctors who want to earn a few extra dollars during their off-hours.[4]

But the potential impact of the platform model on medicine goes far deeper than such basic one-off interactions. In fact, the platform revolution offers huge opportunities to remedy many of the problems that plague American health care. Connecting all suppliers—as well as health care consumers themselves—in a hyperefficient platform has the potential to revolutionize the system.

One of the early harbingers of the kind of change we can expect in the decades to come is the enormous popularity of mobile health care apps and wearable fitness devices linked to networks that provide analysis and information based on the personal data generated. Millions of Americans are already demonstrating that they are comfortable having electronic tools measuring their pulse, blood pressure, activity levels, sleeping patterns, and other health indicators, as well as sharing this information with a software package that can offer diagnostic readings and customized advice. Expanding and enhancing this approach can help shift the emphasis of the health care system from curing or managing illnesses—often diagnosed late and treated at very high cost—to preventing them.

It's also easy to envision a platform that could help individuals manage such chronic—and costly—health care problems as diabetes, hypertension, heart disease, asthma, allergies, and obesity. For example, a wearable device could track a diabetic's nutrition intake, exercise regimen, and blood glucose levels; use the data to describe and explain recommended treatments based on past medical experience and history; and alert a clinician when warning signs of an impending medical crisis arise. One analyst estimates that such a platform could reduce the national investment in diabetes management by at least $100 billion per year.[5] Extend the same logic to the other chronic illnesses that affect tens of millions of Americans—and which our current pay-for-service health care system manages poorly—and the potential cost savings could skyrocket . . . to say nothing of the thousands of lives that would be extended and improved.

Even greater benefits will be realized when one or more platforms emerge that are capable of integrating a wide range of health care data from multiple sources—not just wearable sensors but also patient input and electronic health records generated and maintained by service providers. Developing a platform that is accessible both to patients and to an array of professionals—physicians, nurses, technicians, therapists, pharmacists, insurance carriers, and others—while still protecting patient confidentiality will represent a crucial challenge. As health care consultant Vince Kuraitis notes:

> Many healthcare value propositions will be dependent on broad networks and platforms. If you had high blood pressure and needed to manage your own care with support from your physician, what good would it be if your lab values were on one platform and your medications were listed on another, non-interoperable platform? If you were traveling and went to a hospital emergency room, what good would it do you if your health data was stored on a network not accessible by the hospital?[6]

Many of today's leading technology companies are already beginning to position themselves for the coming battle to dominate the health care platform business. Microsoft, Amazon, Sony, Intel, Facebook, Google, and Samsung have all launched platforms designed to stake out at least one corner of the rapidly growing fitness–health care space.

One intriguing entrant is Apple's HealthKit app, announced in mid-2014, which allows a range of health and fitness apps—including those from outside providers like Nike—to share data with one another. Apple announced plans to work with the famous Mayo Clinic and other health care companies to develop systems that would allow data from HealthKit to be shared with physicians and other caregivers (with appropriate privacy safeguards). And in early 2015, Apple unveiled its new Apple Watch, which boasts an array of health and fitness tracking, measurement, and communication tools.

Under the circumstances, it's not surprising that, according to consultant Kuraitis, Apple has been hiring a large number of professionals to staff up its health platform business—including many with MD and PhD degrees. It seems clear that, within the next decade or two, at least one giant platform business will become a major player in the U.S. health industry. Apple is one of the companies with its eyes fixed on that goal.

The transition from today's fragmented health care system to an efficient platform-based system will not be easy. The barriers to health care platform development include economic and managerial forces that discourage the sharing of patient data and services. These forces help to explain, for example, why the implementation of electronic medical records mandated by the Affordable Care Act (2010) has been poorly managed, with record systems so customized by institution that two hospitals in the same community are often unable to share data regarding the same patient. The problem is exacerbated by the financial incentives for health care organizations to keep each patient within a single medical "home." Many patients are mandated by their insurance carriers to seek services within one health care system, usually defined by geography—an approach that is untenable for patients who are highly mobile or transient, like many young adults.

Furthermore, there is huge variability in how clinicians interact with the health care system. Some are employed by hospitals or other large institutions, which means they usually enjoy relatively easy access to platform data. Others are employed by the government, which means that the platform data they generate are accessible to the government but not to others. Still others are privately employed, which means that the platform data they produce are extremely fragmented.

Until financial incentives are aligned to encourage universal sharing of patient services and data, the growth of platforms within health care may be slow. Helping to bring about this alignment should be a key focus of regulators and industry leaders.

ENERGY: FROM SMART GRID TO MULTIDIRECTIONAL PLATFORM

In a world driven by vast amounts of energy—and in which the supply and usage of energy are intimately linked to such crucial factors as global climate change and international geopolitical conflict—we can't afford to squander the energy supplies we have or use them in ways that harm the natural environment. That's where platform technologies can make a big difference. The electrical energy grid, fueled by sources that include coal, gas, oil, water, wind, solar, and nuclear power, has long been a giant interconnected network of complex technologies. However, it's a network plagued by numerous costly inefficiencies, such as the mismatch between supply and demand caused by variability of energy use over the course of a day and across seasons of the year. The more fully we can convert this network into an intelligent, interactive ecosystem of participants who can produce, share, conserve, store, and manage energy wisely together, the greater the value we can extract from our energy resources—and the healthier the world we'll pass on to future generations.

Today, energy companies and government authorities around the world are working with scientists and engineers to implement "smart grid" technologies that are improving the use and control of energy through digital systems for measuring, communicating, analyzing, and responding to vast amounts of data. Enhanced electrical metering tools are making it easier to implement variable pricing systems that improve the responsiveness of the system to variations in demand, encourage conservation, and smooth out fluctuations in energy availability and use. Decentralization is reducing the grid's reliance on a few vast production facilities, increasing reliability, decreasing vulnerability to sabotage or disaster, and making it easier to distribute energy produced by consumers using wind turbines, photovoltaic panels, and other small-scale systems.

These changes prefigure the interactive network that is likely to shape tomorrow's global energy marketplace. In effect, we're migrating from the one-way pipeline model of energy production and distribution to a platform model, in which millions of individuals and organizations are interconnected and able to play varying roles as circumstances change—consuming energy one moment, producing and selling it the next. Centralized production and control of energy by a few massive utilities will in time give way to millions of small producer-consumers, many as modest as a single solar panel on a family's rooftop.

Continued technological breakthroughs will drive this transformation. Battery technology, for example, will play a crucial role. The leading sources of renewable energy, wind and solar, are both intermittent, which leads to mismatches between supply and demand. More efficient rechargeable electrical storage batteries could provide an answer. Tesla, most famous for its electric vehicles, is currently building a so-called gigafactory in Nevada that is expected to manufacture a new generation of powerful batteries that are capable of supplying energy to a home for up to two days. Sister company Solar-City—run by a cousin of Tesla chairman Elon Musk—which already controls 39 percent of the residential solar market, has announced that, within a decade, all of its power units will come complete with battery storage.

The disruptive potential of this technology for the traditional utility industry is enormous; in fact, a 2013 report by the Edison Electric Institute warned, "One can imagine a day when battery storage technology or micro turbines could allow customers to be electric grid independent." Energy analyst Ravi Manghani foresees a day when today's energy utilities become "something closer to service providers and minders of an increasingly distributed grid rather than the centralized power producers they are today."[7]

It's a pattern we've seen being played out in every corner of the world of platforms: power, which once flowed in a single direction from a central source, is increasingly shared and controlled by millions of market participants. The shift applies to the literal power that flows through electrical lines as well as to the metaphorical kinds of power traditionally wielded by corporate chieftains.

The missing link in the transformation of the energy industry has been a platform that permits large-scale energy transactions. That is beginning to change. The state of California now allows bundlers of distributed energy resources to offer those resources on the wholesale market, and, as we discussed in chapter 4, the state of New York is considering the development of a platform dedicated to the management of distributed energy resources. By mobilizing existing distributed resources, systems like these should facilitate the integration of clean renewable power to accommodate the inherent variability in energy demand.

What is unclear is whether current stakeholders in the energy industry will embrace the emergence of energy platforms or engage in drawn-out regulatory battles in an effort to preserve their current advantages. The challenge for regulators will be to design a system that benefits as many stakeholders as possible—including the future generations that are counting on us to leave them with both adequate supplies of energy and a clean, healthy environment.

FINANCE: MONEY GOES DIGITAL

In a sense, the earliest forms of money—historically documented at least as far back as the Babylonian Code of Hammurabi in the second millennium BCE—represented the first platform businesses. Money is a form of value accepted by all the participants in a particular economic system, who thereby constitute an interactive network able to engage in transactions with one another for mutual benefit. So the world of finance—payment, currency, credit, investment, and the myriad transactions these generate—has always involved platform-like behavior.

Today, online financial platforms like PayPal and Square have created new ways of conducting payment transactions (online in the case of PayPal, mobile and app-based in the case of Square), which in turn open doors to the creation of new categories of merchants. Just as the invention of money some four thousand years ago facilitated astonishing new flexibility and economic growth, the new digital platforms for financial transactions are encouraging thousands of participants to become producers and sellers as well as consumers.

Financial platform companies are also working on unlocking new forms of value hidden within transaction data itself—something that only the new digital tools for gathering and analyzing that data make possible. Knowing who has transacted with whom can help companies discover consumer tastes and spending habits, information they can leverage to generate still more economic activity. For example, MasterCard is a venerable platform business that today operates a financial ecosystem linking two billion cardholders to 25,000 banks and more than 40 million merchants around the world. Now its technology R & D division, known as MasterCard Labs, is experimenting with payment mechanisms that are focused on creating new opportunities to expand the platform's usefulness. Leveraging contextual data captured on the platform, these new tools encourage users to transact by determining the next possible payment opportunity, prompting the user toward it, and facilitating the interaction. ShopThis!, for instance, is a MasterCard Labs innovation that lets magazine readers click on an embedded app to instantly purchase an item they've read about from an affiliated retailer, such as Saks Fifth Avenue.[8]

Other familiar financial platforms—many of them traditionally quite conservative in their business culture as well as significantly constrained by regulation—will be pushed to develop innovations based on the latest platform technologies. Commercial bankers, for instance, have been closely monitoring the rise of online peer-to-peer lending communities like Zopa and Lending Club, which are facilitating billions of dollars' worth of financial transactions and providing credit while bypassing traditional gatekeepers. Peer-to-peer lending platforms have the potential to be particularly disruptive because of their ability to identify patterns in lending and borrowing from the troves of digital data they collect. Using these patterns, these platforms may be able to do a better job of identifying behaviors that predict defaults and fraud than traditional banks that rely on a static set of data markers. Partly for this reason, Lending Club is able to offer most borrowers a lower interest rate on their loans than that available from a traditional bank—while lenders earn a higher return than they would get from most conventional investments.[9] Over time, commercial banks will be driven to adapt the same big-data tools that peer-to-peer lending platforms are using to measure and control risk.

Alternative sources of funding for businesses are also creating new competition for banks. Platforms such as AngelList allow investors to join syndicates that offer funding to early-stage startups in exchange for equity participation. While these applications are themselves still at an early stage of development, they suggest the kinds of new investment models that platforms are making possible.

Platform-based data analysis tools can also be used to enhance the marketing of financial products. Personal finance platforms such as Mint have begun gathering and analyzing data about users' financial status, challenges, and goals that can enable financial institutions to target them with products designed to cater to their specific needs. Well-designed financial platforms can do a better job of consummating mutually beneficial matches between financial services and the consumers who need them than traditional sales and marketing channels have done.

Even more important, traditional financial institutions are beginning to use platform models to expand the reach of their services to segments of the economy that they formerly could not touch. For example, banks are leveraging platforms to tap the cash economy, which they see as a huge future source of growth, particularly in Asia. To gain a foothold in this arena, banks are building invoicing and payment platforms that enable small businesses in the cash economy to better conduct business with one another while capturing data about their interactions in the process. The analytics derived from this data will help banks target small businesses with financial products for the first time in a highly relevant manner. Likewise, some banks are offering digital services to assist consumers with real estate searches in the hope of gathering data that could indicate lending opportunities.

Insurance is another space that is set to be rapidly transformed in the age of data platforms. Connected cars are now gathering real-time data about driving behavior, and insurance companies are leveraging such data to offer customized premium pricing based on user-specific driving habits. The growing popularity of wearable devices for tracking health and wellness indicators will create opportunities for health insurance companies to offer similarly customized insurance packages.

Still another potential source of future growth is the hundreds of millions of "unbanked" people, both in the developing world and in less affluent neighborhoods in the U.S. and other developed countries, who currently have no access to tools that can help them pay their bills, borrow money, save, and make investments. Because they live in areas without bank branches and lack the capital needed to qualify for a traditional bank account or line of credit, the unbanked are forced to rely on costly, inconvenient, and sometimes fraudulent alternatives like check-cashing services, money order businesses, payday loan companies, and illegal loan sharks. These substandard financial operators represent another barrier to self-sufficiency that makes it harder for the poor to escape poverty.

Now that millions of these less affluent consumers have access to mobile technology in the form of cell phones, the possibility of creating affordable online financial platforms customized to their needs has become a reality. Naturally, each of these poor or near-poor customers will generate less value for a bank or financial platform operator than a wealthy customer might—but their numbers are so vast that this market represents a huge business opportunity. In sub-Saharan Africa and other developing regions, telecom and technology companies such as Vodafone (through its Safaricom subsidiary) are sparring with traditional financial institutions such as Kenya's

Equity Bank to determine who will control the leading financial platform and its hundreds of millions of potential customers.[10]

In this area, as in many others, the bankers have heard the message that is spreading through one industry after another—disrupt or be disrupted. Increasingly, they are looking to the platform model as the chief disruptive mechanism.

LOGISTICS AND TRANSPORTATION

Logistics and transportation—the business functions by which people and things are moved efficiently from place to place—are resource-intensive industries that were once largely unaffected by the emergence of digital business models. Logistics companies such as FedEx have enjoyed significant competitive advantages because of the huge fixed costs of owning a fleet of cars, trucks, and planes, which create enormous barriers to entry for competitors. But a platform approach doesn't require fleet ownership. Platforms that can aggregate real-time market information on the movement of physical goods and carriers can orchestrate an ecosystem of third-party delivery agents to manage an efficient logistics and delivery system while requiring minimal capital investment.

Specific industries that rely on complex logistical processing are already being transformed by the superior ability of platforms to coordinate the movement of vehicles and resources using highly efficient algorithms to match demand and supply. For example, San Francisco-based Munchery is one of several rapidly growing new food delivery platforms. By aggregating citywide demand according to specific time slots, Munchery's algorithms determine the best truck routes to maximize density of delivery points, thereby minimizing the marginal costs of delivery. In Indonesia, a platform business named Go-Jek allows motorbike drivers to offer rides in a manner similar to Uber. Go-Jek also offers free food delivery throughout the Indonesian capital of Jakarta by leveraging the connected motorbikes and using cleverly designed algorithms to determine the most efficient delivery routes.

LABOR AND PROFESSIONAL SERVICES:
PLATFORMS REDEFINE THE NATURE OF WORK

As we've discussed, some of the most dramatic examples of platform advances have involved labor markets. Every indication is that the transformation of work by the world of platforms is likely to continue in the decades to come, with some implications that are easy to foresee—and others that may take the world by surprise.

One assumption that is already being shattered is the idea that only routine, semi-skilled jobs like taxi driving, food delivery, or household chores are susceptible. Even traditional professions like medicine and law are proving to be susceptible to platform models. We've already mentioned Medicast, which applies an Uber-like model to finding a doctor. Several platform companies are providing online venues where legal services are available with comparable ease, speed, and convenience. Axiom Law has built a $200 million platform business by using a combination of data-mining software and freelance law talent to provide legal guidance and services to business clients; InCloudCounsel claims it can process basic legal documents such as licensing forms and nondisclosure agreements at a savings of up to 80 percent compared with a traditional law firm.[11]

In the decades to come, it seems likely that the platform model will be applied—or at least tested—in virtually every market for labor and professional services. How will this trend impact the service industries—not to mention the working lives of hundreds of millions of people?

One likely result will be an even greater stratification of wealth, power, and prestige among service providers. Routine and standardized tasks will move to online platforms, where an army of relatively low-paid, self-employed professionals will be available to handle them. Meanwhile, the world's great law firms, medical centers, consulting partnerships, and accounting practices will not vanish, but their relative size and importance will shrink as much of the work they used to do migrates to platforms that can provide comparable services at a fraction of the cost and with far greater convenience. A surviving handful of world-class experts will increasingly focus on a tiny subset of the most highly specialized and challenging assignments, which they can tackle from anywhere in the world using online tools. Thus, at the very highest level of professional expertise, winner-take-all markets are likely to emerge, with (say) two dozen internationally renowned attorneys competing for the splashiest and most lucrative cases anywhere on the globe.

The platform transformation of labor will further accelerate trends that have already made huge inroads into the organization of work. The division of labor into smaller and smaller units of work, which Adam Smith recognized as a key to the productive capability of organizations almost three centuries ago, is likely to continue, powered by increasingly smart algorithms that are capable of breaking down a complex job into tiny, simple tasks to be handled by hundreds of workers, then reassembling the results into a unified whole. Amazon's Mechanical Turk already applies this logic to many assignments.

The trend toward freelance work, self-employment, contract labor, and nontraditional career paths will also continue to accelerate. The Freelancers Union estimates that one in three American workers already does some freelance work; that percentage is likely to increase in the years to come. Of course, this will be a mixed blessing. Many people who want flexibility and freedom to set their own working hours and conditions—artists, students, travelers, working moms, the semi-retired—will thrive in this new environment. Those who prefer stability and predictability in their work—or who are accustomed to relying on an employer for vital benefits such as health insurance and a retirement plan—will find the transition challenging, even painful. Traditional labor unions, which organized and defended the rights of the vast armies of workers that big corporations once employed, will continue to decline, leaving individuals to scramble for security on their own.

As we noted when discussing the regulation of platforms in chapter 11, the growing dominance of the world of platforms will create genuine challenges for society. Traditional corporate employment once provided a safety net for millions of workers and their families. As the platform revolution shreds the final vestiges of that safety net, it seems clear that government—or some other new social institution, as yet unenvisioned—will have to find a way to fill the gap.

GOVERNMENT AS PLATFORM

Government, of course, is not an industry in the conventional sense. But it's a major sector of the economy with a huge impact on the life of every citizen. And it certainly has the characteristics of being information-intensive, surrounded by gatekeepers (as anyone who has struggled with an unresponsive government bureaucracy will attest), fragmented (into dozens or hundreds of agencies with overlapping, often mutually contradictory mandates), and marked by information asymmetries (exacerbated by the legal mumbo-jumbo in which laws and regulations are usually written).

So it's understandable that ordinary citizens, along with well-intentioned legislators, elected officials, and civil servants, might be eager to apply the platform model to governments at all levels. Making government processes as transparent, responsive, flexible, user-friendly, and innovative as a well-designed and well-managed platform would be an enormous blessing to the country and could go a long way toward alleviating the cynicism and negativity with which many citizens currently view government.

Of course, transforming government is easier said than done. Constitutional and legal restrictions, conflicting pressures from interest groups and lobbyists, partisan hostilities, budgetary constraints, the complex challenges inherent in developing services suitable for all citizens rather than just a self-selected subset, and the sheer inertia built into any organization that has grown through accretion over more than two centuries—all of these factors pose huge challenges to leaders who want to apply principles from the for-profit sector to streamlining government along platform lines.

Yet despite these difficulties, local, regional, and national governments around the world are beginning to incorporate some of the benefits of the platform model into their daily operations. Perhaps not surprisingly, one of the leading examples is the city of San Francisco, perched at the northern end of Silicon Valley. The city's Open Data policy, originally launched in 2009 for implementation through the Mayor's Office of Civic Innovation, is designed to promote the sharing of city data through an open-access portal, the creation of public–private partnerships to facilitate the development of value-creating tools that citizens and companies can use, and the promotion of data-based initiatives intended to improve the quality of life for everyone living in and around the San Francisco Bay area.

The city's data platform, dubbed DataSF, contains a vast array of information about the city, gleaned from both public and private sources, as well as an application programming interface and tips for outside developers who want to use the data to create apps. To encourage creative use of the platform, the city government has sponsored a series of Data Jams, Hackathons, and app competitions centered on specific civic challenges, from transportation to sustainable development. For example, in June 2013, San Francisco's City Hall was the site of a Housing Data Jam in which fifty local entrepreneurs took a deep dive into issues related to local housing—homelessness, affordable home finance, building safety, energy efficiency, and more. By October, ten privately created apps had been launched using information from DataSF to create tools for improving housing conditions in the city. They included Neighborhood Score, a mobile app that provides a block-by-block health and sustainability score for every area of the city; Buildingeye, a map-based app that makes building and planning information easily accessible; Project Homeless Connect, which uses mobile technology to help people without shelter find the resources they need to get off the streets and into decent housing; and House Fax, a "Carfax for houses," that allows homeowners and residents to access the maintenance history of a particular building.[12]

Ongoing efforts to apply platform thinking to San Francisco city government include a number of other initiatives, including the creation of a single central portal where local businesses can manage all the licensing, regulation, and reporting requirements associated with operating in the city; the Universal City Services Card, which provides a one-stop location for accessing San Francisco services ranging from marriage licenses to golf course discounts; and a partnership with Yelp, the restaurant-rating platform, that will incorporate city health department scores for local eateries into their online Yelp profiles.

While San Francisco has advanced the concept of "government as platform" further than most jurisdictions, similar efforts are underway in cities, states, and regions around the U.S. and the world. The federal government is beginning to travel the same path. Data.gov, launched in 2009, has gradually been expanded, updated, simplified, and enhanced to make large amounts of once inaccessible government data easy to reach for every citizen, as well as providing tools to enable the building of apps using the data.

The burgeoning government platforms that are springing up around the world will only be as open, democratic, and empowering as the sponsoring agencies and our political leaders will allow them to be. (It's not surprising that the National Security Agency and other intelligence organizations are not among the federal offices participating in Data.gov.) Will the platforming of government usher in a new age of universal responsiveness, efficiency, and freedom . . . or will it further advantage the prosperous and the well connected at the expense of the poor and the powerless?

THE INTERNET OF THINGS: A WORLDWIDE PLATFORM OF PLATFORMS

At its core, the platform revolution is about using technology to connect people and provide them with tools they can use to create value together. As digital technology continues to advance—in particular, as chips, sensors, and communication devices continue to grow smaller and more efficient—the number and ubiquity of these connections continue to grow. Many are now being located not in computing devices such as laptops and cell phones but in ordinary machines and appliances—including everything from home thermostats and garage door openers to industrial security systems. With designers and engineers finding more and more ways to usefully link the machines, gadgets, and other devices people interact with daily, a vast new layer of data infrastructure is emerging that has been dubbed the Internet of things. This new universe of networks will have a profound impact on the power of tomorrow's platforms.

A wide range of companies is deeply engaged in the effort to build the Internet of things—and, if possible, to control both the new infrastructure and the ultra-valuable data it will provide. As we've mentioned, industrial firms like GE, Siemens, and Westinghouse are moving to create information links among the turbines, engines, motors, heating and cooling systems, and manufacturing plants they build and operate, hoping to enable tremendous new efficiencies and cost savings. Digital technology firms like IBM, Intel, and Cisco are racing to design the tools and connections that will make the vast new networks possible. And Internet-centered companies like Google and Apple are designing interfaces and operating systems that will enable both technology experts and ordinary people to have easy access to the Internet of things and use it in countless ways we're only beginning to imagine and explore.

What's more, the potential power of the Internet of things will only continue to grow as the varieties of devices available to us and their capabilities continue to expand. To mention just a few examples, consider the transformative power of such just-around-the-corner technologies as driverless cars, cheap and powerful electrical storage batteries for the home, and easy-to-use 3D printers for quickly replicating useful objects. As these and other new tools become widely available, they'll also quickly be linked to the Internet of things, making even more powerful value-creating platforms possible.

Applied to the Internet of things, platform economics will dramatically alter the business models associated with countless familiar goods and services. Take, for example, the familiar lightbulb. Originally patented by Thomas Edison in 1878, the basic engineering of the incandescent bulb has scarcely changed since then, which is why the typical bulb retails for just 40 cents and provides its maker with virtually no profit margin. It's also highly inefficient, wasting more than 95 percent of the energy it uses in the form of heat.

Improved products such as the compact fluorescent bulb and the light emitting diode (LED) have made lighting technology much more efficient as well as more profitable. But when home lighting systems are connected to the Internet of things, the very purpose of the lightbulb is transformed. Lights can be programmed for intruder alerts; they can flash to warn parents when a toddler is wandering near the stairs or the stove; they can blink to remind grandma to take her medication. Lights with wireless connectivity can track the energy consumption of other appliances, enabling lightbulb vendors to offer energy management services to homeowners and utility companies. Suddenly, the lightbulb maker can afford to give away a $40 LED in exchange for a share of the ongoing revenues provided by networked services.

Platform-based connections among household and personal devices have attracted much of the publicity surrounding the Internet of things. But the potential for transformation in the B2B world is, if anything, even greater. David Mount, a partner at the high-tech investment firm of Kleiner Perkins Caufield and Byers, refers to the coming wave of innovation as the Industrial Awakening. He lists eight markets with the potential to generate new multi-billion-dollar industries based on smart connections among industrial devices:

- **Security:** using platform-based networks to protect industrial assets from attacks
- **Network:** designing, building, and servicing the networks that will link and control industrial tools
- **Connected services:** developing software and systems to manage the new networks
- **Product as a service:** transitioning industrial companies from selling machines and tools to selling services facilitated by platform connections
- **Payments:** implementing new ways to create and capture value from industrial equipment
- **Retrofits:** equipping the $6.8 trillion worth of existing industrial machinery in the U.S. to participate in the new industrial Internet

- **Translation:** teaching a wide array of devices and software systems to share data and communicate with one another
- **Vertical applications:** finding ways to connect industrial tools at various places in the value chain to solve specific problems

In total, Mount concludes (drawing on data from a World Economic Forum report) that the Industrial Awakening will generate $14.2 trillion of global output by 2030.[13]

Economist Jeremy Rifkin has deftly summarized this development, as well as some of its broader implications:

> There are now 11 billion sensors connecting devices to the internet of things. By 2030, 100 trillion sensors will be [in place] . . . continually sending big data to the communications, energy and logistics internets. Anyone will be able to access the internet of things and use big data and analytics to develop predictive algorithms that can speed efficiency, dramatically increase productivity and lower the marginal cost of producing and distributing physical things, including energy, products and services, to near zero, just as we now do with information goods.[14]

We may not be on the verge of seeing the majority of physical goods priced at or even near to zero—not yet. But it seems safe to say that we've barely begun to imagine the transformative potential of the platform model.

A CHALLENGING FUTURE

Having read this far, you've undoubtedly recognized that the authors of this book are, in many ways, enthusiastic about the economic and social changes being wrought by the rise of the platform. The remarkable efficiency improvements, innovative capabilities, and enhanced consumer options that platforms make possible have already begun to create amazing new forms of value for millions of people in many walks of life.

But every revolutionary change has its dangers, and every major social and economic disruption creates both winners and losers. The platform revolution is no exception. We've already seen the problems some long-established industries are suffering as their familiar business models are upended by the advent of platforms. From newspaper publishers to record producers, taxi companies to hotel chains, travel agents to department stores, numerous businesses have seen their market shares, revenues, and profitability plummet in the face of platform competition. The fallout inevitably includes uncertainty, loss, and suffering on the part of countless individuals and even some entire communities.

It's easy for pundits and consultants to call for business leaders to "adapt and adjust" to a transformed business environment. But the process of adaptation is often lengthy, confusing, and painful, and some companies and workers will never find their way in the emerging platform-dominated world. It's an unfortunate reality that society must recognize and deal with.

Society must also respond to the structural changes that the platform revolution is creating. We examined some of these in chapter 11, including the unprecedented access to personal and business information enjoyed by the largest platform businesses; the massive shift from traditional forms of employment to more flexible yet uncertain modes of contingent, freelance work; the unpredictable external impacts, positive and negative, that platforms have on the communities in which they operate; and the potential for manipulation of individuals and entire markets by powerful platforms.

Traditional forms of government regulation developed for pipeline businesses are inadequate to addressing the social challenges these platform-based upheavals will bring. But it will take time for policy-makers to fully understand the nature of the changes and to develop regulatory responses that protect citizens from the most serious dangers posed by the platform revolution without unduly stifling beneficial innovations. It will take even longer for ordinary people and the civil society organizations they support and rely upon to absorb the nature of the platform revolution and create appropriate institutional responses.

History shows that it took generations for Western societies to develop effective responses to the dislocations and abuses associated with the Industrial Revolution of the eighteenth and nineteenth centuries—responses that included the union movement, the building of a modern skills-based educational system to prepare workers for new forms of employment, and the funding of a social safety net to care for those who fell through the cracks. In the same way, it will take time for contemporary societies to figure out what they need to do to respond appropriately to the shifts in economic, social, and political power being generated by the platform revolution—which is why we need to begin thinking about these issues *now*, as the contours of the revolution are beginning to emerge.

One inevitable by-product of dramatic technological change seems to be hyperbole. From the popularizing of the term automation in the 1930s (when predictions about the obsolescence of work were common) to the dot-com and Internet booms of the 1990s and 2000s, there's been no shortage of enthusiasts and hucksters breathlessly describing the latest innovations and declaring, "This changes everything!"

We hope that, in this book, we've provided abundant evidence to document our belief that the platform revolution is indeed transforming our world in a host of significant and exciting ways. But there's one thing the platform revolution will not change—namely, the ultimate goal that technology, business, and the entire economic system need to serve. The purpose of all these human constructs should be the unlocking of individual potential and the building of a society in which everyone has the opportunity to live a rich, fulfilling, creative, and abundant life. It's up to all of us—business leaders, professionals, working people, policy-makers, educators, and ordinary citizens—to play our part in making sure that the platform revolution brings us closer to that objective.

TAKEAWAYS FROM CHAPTER TWELVE

❏ Industries that are most prone to platform transformation in the near future include those that are information-intensive, those with unscalable gatekeepers, those that are highly fragmented, and those characterized by extreme information asymmetries.

❏ Industries that are less likely to be transformed by platforms in the short run include those with high regulatory control and high failure costs as well as those that are resource-intensive.

❏ It's possible to foresee some of the specific changes that are likely to impact selected industries in the decades ahead, including education, health care, energy, and finance.

❏ The platform model will continue to shape transformations in the markets for labor and professional services as well as the operations of government.

❏ The burgeoning Internet of things will add a new layer of connectivity and power to the platforms of the future, linking people and devices to one another in new value-creating ways.

❏ The platform revolution will ultimately transform our world in unpredictable ways, calling for society as a whole to develop creative, humane responses to the challenges this change will produce.

ACKNOWLEDGMENTS

The creation of a book is a team effort to which many people contribute. A few members of our publishing team have been particularly important to all three coauthors of *Platform Revolution*.

We want to thank our editorial advisor, Karl Weber, for his tremendous skill in unifying the voices of three authors. Karl, your patience, wisdom, and experience have been essential.

We want to thank our agent, Carol Franco, for her wise counsel at every stage of this project. And we are grateful to our editor at W. W. Norton, Brendan Curry, and to the rest of the Norton team for their enthusiasm and belief in this book.

We would like to thank the many companies and organizations that have provided research funding and have made their employees available to us in support of our effort to better understand network business models. Geoff Parker and Marshall Van Alystne are grateful to organizations that include Accenture, AT&T, British Telecom, the California ISO, Cellular South, Cisco, Commonwealth Bank of Australia, Dun & Bradstreet, France Telecom, GE, Goldman Sachs, Haier Group, Houghton Mifflin Harcourt, IBM, Intel, the International Post Corporation, Law & Economics Consulting Group, Mass Mutual, Microsoft, Mindtree, Mitsubishi Bank, NetApp, PIM Interconnection, the State of New York, Pearson, Pfizer, SAP, Telecom Italia, Thomson Reuters, the U.S. Postal Service, and the U.S. Office of the Inspector General. This book is richer for the generosity of their support.

Sangeet Choudary would like to thank the various companies he has worked with in advisory positions and on commissioned research, including the Centre for Global Enterprise, the INSEAD Business School, Intuit, Yahoo, Schibsted Media, Spotify, Commonwealth Bank of Australia, 500Startups, JFDI Asia, Autodesk, Adobe, Accenture, Dun & Bradstreet, Webb Brazil, BHP Billiton, Philips, Shutterstock, SWIFT, the iSpirit foundation, and Telkom Indonesia. All these experiences have proven extremely valuable in building up Sangeet's body of work on platforms.

In addition, each of the authors has a personal list of friends, colleagues, advisors, and supporters they wish to acknowledge.

GEOFFREY G. PARKER

I thank my wife, Debra, my father, Don, and my children, Benjamin and Elizabeth, for their wonderful support and feedback during the process of writing this book.

I thank my advisors and mentors at MIT—Arnold Barnett, Steve Connors, Richard DeNeufville, Charles Fine, Gordon Hamilton, Richard Lester, Richard Tabors, and Daniel Whitney—for their support, guidance, and enthusiasm. They truly opened up a new world to me.

At MIT, I was fortunate to meet a group of lifelong collaborators: Edward Anderson, Nitin Joglekar, and Marshall Van Alstyne. I could not ask for a finer set of colleagues and friends.

In the process of teaching and learning about platforms, I came to meet Tom Eisenmann, who has been a great friend and collaborator. His ideas have contributed significantly to this work.

I was also fortunate to meet our coauthor Sangeet Choudary, who has worked at and consulted with numerous platform firms. His experience has been wonderfully complementary to my own.

I thank Erik Brynjolfsson, Andy McAfee, Dave Verrill, and the great team at the MIT Initiative on the Digital Economy (IDE). The IDE has been instrumental in hosting the MIT Platform Summit and providing Marshall and me with the opportunity to work with multiple companies as part of our effort to bridge practice and academia.

Peter Evans has inspired me with his insatiable curiosity and drive to measure the growing platform economy. I have also been fortunate to be part of a large community of like-minded scholars who are interested in the economics of information systems, and I am grateful for the regular interaction.

I am grateful to my colleagues at Tulane University, who have provided a sounding board for me to test and strengthen the ideas presented in this book. I have also been fortunate to teach wonderful students at Tulane, who have eagerly helped to refine earlier versions of this material.

I wish to acknowledge the National Science Foundation, the Department of Energy, and the Louisiana Board of Regents for their generous support of my research agenda.

Finally, I again thank Marshall, who has joined me on a nearly twenty-year odyssey to try to understand the rules of the world we are living in and how to navigate its ever-changing waters. I look forward to many more years of entertainment and fascination as we continue the journey.

MARSHALL W. VAN ALSTYNE

Thank you, Erik and Alexander, for your love, support, and patience while Dad worked on this book. Thank you, Joyce, for carrying through on a project that's finally over. Family will always matter most.

I thank my advisors at MIT: Erik Brynjolfsson, Chris Kemerer, Stuart Madnick, Thomas Malone, Wanda Orlikowski, and Lones Smith. The standards you set were remarkable. I also thank the MIT community for letting me be a part of it, for its openness, and for its joy in experimentation. There is a reason that Open CourseWare, edX, PET scans, RSA encryption, spreadsheets, and condensed soup sprang from people in this environment. It is one of the most grueling and at the same time one of the best intentioned and most rewarding places anywhere.

I join Geoff in thanking the members of the great team at the MIT Initiative on the Digital Economy, including Dave Verrill, Erik Brynjolfsson, Andy McAfee, Glenn Urban, Tommy Buzzell, and Justin Lockenwitz. Thank you Michael Schrage for good wine and deep thoughts. You all are where great ideas gain great influence.

Our work on platforms draws heavily on that of Tom Eisenmann and Andrei Hagiu at Harvard Business School, whose teaching materials are excellent. Tom in particular taught me how much theory really does need application, and his contributions as a collaborator have led to many successful papers.

When it comes to understanding startups and social aspects of platforms, few could be better than our coauthor Sangeet Choudary, who has worked at and consulted with numerous platform firms. His experience is wonderful, and he could not be a better addition to our team.

Recently, Peter Evans has inspired us with his ability to build a community of platform scholarship and deliver new data analytic insights into the behaviors of the network economy.

At Boston University, I thank the research rebels—Erol Pekoz, Stine Grodal, and Chris Dellarocas—who meet regularly over lunch to discuss research, swap stories, and poke fun at each other's ideas. As head of the digital learning initiative, Chris practices what we discuss here. Paul Carlile, the whole school and I owe you thanks for helping to create such a supportive and collaborative academic culture. Maria Anderson and Brett Marks, thank you for making everything work.

In teaching, I owe much to my many students, especially those in IS710, IS827, and IS912, who helped me fully cook my half-baked ideas. It's wonderful to see so many of you start companies and take leadership roles—please keep in touch with me as your careers blossom. Sinan Aral, a remarkable MIT student turned faculty member, helped sharpen some of my key ideas on networks. Students like Tushar Shanker, now at Airbnb, are the best reason to teach.

The National Science Foundation deserves special credit for helping to launch my academic career with a CAREER Award, as well as providing numerous grants along the way via the IOC, SGER, iCORPS, and SBIR programs.

Geoff Parker, it's hard to imagine any of this without you. You've been a friend, collaborator, drinking buddy, and sparring partner—contributing to my growth in all the ways that mattered. It's been almost two decades of output, but we're just getting started. My best work has been possible because of you. Thank you.

SANGEET PAUL CHOUDARY

First and foremost, I thank my wife, Devika, and my parents, Varu and Effie, for supporting every decision I've ever taken, including the decision to quit a traditional career and devote my life's work to understanding how connected systems transform the world. Out of this curiosity emerged the focus on researching platforms.

I also thank my parents-in-law, Payal and Arun Sikka, for their enthusiasm and support at every step of this journey. I thank my friends Yow Kin Cheong, David Dayalan, L. T. Jeyachandran, and many others who have enthusiastically partnered on this journey with me.

I want to especially thank my coauthors, Geoffrey Parker and Marshall Van Alstyne, for being the best allies and partners I could ever have asked for on this journey to understanding the impact of technology and connectivity on today's economy. It's been a privilege to have partnered with them in further building the body of work that explains this field.

Finally, I am grateful to everyone who has followed my work on platforms on the Internet and across different research and media channels, embracing the principle of connected business models and my work on this topic as they work to transform their businesses. It is that large-scale proof of concept—multiple businesses globally applying this work and achieving important results—that drives me daily to build our understanding of this field further.

GLOSSARY

Adjacent platforms. Platforms that serve similar or overlapping user bases.

Application programming interface (API). A standardized set of routines, protocols, and tools for building software applications that makes it easy for an outside programmer to write code that will connect seamlessly with the platform infrastructure.

Brand effects. The power of a highly positive brand image to attract consumers and lead to rapid growth of a business. Not to be confused with *network effects*.

Convex growth. See *Metcalfe's law*.

Core developers. Programmers and designers who create the core platform functions that provide value to platform participants. These developers are generally employed by the platform managers—the brand names that are familiar to users, such as Apple, Samsung, Airbnb, Uber, and many others. Their main job is to get the platform into user hands and to deliver value through tools and rules that make the core interaction easy and mutually satisfying.

Core interaction. The single most important form of activity that takes place on a platform—the exchange of value that attracts most users to the platform in the first place. Therefore, platform design generally starts with the design of the core interaction. The core interaction involves three key components: the participants, the *value unit*, and the filter. All three must be clearly identified and carefully designed to make the core interaction as easy, attractive, and valuable to users as possible.

Cross-side effects. In a two-sided market, network effects created by the impact of user from one side of the market on users from the other side of the market—for example, the effects that consumers have on producers and the effects that producers have on consumers. Cross-side effects can be positive or negative, depending on the design of the system and the rules put in place.

Curation. The process by which a platform filters, controls, and limits the access of users to the platform, the activities they participate in, and the connections they form with other users. When the quality of a platform is effectively curated, users find it easy to make matches that produce significant value for them; when curation is nonexistent or poorly handled, users find it difficult to identify potentially valuable matches amid a flood of worthless matches.

Curation of participants. See *Trust*.

Data aggregators. Outside developers that enhance the matching function of the platform by adding data from multiple sources. Under license from the platform management, they "vacuum up" data about platform users and the interactions they engage in, which they generally resell to other companies for purposes such as advertising placement. The platform that is the source of the data shares a portion of the profits generated.

Enhanced access. The provision of tools that enable a producer to stand out above the crowd and be noticed on a two-sided platform, despite an abundance of rival producers and the resulting intense competition to attract consumer attention. Platforms that charge producers fees for better-targeted messages, more attractive presentations, or interactions with particularly valuable users are using enhanced access as a monetization technique.

Envelopment. The process by which one platform effectively absorbs the functions—and often the user base—of an adjacent platform.

Excess inertia. The power of network effects to slow or prevent the adoption of new, perhaps better, technologies. When one or a few platforms are able to dominate a particular market because of the power of network effects, they may choose to resist beneficial innovations in order to protect themselves from the costs of change and other disruptive effects.

Feedback loop. In platforms, any pattern of interactions that serves to create a constant stream of self-reinforcing activity. In the typical feedback loop, a flow of value units is delivered to the participant which generates a response from him or her. If the units are relevant and interesting, the user will be drawn to the platform repeatedly, generating a further flow of value units and prompting more interactions. Effective feedback loops help to swell the network, increase value creation, and enhance network effects.

Filter. An algorithmic, software-based tool used by the platform to enable the exchange of appropriate units of information between users. A well-designed filter ensures that platform users receive only units of information that are relevant and valuable to them; a poorly-designed filter (or no filter at all) means users may be flooded with units of information they find irrelevant and valueless, driving them to abandon the platform.

Frictionless entry. The ability of users to quickly and easily join a platform and begin participating in the value creation that the platform facilitates. Frictionless entry is a key factor in enabling a platform to grow rapidly.

Linear value chain. See *Pipeline*.

Liquidity. A state in which there are a minimum number of producers and consumers in a platform marketplace and a high level of interactions taking place. When liquidity is achieved, interaction failure is minimized, and the intent of users to interact is consistently satisfied within a reasonable period of time. Achieving liquidity is the first and most important milestone in the life cycle of a platform.

Market aggregation. The process whereby platforms provide centralized markets to serve widely dispersed individuals and organizations. Market aggregation provides information and power to platform users who formerly engaged in interactions in a haphazard fashion, often without access to reliable or up-to-date market data.

Matching quality. The accuracy of the search algorithm and the intuitiveness of the navigation tools offered to users as they seek other users with whom they can engage in value-creating interactions. Matching quality is critical to delivering value and stimulating the long-term growth and success of a platform. It is achieved through excellence in product or service *curation.*

Metcalfe's law. A principle formulated by Robert Metcalfe which states that the value of a network grows nonlinearly as the number of users of the network increases, making more connections among users possible (a type of growth also known as *convex growth*). Specifically, Metcalfe's law posits that the value of a network with n connected users is proportional to the square of the number of users (n^2).

Multihoming. The phenomenon of users engaging in similar types of interaction on more than one platform. A freelance professional who presents his credentials on two or more service marketing platforms, a music fan who downloads, stores, and shares tunes on more than one music site, and a driver who solicits rides through both Uber and Lyft all illustrate the phenomenon of multihoming. Platform businesses seek to discourage multihoming, since it facilitates *switching*—the abandonment by users of one platform in favor of another.

Network effects. The impact that the number of users of a platform has on the value created for each user. "Positive network effects" refers to the ability of a large, well-managed platform community to produce significant value for each user of the platform. "Negative network effects" refers to the possibility that the growth in numbers of a poorly managed platform community can *reduce* the value produced for each user.

Pipeline. The structure of a traditional (non-platform) business, in which a firm first designs a product or service, then manufactures the product and offers it for sale or puts in place a system to deliver the service. Finally, a customer shows up and purchases the product or service. This step-by-step arrangement for creating and transferring value can be viewed as a kind of pipeline, with producers at one end and consumers at the other. Also known as a *linear value chain*.

Platform. A business based on enabling value-creating interactions between external producers and consumers. The platform provides an open, participative infrastructure for these interactions and sets governance conditions for them. The platform's overarching purpose: to consummate matches among users and facilitate the exchange of goods, services, or social currency, thereby enabling value creation for all participants.

Platform envelopment. The process whereby one platform effectively absorbs the functions—and the user base—of an *adjacent platform*.

Price effects. The power of extremely low prices for goods or services to (temporarily) attract consumers and lead to rapid growth of a business. Not to be confused with *network effects*.

Product or service curation. See *Matching quality*.

Re-intermediation. The process whereby platforms introduce new kinds of middlemen into markets. Typically, re-intermediation involves replacing non-scalable and inefficient agent intermediaries with online, often automated tools and systems that offer valuable new goods and services to participants on both sides of the platform.

Same-side effects. In a two-sided market, network effects created by the impact of users from one side of the market on other users from the same side of the market—for example, the effects that consumers have on other consumers and the effects that producers have on other producers. Same-side effects can be positive or negative, depending on the design of the system and the rules put in place.

Sharing economy. The growing sector of the economy in which products, services, and resources are shared among people and organizations rather than having their availability limited to one proprietor. Often facilitated by platform businesses, sharing economy systems have the potential to unlock hidden or untapped sources of value and to reduce waste.

Side switching. The phenomenon of platform users from one side of the platform joining the opposite side—for example, when those who consume goods or services produced on the platform begin to produce goods and services for others to consume. On some platforms, users engage in side switching easily and repeatedly.

Spreadable value unit. See *Value unit.*

Supply economies of scale. Economic advantages driven by production efficiencies, which reduce the unit cost of creating a product or service as the quantities produced increase. These supply economies of scale can give the largest company in an industrial economy a cost advantage that is extremely difficult for competitors to overcome.

Switching. The abandonment by users of one platform in favor of another.

Switching costs. The costs incurred by users when they abandon one platform in favor of another. These may be financial costs (for example, cancellation fees) or costs in terms of time, effort, and inconvenience (for example, the need to move information files from one platform to another).

Trust. The degree to which users of a platform feel comfortable with the level of risk associated with engaging in interactions on the platform. Trust is achieved through excellent curation of participants in the platform.

Value unit. The most basic item of value that may be exchanged by users on a platform—for example, a photo on Instagram, a video on YouTube, a craft product on Etsy, or a freelance project on Upwork. When a value unit is *spreadable*, it can be easily distributed by users both on and off the platform, thereby helping to fuel *viral growth.*

Viral growth. A pull-based process that encourages users to spread the word about the platform to other potential users. When users themselves encourage others to join the network, the network becomes the driver of its own growth.

Virality. The tendency of an idea or brand to be circulated rapidly and widely from one Internet user to another. Virality can attract people to a network, but network effects keep them there. Virality is about stimulating growth among people off-platform, while network effects are about increasing value among people on-platform.

Winner-take-all market. A market in which specific forces conspire to encourage users to gravitate toward one platform and to abandon others. The four forces that most often characterize winner-take-all markets are supply economies of scale, strong network effects, high multihoming or switching costs, and lack of niche specialization.

NOTES

CHAPTER 1: TODAY

1. Bill Gurley, "A Rake Too Far: Optimal Platform Pricing Strategy," *Above the Crowd*, April 18, 2013, http://abovethecrowd .com/2013/04/18/a-rake-too-far-optimal-platformpricing-strategy/.
2. Thomas Steenburgh, Jill Avery, and Naseem Dahod, "HubSpot: Inbound Marketing and Web 2.0," Harvard Business School Case 509-049, 2009.
3. Tom Goodwin, "The Battle Is for the Customer Interface," *TechCrunch*, March 3, 2015, http://techcrunch.com/2015/03/03/in-the-age-of-disintermediation-the-battle-is-all-for-the-customer-interface/.

CHAPTER 2: NETWORK EFFECTS

1. Aswath Damodaran, "Uber Isn't Worth $17 Billion," *FiveThirtyEightEconomics*, June 18, 2014, http://fivethirtyeight.com/features/uber-isnt-worth-17-billion/.
2. Bill Gurley, "How to Miss By a Mile: An Alternative Look at Uber's Potential Market Size," *Above the Crowd*, July 11, 2014, http://abovethecrowd.com/2014/07/11/how-to-miss-by-a-mile-an-alternative-look-at-ubers-potential-market-size/.
3. W. Brian Arthur, "Increasing Returns and the Two Worlds of Business," *Harvard Business Review* 74, no. 4 (1996): 100–9; Michael L. Katz and Carl Shapiro, "Network Externalities, Competition, and Compatibility," *American Economic Review* 75, no. 3 (1985): 424–40.
4. Carl Shapiro and Hal R. Varian, *Information Rules* (Cambridge, MA: Harvard Business School Press, 1999).
5. Thomas Eisenmann, Geoffrey Parker, and Marshall Van Alstyne, "Strategies for Two-Sided Markets," *Harvard Business Review* 84, no. 10 (2006): 92–101.
6. Sarah Needleman and Angus Loten, "When Freemium Fails," *Wall Street Journal*, August 22, 2012.

7. Saul Hansell, "No More Giveaway Computers. Free-PC To Be Bought by eMachines," *New York Times*, November 30, 1999, http://www .nytimes.com/1999/11/30/business/no-more-giveaway-computers-free-pc-to-be-bought-by-emachines.html.

8. Dashiell Bennett, "8 Dot-Coms That Spent Millions on Super Bowl Ads and No Longer Exist," *Business Insider*, February 2, 2011, http://www.businessinsider.com/8-dot-com-super-bowl-advertisers -that-no-longer-exist-2011-2.

9. "The Greatest Defunct Web Sites and Dotcom Disasters," *Crave*, cnet .co.uk, June 5, 2008, http://web.archive.org/web/20080607211840/ http://crave.cnet.co.uk/0,39029477,49296926-6,00.htm.

10. Geoffrey Parker and Marshall Van Alstyne, "Information Comple-ments, Substitutes and Strategic Product Design," *Proceedings of the Twenty-First International Conference on Information Systems* (Association for Information Systems, 2000), 13–15; Geoffrey Parker and Marshall Van Alstyne, "Internetwork Externalities and Free Information Goods," *Proceedings of the Second ACM Conference on Electronic Commerce* (Association for Computing Machinery, 2000), 107–16; Geoffrey Parker and Marshall Van Alstyne, "Two-Sided Net-work Effects: A Theory of Information Product Design," *Management Science* 51, no. 10 (2005): 1494–1504.

11. M. Rysman, "The Economics of Two-Sided Markets," *Journal of Eco-nomic Perspectives* 23, no. 3 (2009): 125–43.

12. Paul David, "Clio and the Economics of QWERTY," *American Eco-nomic Review* 75 (1985): 332–7.

13. UN Data: https://data.un.org/Host.aspx?Content=Tools.

14. Christian Rudder, "Your Looks and Your Inbox," OkCupid, http://blog .okcupid.com/index.php/your-looks-and-online-dating/.

15. Jiang Yang, Lada A. Adamic, and Mark S. Ackerman, "Crowdsourcing and Knowledge Sharing: Strategic User Behavior on taskcn," *Proceed-ings of the Ninth ACM Conference on Electronic Commerce* (Associ-ation for Computing Machinery, 2008), 246–55; Kevin Kyung Nam, Mark S. Ackerman, and Lada A. Adamic, "Questions In, Knowledge In?: A Study of Naver's Question Answering Community," *Proceed-ings of the SIGCHI Conference on Human Factors in Computing Sys-tems* (Special Interest Group on Computer–Human Interaction, 2009), 779–88.

16. Barry Libert, Yoram (Jerry) Wind, and Megan Beck Fenley, "What Airbnb, Uber, and Alibaba Have in Common," *Harvard Business*

Review, November 20, 2014, https://hbr.org/2014/11/what-airbnb-uber
-and-alibaba-have-in-common.

17. Andrei Hagiu and Julian Wright, "Marketplace or Reseller?" *Management Science* 61, no. 1 (January 2015): 184–203.

18. Clay Shirky, *Here Comes Everybody: The Power of Organizing Without Organizations* (New York: Penguin, 2008).

19. Henry Chesbrough, *Open Innovation: The New Imperative for Creating and Profiting from Technology* (Cambridge, MA: Harvard Business School Press, 2003).

CHAPTER 3: ARCHITECTURE

1. Charles B. Stabell and Øystein D. Fjeldstad, "Configuring Value for Competitive Advantage: On Chains, Shops, and Networks," *Strategic Management Journal* 19, no. 5 (1998): 413–37.

2. Rajiv Banker, Sabyasachi Mitra, and Vallabh Sambamurthy, "The Effects of Digital Trading Platforms on Commodity Prices in Agricultural Supply Chains," *MIS Quarterly* 35, no. 3 (2011): 599–611.

3. "Hop In and Shove Over," *Businessweek,* February 2, 2015.

4. Mark Scott and Mike Isaac, "Uber Joins the Bidding for Here, Nokia's Digital Mapping Service," *New York Times,* May 7, 2015.

5. Adam Lashinsky, "Uber Banks on World Domination," *Fortune,* October 6, 2014.

6. J. H. Saltzer, D. P. Reed, and D. D. Clark, "End-to-End Arguments in System Design," *ACM Transactions on Computer Systems* 2, no. 4 (1984): 277–88.

7. Steve Lohr, "First the Wait for Microsoft Vista; Now the Marketing Barrage," *New York Times,* January 30, 2007.

8. Denise Dubie, "Microsoft Struggling to Convince about Vista," *Computerworld UK,* November 19, 2007, http://www.computerworlduk.com/news/it-vendors/microsoft-struggling-to-convince-about-vista-6258/.

9. Robin Bloor, "10 Reasons Why Vista is a Disaster," *Inside Analysis,* December 18, 2007, http://insideanalysis.com/2007/12/10-reasons-why-vista-is-a-disaster/2/.

10. See https://en.wikipedia.org/wiki/Windows_Vista and https://en.wikipedia.org/wiki/Windows_XP .

11. Steve Lohr and John Markoff, "Windows Is So Slow, but Why?" *New York Times,* March 27, 2006, http://www.nytimes.com/2006/03/27/technology/27soft.html?_r=1.

12. Carliss Young Baldwin and Kim B. Clark, *Design Rules: The Power of Modularity*, vol. 1 (Cambridge, MA: MIT Press, 2000).

13. Robert S. Huckman, Gary P. Pisano, and Liz Kind, "Amazon Web Services," Harvard Business School Case 609-048, 2008.

14. Carliss Young Baldwin and Kim B. Clark, "Managing in an Age of Modularity," *Harvard Business Review* 75, no. 5 (1996): 84–93.

15. Carliss Young Baldwin and C. Jason Woodard, "The Architecture of Platforms: A Unified View," Harvard Business School Working Paper 09-034, http://www.hbs.edu/faculty/Publication%20Files/09-034_149607b7-2b95-4316-b4b6-1df66dd34e83.pdf.

16. Daniel Jacobson, Greg Brail, and Dan Woods, *APIs: A Strategy Guide* (Cambridge, MA: O'Reilly, 2012).

17. Peter C. Evans and Rahul C. Basole, "Decoding the API Economy with Visual Analytics," Center for Global Enterprise, September 2, 2015, http://thecge.net/decoding-the-api-economy-with-visual-analytics/.

18. Michael G. Jacobides and John Paul MacDuffie, "How to Drive Value Your Way," *Harvard Business Review* 91, no. 7/8 (2013): 92–100.

19. Amrit Tiwana, *Platform Ecosystems: Aligning Architecture, Governance, and Strategy* (Burlington, MA: Morgan Kaufmann, 2013), ch. 5.

20. Steven Eppinger and Tyson Browning, *Design Structure Matrix Methods and Applications* (Cambridge, MA: MIT Press, 2012).

21. Alan MacCormack and Carliss Young Baldwin, "Exploring the Structure of Complex Software Designs: An Empirical Study of Open Source and Proprietary Code," *Management Science* 52, no. 7 (2006): 1015–30.

22. Andy Grove, *Only the Paranoid Survive* (New York: Doubleday, 1996).

23. Michael A. Cusumano and Annabelle Gawer, "The Elements of Platform Leadership," *MIT Sloan Management Review* 43, no. 3 (2002): 51.

24. Edward G. Anderson, Geoffrey G. Parker, and Burcu Tan, "Platform Performance Investment in the Presence of Network Externalities," *Information Systems Research* 25, no. 1 (2014): 152–72.

25. Interested readers who wish to learn more might begin with the following managerial works: Charles H. Fine, *Clockspeed: Winning Industry Control in the Age of Temporary Advantage* (New York: Basic Books, 1998); N. Venkatraman and John C. Henderson, "Real Strategies for Virtual Organizing," *MIT Sloan Management Review* 40, no. 1 (1998): 33; and Daniel E. Whitney, "Manufacturing by Design," *Harvard Business Review* 66, no. 4 (1988): 83–91. There is also a tremendous volume of

academic work on modularity. Readers who wish to explore the subject might start with the following academic works: Baldwin and Clark, *Design Rules*; Timothy F. Bresnahan and Shane Greenstein, "Technological Competition and the Structure of the Computer Industry," *Journal of Industrial Economics* 47, no. 1 (1999): 1–40; Viswanathan Krishnan and Karl T. Ulrich, "Product Development Decisions: A Review of the Literature," *Management Science* 47, no. 1 (2001): 1–21; Ron Sanchez and Joseph T. Mahoney, "Modularity, Flexibility, and Knowledge Management in Product and Organization Design," *Strategic Management Journal* 17, no. S2 (1996): 63–76; Melissa A. Schilling, "Toward a General Modular Systems Theory and Its Application to Interfirm Product Modularity," *Academy of Management Review* 25, no. 2 (2000): 312–34; Herbert A. Simon, *The Sciences of the Artificial* (Cambridge, MA: MIT Press, 1969); and Karl Ulrich, *Fundamentals of Product Modularity* (Heidelberg, Germany: Springer Netherlands, 1994).

CHAPTER 4: DISRUPTION

1. Chris Gayomali, "The Two Startups that Joined the $40 Billion Club in 2014," *Fast Company*, December 30, 2014, http://www.fastcompany.com/3040367/the-two-startups-that-joined-the-40-billion-club-in-2014.

2. Kara Swisher, "Man and Uber Man," *Vanity Fair*, December 2014; Jessica Kwong, "Head of SF Taxis to Retire," *San Francisco Examiner*, May 30, 2014; Alison Griswold, "The Million-Dollar New York City Taxi Medallion May Be a Thing of the Past," *Slate*, December 1, 2014, http://www.slate.com/blogs/moneybox/2014/12/01/new_york_taxi_medallions_did_tlc_transaction_data_inflate_the_price_of_driving.html.

3. Swisher, "Man and Uber Man."

4. Zack Kanter, "How Uber's Autonomous Cars Will Destroy 10 Million Jobs and Reshape the Economy by 2025," CBS SF Bay Area, sanfrancisco.cbslocal.com/2015/01/27/how-ubers-autonomous-cars-will-destroy-10-million-jobs-and-reshape-the-economy-by-2025-lyft-google-zack-kanter/.

5. Swisher, "Man and Uber Man."

6. Marc Andreessen, "Why Software Is Eating the World," *Wall Street*

Journal, August 20, 2011, http://www.wsj.com/articles/SB1000142405
31119034809045765122509156829460.

7. Phil Simon, *The Age of the Platform: How Amazon, Apple, Facebook, and Google Have Redefined Business* (Henderson, NV: Motion Publishing, 2011).

8. Feng Zhu and Marco Iansiti, "Entry into Platform-Based Markets," *Strategic Management Journal* 33, no. 1 (2012): 88–106.

9. Jason Tanz, "How Airbnb and Lyft Finally Got Americans to Trust Each Other," *Wired,* April 23, 2014, http://www.wired.com/2014/04/trust-in-the-share-economy/.

10. Arun Sundararajan, "From Zipcar to the Sharing Economy," *Harvard Business Review,* January 3, 2013, https://hbr.org/2013/01/from-zipcar-to-the-sharing-eco/.

11. Dan Charles, "In Search of a Drought Strategy, California Looks Down Under," *The Salt,* NPR, August 19, 2015, http://www.npr.org/sections/thesalt/2015/08/19/432885101/in-search-of-salvation-from-drought-california-looks-down-under.

12. Simon, *The Age of the Platform.*

13. Hemant K. Bhargava and Vidyanand Choudhary, "Economics of an Information Intermediary with Aggregation Benefits," *Information Systems Research* 15, no. 1 (2004): 22–36.

14. Marco Ceccagnoli, Chris Forman, Peng Huang, and D. J. Wu, "Cocreation of Value in a Platform Ecosystem: The Case of Enterprise Software," *MIS Quarterly* 36, no. 1 (2012): 263–90.

15. DC Rainmaker blog, "Under Armour (owner of MapMyFitness) buys both MyFitnessPal and Endomondo," February 4, 2015, http://www.dcrainmaker.com/2015/02/mapmyfitness-myfitnesspal-endomondo.html.

16. Peter C. Evans and Marco Annunziata, "Industrial Internet: Pushing the Boundaries of Minds and Machines," General Electric , November 26, 2012, http://www.ge.com/docs/chapters/Industrial_Internet.pdf.

17. Accenture Technology, "Vision 2015 – Trend 3: Platform (R)evolution," http://techtrends.accenture.com/us-en/downloads/Accenture_Technology_Vision%202015_Platform_Revolution.pdf. Accessed October 13, 2015.

18. Barry Wacksman and Chris Stutzman, *Connected by Design: Seven Principles for Business Transformation Through Functional Integration* (New York: John Wiley and Sons, 2014).

CHAPTER 5: LAUNCH

1. Eric M. Jackson, "How eBay's purchase of PayPal changed Silicon Valley," *VentureBeat,* October 27, 2012, http://venturebeat.com/2012/10/27/how-ebays-purchase-of-paypal-changed-silicon-valley/.
2. Blake Masters, "Peter Thiel's CS183: Startup—Class 2 Notes Essay," Blake Masters blog, April 6, 2012, http://blakemasters.com/post/20582845717/peter-thiels-cs183-startup-class-2-notes-essay. Copyright 2014 by David O. Sacks. Reprinted by permission.
3. Eric M. Jackson, *The PayPal Wars: Battles with eBay, the Media, the Mafia, and the Rest of Planet Earth* (Los Angeles: WND Books, 2012).
4. Andrei Hagiu and Thomas Eisenmann, "A Staged Solution to the Catch-22," *Harvard Business Review* 85, no. 11 (2007): 25–26.
5. Annabelle Gawer and Rebecca Henderson, "Platform Owner Entry and Innovation in Complementary Markets: Evidence from Intel," *Journal of Economics and Management Strategy* 16, no. 1 (2007): 1–34.
6. Joel West and Michael Mace, "Browsing as the Killer App: Explaining the Rapid Success of Apple's iPhone," *Telecommunications Policy* 34, no. 5 (2010): 270–86.
7. K. J. Boudreau, "Let a Thousand Flowers Bloom? An Early Look at Large Numbers of Software App Developers and Patterns of Innovation," *Organization Science* 23, no. 5 (2012): 1409–27.
8. Ciara O'Rourke, "Swiss Postal Service Is Moving Some Mail Online," *New York Times,* July 13, 2009.
9. Ellen Wallace, "Swiss Post Set to Become Country's Largest Apple Seller," *Genevalunch,* June 28, 2012, http://genevalunch.com/2012/06/28/swiss-post-set-to-become-countrys-largest-apple-seller/.
10. Mark Suster, "Why Launching Your Startup at SXSW Is a Bad Idea," *Fast Company,* February 13, 2013.
11. "Instagram Tips: Using Hashtags," Instagram blog, http://blog.instagram.com/post/17674993957/instagram-tips-using-hashtags.

CHAPTER 6: MONETIZATION

1. *Research Network,* September 12, 2012, http://papers.ssrn.com/sol3/papers.cfm?abstract_id=1676444.
2. Parker and Van Alstyne, "Internetwork Externalities and Free Information Goods"; Geoffrey G. Parker and Marshall Van Alstyne, "Two-Sided Network Effects: A Theory of Information Product Design," *Manage-*

ment Science 51, no. 10 (2005); Eisenmann, Parker, and Van Alstyne, "Strategies for Two-Sided Markets."

3. Jean-Charles Rochet and Jean Tirole, "Platform Competition in Two-Sided Markets," *Journal of the European Economic Association* 1, no. 4 (2003): 990–1029.

4. Rob Hof, "Meetup's Challenge," *Businessweek*, April 14, 2005, http://www.businessweek.com/stories/2005-04-13/meetups-challenge.

5. Matt Linderman, "Scott Heiferman Looks Back at Meetup's Bet-the-Company Moment," *Signal v. Noise,* January 25, 2011, https://signalvnoise.com/posts/2751-scott-heiferman-looks-back-at-meetups-bet-the-company-moment-.

6. Stuart Dredge, "MySpace—What Went Wrong," *Guardian*, March 6, 2015.

CHAPTER 7: OPENNESS

1. Nigel Scott, "Wikipedia: Where Truth Dies Online," *Spiked*, April 29, 2014, http://www.spiked-online.com/newsite/article/wikipedia-where-truth-dies-online/14963#.U7RzHxbuSQ2.

2. Thomas R. Eisenmann, Geoffrey G. Parker, and Marshall Van Alstyne, "Opening Platforms: How, When and Why?" chapter 6 in *Platforms, Markets and Innovation*, edited by Annabelle Gawer (Cheltenham, UK, and Northampton, MA: Edward Elgar, 2009).

3. Kevin Boudreau, "Open Platform Strategies and Innovation: Granting Access Versus Devolving Control," *Management Science* 56, no. 10 (2010): 1849–72.

4. Andrei Hagiu and Robin S. Lee, "Exclusivity and Control," *Journal of Economics and Management Strategy* 20, no. 3 (Fall 2011): 679–708.

5. Joel West, "How Open Is Open Enough? Melding Proprietary and Open Source Platform Strategies," *Research Policy* 32, no. 7 (2003): 1259–85; Henry William Chesbrough, *Open Innovation: The New Imperative for Creating and Profiting from Technology* (Cambridge, MA: Harvard Business School Press, 2006).

6. Felix Gillette, "The Rise and Inglorious Fall of Myspace," *Businessweek*, June 22, 2011.

7. Simon, *The Age of the Platform.*

8. Catherine Rampell, "Widgets Become Coins of the Social Realm," *Washington Post*, November 3, 2011, D01.

9. Peng Huang, Marco Ceccagnoli, Chris Forman, and D. J. Wu, "Appro-

priability Mechanisms and the Platform Partnership Decisic dence from Enterprise Software," *Management Science* 59, (2013): 102–21.

10. Thomas R. Eisenmann, "Managing Proprietary and Shared Platforms, *California Management Review* 50, no. 4 (2008): 31–53.

11. Eisenmann, Parker, and Van Alstyne, "Opening Platforms."

12. "Android and iOS Squeeze the Competition, Swelling to 96.3% of the Smartphone Operating System Market for Both 4Q14 and CY14, According to IDC," press release, International Data Corporation, February 24, 2015, http://www.idc.com/getdoc.jsp?containerId=prUS25450615.

13. Matt Rosoff, "Should Google Ditch Android Open Source?" *Business Insider*, April 10, 2015, http://www.businessinsider.com/google-should-ditch-android-open-source-2015-4; Ron Amadeo, "Google's Iron Grip on Android—Controlling Open Source By Any Means Necessary," *Arstechnica*, October 20, 2013, http://arstechnica.com/gadgets/2013/10/googles-iron-grip-on-android-controlling-open-source-by-any-means-necessary/.

14. Rahul Basole and Peter Evans, "Decoding the API Economy with Visual Analytics Using Programmable Web Data," Center for Global Enterprise, September 2015, http://thecge.net/decoding-the-api-economy-with-visual-analytics/.

15. Shannon Pettypiece, "Amazon Passes Wal-Mart as Biggest Retailer by Market Cap," *BloombergBusiness*, July 23, 2015, http://www.bloomberg.com/news/articles/2015-07-23/amazon-surpasses-wal-mart-as-biggest-retailer-by-market-value.

16. Bala Iyer and Mohan Subramaniam, "The Strategic Value of APIs," *Harvard Business Review*, January 7, 2015, https://hbr.org/2015/01/the-strategic-value-of-apis.

17. Charles Duhigg, "How Companies Learn Your Secrets," *New York Times*, February 16, 2012, http://www.nytimes.com/2012/02/19/magazine/shopping-habits.html?pagewanted=all.

18. Wade Roush, "The Story of Siri, from Birth at SRI to Acquisition by Apple—Virtual Personal Assistants Go Mobile," *xconomy*, June 14, 2010, http://www.xconomy.com/san-francisco/2010/06/14/the-story-of-siri-from-birth-at-sri-to-acquisition-by-apple-virtual-personal-assistants-go-mobile/?single_page=true.

19. "A letter from Tim Cook on Maps," Apple, http://www.apple.com/letter-from-tim-cook-on-maps/.

20. Amadeo, "Google's Iron Grip on Android."

CHAPTER 8: GOVERNANCE

1. Josh Dzieza, "Keurig's Attempt to DRM Its Coffee Cups Totally Backfired," *The Verge,* February 5, 2015, http://www.theverge .com/2015/2/5/7986327/keurigs-attempt-to-drm-its-coffee-cups -totally-backfired.

2. Geoffrey G. Parker and Marshall Van Alstyne, "Innovation, Openness and Platform Control," October 3, 2014, available at SSRN at http:// ssrn.com/abstract=1079712.

3. Tiwana, *Platform Ecosystems*; Youngin Yoo, Richard J. Boland, Kalle Lyytinen, and Ann Majchrzak, "Organizing for Innovation in the Digitized World," *Organization Science* 23, no. 15 (2012): 1398–1408.

4. J. R. Raphael, "Facebook Privacy: Secrets Unveiled," *PCWorld,* May 16, 2010, http://www.pcworld.com/article/196410/Facebook_Privacy_ Secrets_Unveiled.html.

5. Brad McCarty, "LinkedIn Lockout and the State of CRM," *Full Contact,* March 28, 2014, https://www.fullcontact.com/blog/ linkedin-state-of-crm-2014/.

6. Nitasha Tiku and Casey Newton, "Twitter CEO: 'We Suck at Dealing with Abuse,'" *The Verge,* February 4, 2015, http://www .theverge.com/2015/2/4/7982099/twitter-ceo-sent-memo-taking -personal-responsibility-for-the.

7. Juro Osawa, "How to Understand Alibaba's Business Model," *MarketWatch,* March 15, 2014, http://www.marketwatch.com/story/ how-to-understand-alibabas-business-model-2014-03-15-94855847.

8. Brad Burnham, "Web Services as Governments," Union Square Ventures, June 10, 2010, https://www.usv.com/blog/web-services-as-governments.

9. Wolfram Knowledgebase, https://www.wolfram.com/knowledgebase/. Accessed May 30, 2015.

10. "Politicians," Corrupt Practices Investigation Bureau, https://www.cpib .gov.sg/cases-interest/cases-involving-public-sector-officers/politicians. Accessed October 13, 2015.

11. "Corrupt Perceptions Index," *Wikipedia,* http://en.wikipedia.org/wiki/ Corruption_Perceptions_Index, accessed October 13, 2015; B. Podobnik, J. Shao, D. Njavro, P. C. Ivanov, and H. E. Stanley, "Influence of Corruption on Economic Growth Rate and Foreign Investment," *European Physical Journal B-Condensed Matter and Complex Systems* 63, no. 4:547–50.

12. Estimate based on data from Wolfram Knowledgebase. Accessed October 13, 2015.

13. Daron Acemoglu, Simon Johnson, and James A. Robinson, "The Colonial Origins of Comparative Development: An Empirical Investigation," *American Economic Review* 91, no. 5 (2001): 1369–1401; D. Acemoglu, S. Johnson, and J. A. Robinson, "Reversal of Fortune: Geography and Institutions in the Making of the Modern World Income Distribution," *Quarterly Journal of Economics* 117, no. 4 (2002): 1231–94; Gavin Clarkson and Marshall Van Alstyne, "The Social Efficiency of Fairness," Gruter Institute Squaw Valley Conference: Innovation and Economic Growth, October 2010.

14. Roger Protz, "Arctic Ale, 1845," *Beer Pages*, March 23, 2011, http://www.beer-pages.com/stories/arctic-ale.htm; Jeremy Singer-Vine, "How Long Can You Survive on Beer Alone?" *Slate*, April 28, 2011, http://www.slate.com/articles/news_and_politics/explainer/2011/04/how_long_can_you_survive_on_beer_alone.html.

15. "Allsopp's Arctic Ale, The $500,000 eBay Typo," *New Life Auctions*, http://www.newlifeauctions.com/allsopp.html, accessed October 13, 2015. In fact, the winning bid was $503,300, but it is unclear whether anyone actually paid this amount.

16. Hillel Aron, "How eBay, Amazon and Alibaba Fuel the World's Top Illegal Industry—The Counterfeit Products Market," *LA Weekly*, December 3, 2014, http://www.laweekly.com/news/how-ebay-amazon-and-alibaba-fuel-the-worlds-top-illegal-industry-the-counterfeit-products-market-5261019.

17. Andrei Shleifer and Robert W. Vishny, "A Survey of Corporate Governance," *Journal of Finance* 52, no. 2 (1997): 737–83, esp. 737.

18. Steve Denning, "The Dumbest Idea in the World: Maximizing Shareholder Value," *Forbes*, November 28, 2011, http://www.forbes.com/sites/stevedenning/2011/11/28/maximizing-shareholder-value-the-dumbest-idea-in-the-world/.

19. Alvin E. Roth, "The Art of Designing Markets," *Harvard Business Review* 85, no. 10 (2007): 118.

20. Lawrence Lessig, *Code and Other Laws of Cyberspace* (New York: Basic Books, 1999).

21. Dana Sauchelli and Bruce Golding, "Hookers Turning Airbnb Apartments into Brothels," *New York Post*, April 14, 2014, http://nypost.com/2014/04/14/hookers-using-airbnb-to-use-apartments-

for-sex-sessions/; Amber Stegall, "Craigslist Killers: 86 Murders Linked to Popular Classifieds Website," WAFB 9 News, Baton Rouge, LA, April 9, 2015, http://www.wafb.com/story/28761189/craigslist-killers-86-murders-linked-to-popular-classifieds-website.

22. Apple, "iTunes Store—Terms and Conditions," http://www.apple.com/legal/internet-services/itunes/us/terms.html. Accessed May 20, 2015.

23. Apple, "iOS Developer Program License Agreement," https://developer.apple.com/programs/terms/ios/standard/ios_program_standard_agreement_20140909.pdf. Accessed May 20, 2015.

24. Stack Overflow, "Privileges," Stack Overflow help page, http://stackoverflow.com/help/privileges. Accessed May 20, 2015.

25. Rebecca Grant and Meghan Stothers, "iStockphoto.Com: Turning Community Into Commerce," Richard Ivey School of Business Case 907E13, 2011.

26. Michael Dunlop, "Interview With Bruce Livingstone—Founder and CEO of iStockphoto," *Retire at 21,* http://www.retireat21.com/interview/interview-with-bruce-livingstone-founder-of-istockphoto.

27. Grant and Stothers, "iStockphoto.Com," 3.

28. Nir Eyal, *Hooked: How to Build Habit-Forming Products* (Toronto: Penguin Canada, 2014).

29. Nir Eyal, "Hooks: An Intro on How to Manufacture Desire," *Nir & Far,* http://www.nirandfar.com/2012/03/how-to-manufacture-desire.html. Accessed October 13, 2015.

30. Elinor Ostrom, *Governing the Commons: The Evolution of Institutions for Collective Action* (New York: Cambridge University Press, 1990).

31. Jeff Jordan, "Managing Tensions In Online Marketplaces," *Tech-Crunch,* February 23, 2015, http://techcrunch.com/2015/02/23/managing-tensions-in-online-marketplaces/.

32. Ibid.

33. Charles Moldow, "A Trillion Dollar Market, By the People, For the People," Foundation Capital, https://foundationcapital.com/downloads/FoundationCap_MarketplaceLendingWhitepaper.pdf.

34. Sangeet Choudhary, "Will Peer Lending Platforms Disrupt Banking?" *Platform Thinking,* http://platformed.info/peer-lending-platforms-disrupt-banking/.

35. Michael Lewis, *Flash Boys: A Wall Street Revolt* (New York: Norton, 2014); P. Martens, "Goldman Sachs Drops a Bombshell on Wall Street," *Wall Street on Parade,* April 9, 2014, http://wallstreetonparade.com/2014/04/goldman-sachs-drops-a-bombshell-on-wall-street/.

9. Eisenmann, Parker, and Van Alstyne, "Strategies for Two-Sided Markets"; Croll and Yoskovitz, *Lean Analytics*.
10. Francis J. Mulhern, "Customer Profitability Analysis: Measurement, Concentration, and Research Directions," *Journal of Interactive Marketing* 13, no. 1 (1999): 25–40; Nicolas Glady, Bart Baesens, and Christophe Croux, "Modeling Churn Using Customer Lifetime Value," *European Journal of Operational Research* 197, no. 1 (2009): 402–11.
11. Minter Dial, "Best of the Web or Death by Aggregation? Why Don't Brands Curate the News?" *Myndset,* December 16, 2014, http://themyndset.com/2014/12/aggregation-curation/.
12. Nidhi Subbaraman, "Airbnb's Small Army of Photographers Are Making You (and Them) Look Good," *Fast Company,* October 17, 2011, http://www.fastcompany.com/1786980/airbnbs-small-army-photographers-are-making-you-and-them-look-good.
13. Ruimin Zhang interview by Geoffrey Parker and Marshall Van Alstyne, December 12, 2014.
14. Tiwana, *Platform Ecosystems.*
15. Parker and Van Alstyne. "Innovation, Openness, and Platform Control."
16. Guido Jouret interview by Geoffrey Parker and Marshall Van Alstyne, September 8, 2006.
17. Gary Swart, "7 Things I Learned from Startup Failure," *In,* September 23, 2013, https://www.linkedin.com/pulse/20130923123247-758147-7-things-i-learned-from-startup-failure.
18. Eric Ries, *The Lean Startup: How Today's Entrepreneurs Use Continuous Innovation to Create Radically Successful Businesses* (New York: Random House, 2011).

CHAPTER 10: STRATEGY

1. David J. Teece, "Next Generation Competition: New Concepts for Understanding How Innovation Shapes Competition and Policy in the Digital Economy," *Journal of Law Economics and Policy* 9, no. 1 (2012): 97–118.
2. David B. Yoffie and Michael A. Cusumano, *Strategy Rules: Five Timeless Lessons from Bill Gates, Andy Grove, and Steve Jobs* (New York: HarperCollins, 2015); F. F. Suarez and J. Kirtley, "Innovation Strategy—Dethroning an Established Platform," *MIT Sloan Management Review* 53, no. 4 (2012): 35.

3. David Barboza, "China's Internet Giants May Be Stuck There," *New York Times*, March 23, 2010, http://www.nytimes.com/2010/03/24/business/global/24internet.html.

4. Brad Stone, "Alibaba's IPO May Herald the End of U.S. E-Commerce Dominance," *Businessweek,* August 7, 2014, http://www.bloomberg.com/bw/articles/2014-08-07/alibabas-ipo-may-herald-the-end-of-u-dot-s-dot-e-commerce-dominance.

5. Sarit Markovich and Johannes Moenius, "Winning While Losing: Competition Dynamics in the Presence of Indirect Network Effects," *International Journal of Industrial Organization* 27, no. 3 (2009): 346–57.

6. Stone, "Alibaba's IPO."

7. Michael E. Porter, "How Competitive Forces Shape Strategy," *Harvard Business Review* 57, no. 2 (1979): 137–45; Michael E. Porter, *Competitive Strategy* (New York: Free Press, 1980).

8. Birger Wernerfelt, "A Resource-Based View of the Firm," *Strategic Management Journal* 5 (1984): 171–80.

9. Paul Zimnisky, "A Diamond Market No Longer Controlled By De Beers," Kitco Commentary, June 6, 2013, http://www.kitco.com/ind/Zimnisky/2013-06-06-A-Diamond-Market-No-Longer-Controlled-By-De-Beers.html.

10. Richard D'Aveni, *Hypercompetition* (New York: Free Press, 1994), 4.

11. Rita Gunther McGrath, *The End of Competition: How to Keep Your Strategy Moving as Fast as Your Business* (Cambridge, MA: Harvard Business Review Press, 2013).

12. Steve Denning, "What Killed Michael Porter's Monitor Group? The One Force That Really Matters," *Forbes,* November 20, 2012, http://www.forbes.com/sites/stevedenning/2012/11/20/what-killed-michael-porters-monitor-group-the-one-force-that-really-matters/.

13. Ming Zeng, "Three Paradoxes of Building Platforms," Communications of the ACM 58, no. 2 (2015): 27–9, cacm.acm.org/magazines/2015/2/182646-three-paradoxes-of-building-platforms/abstract.

14. Thomas Eisenmann, Geoffrey G. Parker, and Marshall Van Alstyne, "Platform Envelopment," *Strategic Management Journal* 32, no. 12 (2011): 1270–85.

15. Geoffrey G. Parker and Marshall Van Alstyne, "Platform Strategy," *New Palgrave Encyclopedia of Business Strategy* (New York: Macmillan, 2014).

16. Angel Salazar, "Platform Competition: A Research Framework and Synthesis of Game-Theoretic Studies," Social Science Research Net-

work, February 15, 2015, papers.ssrn.com/sol3/papers.cfm?abstract_id=2565337. Mimeo: Manchester Metropolitan University, 2015; Barry J. Nalebuff and Adam M. Brandenburger, *Co-opetition* (London: HarperCollins Business, 1996).

17. Steve Jobs, "Thoughts on Flash," April 2010, http://www.apple.com/hotnews/thoughts-on-flash/.

18. Vardit Landsman and Stefan Stremersch, "Multihoming in Two-Sided Markets: An Empirical Inquiry in the Video Game Console Industry," *Journal of Marketing* 75, no. 6 (2011): 39–54.

19. Ming Zeng, "How Will Big Data and Cloud Computing Change Platform Thinking?", keynote address, MIT Platform Strategy Summit, July 25, 2014, http://platforms.mit.edu/2014.

20. "Top 20 Apps with MAU Over 10 Million," Facebook Apps Leaderboard, AppData, appdata.com/leaderboard/apps?show_na=1. Accessed October 14, 2015.

21. Carl Shapiro and Hal R. Varian, "The Art of Standards Wars," *California Management Review* 41, no. 2 (1999): 8–32.

22. Bill Gurley, "All Revenue Is Not Created Equal: Keys to the 10X Revenue Club," *Above the Crowd*, May 24, 2011, http://abovethecrowd.com/2011/05/24/all-revenue-is-not-created-equal-the-keys-to-the-10x-revenue-club/.

23. Douglas MacMillan, "The Fiercest Rivalry in Tech: Uber vs. Lyft," *Wall Street Journal*, August 11, 2014; C. Newton, "This is Uber's Playbook for Sabotaging Lyft," *The Verge*, August 26, 2014, http://www.theverge.com/2014/8/26/6067663/this-is-ubers-playbook-for-sabotaging-lyft.

CHAPTER 11: POLICY

1. Kevin Boudreau and Andrei Hagiu, *Platform Rules: Multi-Sided Platforms as Regulators* (Cheltenham, UK: Edward Elgar, 2009), 163–89.

2. Malhotra and Van Alstyne, "The Dark Side of the Sharing Economy."

3. Felix Gillette and Sheelah Kolhatkar, "Airbnb's Battle for New York," *Businessweek*, June 19, 2014, http://www.bloomberg.com/bw/articles/2014-06-19/airbnb-in-new-york-sharing-startup-fights-for-largest-market.

4. Ron Lieber, "A Liability Risk for Airbnb Hosts," *New York Times*, December 6, 2014.

5. Georgios Zervas, Davide Proserpio, and John W. Byers, "The Rise of

the Sharing Economy: Estimating the Impact of Airbnb on the Hotel Industry," Boston University School of Management Research Paper 2013-16, http://ssrn.com/abstract=2366898.

6. Brad N. Greenwood and Sunil Wattal, "Show Me the Way to Go Home: An Empirical Investigation of Ride Sharing and Motor Vehicle Homicide," Platform Strategy Research Symposium, Boston, MA, July 9, 2015, http://ssrn.com/abstract=2557612.

7. John Coté, "SF Cracks Down on 'MonkeyParking' Mobile App," *SF Gate,* June 23, 2014, http://blog.sfgate.com/cityinsider/2014/06/23/sf-cracks-down-on-street-parking-cash-apps/.

8. Kevin Roose, "Does Silicon Valley Have a Contract-Worker Problem?" *New York,* September 18, 2014, http://nymag.com/daily/intelligencer/2014/09/silicon-valleys-contract-worker-problem.html.

9. George J. Stigler, "The Theory of Economic Regulation," *Bell Journal of Economics and Management Science* 2, no. 1 (Spring 1971): 3–21.

10. Jean-Jacques Laffont and Jean Tirole, "The Politics of Government Decision-Making: A Theory of Regulatory Capture," *Quarterly Journal of Economics* 106, no. 4 (1991): 1089–1127.

11. Conor Friedersdorf, "Mayors of Atlanta and New Orleans: Uber Will Beat the Taxi Industry," *Atlantic,* June 29, 2014, http://www.theatlantic.com/business/archive/2014/06/mayors-of-atlanta-and-new-orleans-uber-will-beat-the-taxi-cab-industry/373660/.

12. Don Boudreaux, "Uber vs. Piketty," *Cafe Hayek,* August 1, 2015, http://cafehayek.com/2015/08/uber-vs-piketty.html.

13. Andrei Shleifer, "Understanding Regulation," *European Financial Management* 11, no. 4 (2005): 439–51.

14. Jean-Jacques Laffont and Jean Tirole, *Competition in Telecommunications* (Cambridge, MA: MIT Press, 2000).

15. Ben-Zion Rosenfeld and Joseph Menirav, "Methods of Pricing and Price Regulation in Roman Palestine in the Third and Fourth Centuries," *Journal of the American Oriental Society* 121, no. 3 (2001): 351–69; Geoffrey E. Rickman, "The Grain Trade under the Roman Empire," *Memoirs of the American Academy in Rome* 36 (1980): 261–75.

16. Jad Mouawad and Christopher Drew, "Airline Industry Is at Its Safest Since the Dawn of the Jet Age," *New York Times,* February 11, 2013, http://www.nytimes.com/2013/02/12/business/2012-was-the-safest-year-for-airlines-globally-since-1945.html.

17. Simeon Djankov, Edward Glaeser, Rafael La Porta, Florencio Lopez-de-Silanes, and Andrei Shleifer, "The New Comparative

Economics," *Journal of Comparative Economics* 31, no. 4 (2003): 595–619.

18. Shleifer, "Understanding Regulation."

19. KPMG, "China 360: E-Commerce in China, Driving a New Consumer Culture," https://www.kpmg.com/CN/en/IssuesAndInsights/ArticlesPublications/Newsletters/China-360/Documents/China-360-Issue15-201401-E-commerce-in-China.pdf.

20. S. Shankland, "Sun Brings Antitrust Suit Against Microsoft," CNET News, July 20, 2002, http://www.cnet.com/news/sun-brings-antitrust-suit-against-microsoft-1/.

21. Carl Shapiro, "Exclusivity in Network Industries," *George Mason Law Review* 7 (1998): 673.

22. Neil Gandal, "Compatibility, Standardization, and Network Effects: Some Policy Implications," *Oxford Review of Economic Policy* 18, no. 1 (2002): 80–91.

23. Parker and Van Alstyne, "Innovation, Openness, and Platform Control."

24. Parker and Van Alstyne, "Internetwork Externalities and Free Information Goods"; Parker and Van Alstyne, "Two-Sided Network Effects."

25. David S. Evans and Richard Schmalensee, "The Antitrust Analysis of Multi-Sided Platform Businesses," in *The Oxford Handbook of International Antitrust Economics*, vol. 1, edited by Roger D. Blair and D. Daniel Sokol (Oxford: Oxford University Press, 2015).

26. Tom Fairless, Rolfe Winkler, and Alistair Barr, "EU Files Formal Antitrust Charges Against Google," *Wall Street Journal*, April 15, 2015.

27. "Statement of the Federal Trade Commission Regarding Google's Search Practices: In the Matter of Google, Inc.," FTC File Number 111-0163, January 3, 2013, https://www.ftc.gov/public-statements/2013/01/statement-federal-trade-commission-regarding-googles-search-practices.

28. Jeremy Greenfield, "How the Amazon–Hachette Fight Could Shape the Future of Ideas," *Atlantic Monthly*, May 28, 2014.

29. Helen F. Ladd, "Evidence on Discrimination in Mortgage Lending," *Journal of Economic Perspectives* 12, no. 2 (1998): 41–62.

30. Noel Capon, "Credit Scoring Systems: A Critical Analysis," *Journal of Marketing* 46, no. 2 (1982): 82–91.

31. Jim Puzzangher, "Obama to Push Cybersecurity, Identity Theft and Online Access Plans," *Los Angeles Times*, January 10, 2015, http://www.latimes.com/nation/politics/politicsnow/la-pn-obama-cybersecurity-20150110-story.html.

32. Steve Kroft, "The Data Brokers: Selling Your Personal Informa-

tion," *CBS News*, March 9, 2014, http://www.cbsnews.com/news/the
-data-brokers-selling-your-personal-information/.

33. Federal Trade Commission, "Data Brokers: A Call for Transparency and
    Accountability," May 2014, http://www.ftc.gov/system/files/documents/
    reports/data-brokers-call-transparency-accountability-report-federal-
    trade-commission-may-2014/140527databrokerreport.pdf.

34. Lee Rainie and Janna Anderson, "The Future of Privacy," Pew Research
    Center, December 18, 2014, http://www.pewinternet.org/2014/12/18/
    future-of-privacy/.

35. "Who Owns Your Personal Data? The Incorporated Woman,"
    Economist, June 27, 2014, http://www.economist.com/blogs/schum
    peter/2014/06/who-owns-your-personal-data.

36. Lee Rainie and Janna Anderson, "The Future of Privacy: Other
    Resounding Themes," Pew Research Center, December 18, 2014,
    http://www.pewinternet.org/2014/12/18/other-resounding-themes/.

37. Charles Arthur, "Tech Giants May Be Huge, But Nothing Matches
    Big Data," *Guardian*, August 23, 2013, http://www.theguardian.com/
    technology/2013/aug/23/tech-giants-data.

38. James Cook, "Sony Hackers Have Over 100 Terabytes Of Documents.
    Only Released 200 Gigabytes So Far," *Business Insider*, December 16,
    2014, http://www.businessinsider.com/the-sony-hackers-still-have-a-
    massive-amount-of-data-that-hasnt-been-leaked-yet-2014-12.

39. Lisa Beilfuss, "Target Reaches $19 Million Settlement with Master-
    Card Over Data Breach," *Wall Street Journal*, April 15, 2015.

40. Andrew Nusca, "Who Should Own Farm Data?" *Fortune,* December
    22, 2014.

41. We thank Peter Evans, former head of analytics for GE, for his counsel
    on this topic.

42. Email to Marshall Van Alstyne from Peter Evans, Center for Global
    Enterprise, using 2015 Crunchbase data.

43. Avi Goldfarb and Catherine E. Tucker, "Privacy Regulation and Online
    Advertising," *Management Science* 57, no. 1 (2011): 57–71.

44. Robert W. Wood, "Amazon No Longer Tax-Free: 10 Surpris-
    ing Facts As Giant Loses Ground," *Forbes*, August 22, 2013,
    http://www.forbes.com/sites/robertwood/2013/08/22/amazon-no
    -longer-tax-free-10-surprising-facts-as-giant-loses-ground.

45. Bob Egelko, "Court Rules FedEx Drivers in State Are Employees, Not
    Contractors," *SF Gate,* August 28, 2014, http://www.sfgate.com/bayarea/
    article/Court-to-FedEx-Your-drivers-are-full-time-5717048.php.

46. Google search results, "Internet sweatshop," accessed January 28, 2015.

47. Krishnadev Calamur, "Uber's Troubles Mount Even As Its Value Grows," The Two-Way, NPR, December 10, 2014, http://www .npr.org/blogs/the-two-way/2014/12/10/369922099/ubers-trou bles-mount-even-as-its-value-grows.

48. Jeffrey A. Trachtenberg and Greg Bensinger, "Amazon, Hachette End Publishing Dispute," Wall Street Journal, November 13, 2014, http://www.wsj.com/articles/amazon-hachette-end-publishing -dispute-1415898013.

49. Robinson Meyer, "Everything We Know About Facebook's Secret Mood Manipulation Experiment," Atlantic, June 28, 2014, http://www .theatlantic.com/technology/archive/2014/06/everything-we -know-about-facebooks-secret-mood-manipulation-experiment/ 373648/.

50. Robert M. Bond, Christopher J. Fariss, Jason J. Jones, Adam D. I. Kramer, Cameron Marlow, Jaime E. Settle, and James H. Fowler, "A 61-Million-Person Experiment in Social Influence and Political Mobi- lization," Nature 489, no. 7415 (2012): 295–8.

51. Dominic Rushe, "Facebook Sorry—Almost—For Secret Psycho- logical Experiment on User," Guardian, October 2, 2012, http:// www.theguardian.com/technology/2014/oct/02/facebook-sorry -secret-psychological-experiment-users.

52. Alex Rosenblat, "Uber's Phantom Cars," Motherboard, July 27, 2015, http://motherboard.vice.com/read/ubers-phantom-cabs.

53. Nick Grossman, "Regulation, the Internet Way: A Data-First Model for Establishing Trust, Safety, and Security—Regulatory Reform for the 21st Century City," Harvard Kennedy School, ASH Center for Democratic Governance and Innovation, April 8, 2015, http://datasmart.ash.harvard. edu/news/article/white-paper-regulation-the-internet-way-660.

54. Ibid.

55. Tim O'Reilly, Government as a Platform (Cambridge, MA: MIT Press, 2010), 11–40.

56. The social impact of mandated transparency rules has been thoroughly analyzed by three experts from Harvard's Kennedy School of Govern- ment; see Archon Fung, Mary Graham, and David Weil, Full Disclo- sure: The Perils and Promise of Transparency (New York: Cambridge University Press, 2007).

57. See, for example, Richard Stallman, "Why Open Source Misses the Point of Free Software," GNU Operating System, Free Software Foun-

dation, http://www.gnu.org/philosophy/open-source-misses-the-point
.en.html.

58. Carlota Perez, *Technological Revolutions and Financial Capital: The Dynamics of Bubbles and Golden Ages* (Cheltenham, UK: Edward Elgar, 2003).

59. Heli Koski and Tobias Kretschmer, "Entry, Standards and Competition: Firm Strategies and the Diffusion of Mobile Telephony," *Review of Industrial Organization* 26, no. 1 (2005): 89–113.

60. David Evans, "Governing Bad Behavior by Users of Multi-Sided Platforms," *Berkeley Technology Law Journal* 27, no. 12 (Fall 2012), http://scholarship.law.berkeley.edu/cgi/viewcontent .cgi?article=1961&context=btlj.

61. Benjamin Edelman, "Digital Business Models Should Have to Follow the Law, Too," *Harvard Business Review*, January 6, 2015, https://hbr.org/2015/01/digital-business-models-should-have -to-follow-the-law-too.

CHAPTER 12: TOMORROW

1. Brandon Alcorn, Gayle Christensen, and Ezekiel J. Emanuel, "The Real Value of Online Education," *Atlantic Monthly*, September 2014.

2. Luis Von Ahn, "Crowdsourcing, Language and Learning," presentation, MIT Platform Strategy Summit, July 10, 2015, available at http:// platforms.mit.edu/agenda.

3. Graeme Wood, "The Future of College?" *Atlantic Monthly*, September 2014.

4. "There's an App for That," *Economist*, January 3, 2015.

5. Hemant Taneja, "Unscaling the Healthcare Economy," *TechCrunch*, June 28, 2014, http://techcrunch.com/2014/06/28/ software-defined-healthcare/.

6. Vince Kuraitis, "Patient Digital Health Platforms (PDHPs): An Epicenter of Healthcare Transformation?" Healthcare Information and Management Systems Society, June 18, 2014, http://blog.himss .org/2014/06/18/patient-digital-health-platforms-pdhps-an-epicen- ter-of-healthcare-transformation/.

7. Josh Dzieza, "Why Tesla's Battery for Your Home Should Terrify Utilities," *The Verge*, February 13, 2015, http://www.theverge .com/2015/2/13/8033691/why-teslas-battery-for-your-home-should -terrify-utilities.

8. Daniel Roberts, "How MasterCard became a Tech Company," *Fortune*, July 24, 2014.

9. William D. Cohan, "Bypassing the Bankers," *Atlantic Monthly*, September 2014.

10. Matina Stevis and Patrick McGroarty, "Banks Vie for a Piece of Africa's Mobile Banking Market," *Wall Street Journal*, August 15, 2014.

11. Daniel Fisher, "Legal-Services Firm's $73 Million Deal Strips the Mystery from Derivatives Trading," *Forbes*, February 12, 2015; "There's an App for That," *Economist*.

12. San Francisco Mayor's Office of Civic Innovation, "Announcing the First-Ever San Francisco Datapalooza," blog post, October 12, 2013; San Francisco Mayor's Office of Civic Innovation, "Data Jam, 100 Days to Tackle Housing," blog post, June 7, 2013, http://innovatesf.com.

13. David Mount, "The Industrial Awakening: The Internet of Heavier Things," March 3, 2015, http://www.kpcb.com/blog/the-industrial-awakening-the-internet-of-heavier-things.

14. Jeremy Rifkin, "Capitalism Is Making Way for the Age of Free," *Guardian*, March 31, 2014.

INDEX

Page numbers in *italics* refer to figures.

ABOUT THE AUTHORS

Geoffrey G. Parker is a professor of engineering at Dartmouth College (effective July 2016) and has been a professor of management science at Tulane University since 1998. He is also a visiting scholar and research fellow at the MIT Initiative on the Digital Economy. Before joining academia, he held positions in engineering and finance at General Electric. He has made significant contributions to the economics of network effects as codedeveloper of the theory of two-sided networks. Parker's work has been supported by the Department of Energy, the National Science Foundation, and numerous corporations. Parker advises senior leaders in government and business and is a frequent speaker at conferences and industry events. He received his BS from Princeton and his MS and PhD from MIT.

Marshall W. Van Alstyne is a professor at Boston University and a visiting scholar and research fellow at the MIT Initiative on the Digital Economy. Van Alstyne is a world expert on information economics and has made fundamental contributions to IT productivity and to theories of network effects. His coauthored work on two-sided networks is taught in business schools worldwide. In addition, he holds patents in information privacy protection and on spam-prevention methods. Van Alstyne has been honored with six best paper awards and National Science Foundation IOC, SGER, iCORPS, SBIR and Career Awards. He is an advisor to leading executives, a frequent keynote speaker, a former entrepreneur, and a consultant to startups and to Global 100 companies. He received his BA from Yale and his MS and PhD from MIT. Reach him at @InfoEcon.

Sangeet Paul Choudary is a C-level advisor to executives globally on platform business models. He is an Entrepreneur-in-Residence at the INSEAD Business School and a Fellow at the Centre for Global Enterprise. He has been ranked among the top 30 emerging business thinkers globally by Thinkers50. Sangeet writes the popular blog Platformed (platformed.info), and his work has been featured in leading journals and media, including the *Harvard Business Review*, *MIT Technology Review*, *Sloan Management Review*, the *Wall Street Journal*, and *The Economist*. He is a frequent keynote speaker at leading conferences, including the G20 World Summit 2014 and World Economic Forum events.